The Public Space of Social

T0229421

This book addresses how practices contained within contemporary networked publics are situated within a larger history and genealogy of public space. Tierney explores spatial concepts linked to theories of communal identity, civitas and democracy, the fête, and self-expression. Through empirical research, she describes the actual social practices of the participants of networked publics.

Documenting how online counterpublics use the Internet to transmit classified photos, mobilize activists, and challenge the status quo, Tierney argues that their online activities do not stop at online conversations; they are physically grounded through mobile global positioning system (GPS) coordinates, which are then transformed into activities in physical space—the street, the plaza, the places where people have traditionally gathered to demonstrate and express their opinions publicly.

Thérèse F. Tierney is assistant professor of architecture with a designated emphasis in new media at the University of Illinois at Urbana–Champaign, U.S.

Routledge Studies in New Media and Cyberculture

The Public Space of Social Media

Connected Cultures of the Network Society

Thérèse F. Tierney

Routledge
Taylor & Francis Group

NEW YORK AND LONDON

First published 2013
by Routledge
711 Third Avenue, New York, NY 10017

Simultaneously published in the UK
by Routledge
2 Park Square, Milton Park, Abingdon, Oxfordshire OX14 4RN

First issued in paperback 2015

*Routledge is an imprint of the Taylor & Francis Group,
an informa business*

Library of Congress Cataloging-in-Publication Data

Tierney, Therese.
  The public space of social media : connected cultures of the network society /
by Thérèse F. Tierney.
    pages cm. — (Routledge studies in new media and cyberculture ; 13)
    Includes bibliographical references and index.
  1. Online social networks.   2. Social media.   3. Internet—Social
aspects.   I. Title.
    HM742.T54 2013
    006.7'54–dc23
    2013002653

ISBN: 978-1-138-64930-9 (pbk)
ISBN: 978-0-415-63523-3 (hbk)

Typeset in Sabon
by Apex CoVantage, LLC

Contents

Acknowledgments

This book is the result of a nexus of thought between two knowledge centers: Massachusetts Institute of Technology and University of California–Berkeley. These universities have long recognized the value of interdisciplinary research, and not unwisely, because they believe that interdisciplinary work is where significant breakthroughs will occur. Productive concepts often transcend the scope of a single discipline or program, especially prevalent with new media technologies, information and communication technologies, or urban design. The integration of education and research in computer science and the humanities prepares scholars to undertake research challenges in rigorous and innovative ways.

While at MIT, I was grateful for the guidance of Bill Mitchell, who was director of the Media Lab while I was a predoctoral researcher. In spite of his many responsibilities, he always had time to meet and answer my questions. These people were also important in the early stages of the project: John Maeda, Chris Csikszentmihalyi, and Dan Ariely. I'd like to thank Adele Santos and Sanford Kwinter (now at Harvard GSD) in the School of Architecture for their enlightened views; Rosalind Williams and Leo Marx with the Science, Technology, and Society program; and Henry Jenkins and William Uricchio of Comparative Media Studies. And to friends and colleagues who I learned much from: Burak Arikan, Hilary Karls, Saeed Arida, Karrie Karahalios, Ivan Askwith, Ana María León, Yanni Loukissas, James Nadeau, Kelly Norton, Neri Oxman, Noah Paessel, Marc Schwartz, and Noah Vawter. In New York, many thanks to Clay Shirky, Kazy Varnelis, and Mabel O. Wilson, who have inspired my writings.

While completing my doctoral degree at University of California–Berkeley, I was grateful for Jean-Pierre Protzen, Nezar Alsayyad, and Eleanor Rosch, for their insight, comments and suggestions; they were invaluable in developing my skills as a researcher. Special thanks goes to Tara Graham; her keen intelligence and editorial rigor were essential to this project. I'd like to thank Ken Goldberg, who enthusiastically encouraged my research from the beginning. His direction of the Berkeley Center for New Media, as well as the Art, Technology, and Culture Colloquium, introduced me to a world of talented media artists and theorists: Greg Neimeyer, Sonya Rapoport,

Eric Paulos, Julian Stallabrass, Hertha Wong, and colleagues Kris Paulsen and Meredith Hoy. Much appreciation goes to Paul Rabinow for explaining how urgent is the need to observe contemporary publics. At California College of the Arts, I am grateful to my friend and mentor, Mitchell Schwarzer. Thanks also goes to David Meckel, Barry Katz, and Lisa Findley.

I was very fortunate to work with Felisa Salvago-Keyes at Routledge; her extensive knowledge of new media was an immeasurable asset to the book. My gratitude goes to Nick Cronbach for copyediting the final chapters. And much appreciation goes to the entire editorial staff at Routledge for bringing this project to fruition.

Special thanks goes to the Stanford University Archives: The Whole Earth Catalog (1968), Liza Loop papers, (1972–1988), Silicon Valley ephemera, and the staff at University of California–Berkeley Graduate Library; these resources enriched the project; the Dalhousie University Research Board; University of Illinois Research Board, whose grant made it possible for me to take time off from teaching to write this book; Kevin Franklin and HASTAC; and Christian Sandvig for his encouragement. I am grateful for Doug Armato for his comments and suggestions, to Cynthia Joba, Doug Sery, as well as my reviewers Mark Nunes and others unnamed. Much gratitude goes to my research assistants Shantel Martinez and Catherine Macan. I am grateful to all those who assisted me with images; to the people who responded to the study; to friends and colleagues who listened to my explorations and made suggestions: Kathryn Anthony, Anita Chan, Amanda Ciafone, Lynne Dearborn, Marcella Del Signore, Gale Fulton, Harriett Green, Kevin Hamilton, David Hayes, Stewart Hicks, Sharon Irish, Prita Meier, Julie Turnock, and to Tristan d'Estree Sterk, who said that by setting up a framework for human interaction, social media is a kind of architecture.

Figures

Introduction

SOCIAL MEDIA, PLURALISM, AND PLACE

At this moment, a plethora of online conversations are occurring around the globe, most of them unseen and unheard, except by their intended audiences. Blogs, chats, tweets, wikis, and social networking sites—all are part of media communities. Yet due to their newness and invisibility, how much can we say with certainty about those communities? How much do we really know about the conversations, participants, practices, and the meaning these hold for the groups or communities generating them?

This question is even more important today, as societies across the world are increasingly connected to one another via the Internet and mobile technologies. This impacts the traditional social practices surrounding communications, relationships, space, play, and work. Social media in particular has been associated with shaping political activism in the Middle East and North Africa, thus presenting opportunities for what scholars are deeming an expanded public. While a thread of literature already exists that emphasizes the changing nature of time and space brought about by advances in telecommunications, many of those writings focus on the socioeconomic and political conditions of late modernity.[1] Other texts address a postmodern discontinuity between the public and private spheres,[2] as well as increased social fragmentation.[3] Furthermore, empirical studies involving narrow sample groups of 14- to 18-year-olds may be too limited in scope.[4] However significant these contributions are to media studies, few writings have captured the contemporary phenomena of social media, either because they were written prior to the emergence of mobile technologies or their methodological range was too narrow. Missing from this literature is a perspective that encompasses today's dispersed place-based communities and a new understanding about bringing together physically separated individuals under the rubric of social media.

This book addresses the dynamic tension between spatial dispersion and social connection as manifested through networked publics. But instead of analyzing social media through a *utopian* or *dystopian* lens, I more interested in documenting how social media forms connections between human beings and physical space.

With this objective in mind, I draw from Bruno Latour's concept of a sociotechnological system that describes the microagency of shared objects in maintaining a social reality.[5] Furthermore, I suggest that as social communities, networked publics are created through social practices similar to those that shape communities in physical space. Networked publics consist of pluralistic participatory practices existing within an environmental spectrum—interdependent, and thus mutually constituted, with everyday life in the physical world.

My research draws insight from the urban planner Melvin Webber's *Community without Propinquity* (1963), which countered a tendency in sociology to exaggerate the loss of community, a view that opposed the notion of community with structures of complex association.[6] As an alternative, Webber proposed that one could attempt to understand community by identifying the nodes of communal organization that bind individuals together. My work draws on Webber's argument that friendships can be maintained at a distance, and alternative communities can emerge on the basis of affinities. Those principles reveal a deeper understanding of choice, flexibility, and the multiplicity of relational groupings.[7] Webber's conceptions of spatial dispersion and the transcendence of that dispersion emphasize the importance of time-space distancing on theories of community and the public sphere well before the Internet.

Where Webber left off—speaking about networks in a general way and not closely comparing the differences with face-to-face relationships—is the launching point for my own work and this book. Along with a philosophical examination of the public realm, my empirical research extends Manuel Castells's earlier project, *The Rise of the Network Society* (1996). According to Castells, networks constitute a new social morphology for our societies. My research surveys and interviews, conducted over a four-year period, represent an attempt to query those communities and structures of complex association in a more rigorous way. Their results tend to verify that social media typically foster categorical identities to a greater degree than the dense, multiplex, and systematic webs of relationships that have been associated with the term *network*. In addition, the terms *networks, community*, and *public sphere* in themselves can be misleading or conflated, in part because of the political dimensions they imply. This exploration must, therefore, include a history of technology as well as a discourse on media theory—both of which are grounded by empirical research.

Any study of networked publics should be accompanied by more direct attention to the social basis of discursive publics. In response to earlier theories, my intention is to situate social media in a deeper and more specific historical and social context. The problems of power, distribution networks, conflicting senses of history, and the various contingencies surrounding the ideas of subjectivity and political agency are continual reminders of how fraught this moment of communication technologies really is. Social media platforms are participating in shaping political change. As political destabilization presents a threat to established governments, it sparks increased surveillance measures, which in turn allows for the monitoring of civilians in both public spaces and private spheres. At present, the United Nations International Telecommunications Union (ITU) is drafting international legislation that could affect Internet free speech, privacy, and other human rights issues.

Writing from the perspective of an urbanist, I argue that the integration of everyday online social practices into education, work, and leisure has serious implications not only for ongoing social relations but, more importantly, for how we design our cities and, ultimately, how we choose to define public space, whether online or off. To misunderstand social media at this particular juncture will have profound implications for the future of our organizations. Because networked publics possess social, economic, and political dimensions, additional knowledge and understanding are crucial if designers and humanists are to make a timely and significant contribution to guiding their future development.

OVERVIEW

Any examination of social media will necessarily include a multithreaded history of society, culture, and technology, although it is not only a historical examination. The research for this book was organized as an articulated net-like structure. Larger historical trends, such as postmodern and postindustrial theories, inform the overall pattern, but I place geographic nodes linking together ideas, people, and technology. I am most concerned with how larger contextual forces converge with social, psychological, and technological forces to form meaningful connections.

To organize these multiple intellectual threads, the chapters are divided thematically. In Chapter One, "Reappropriating Social Media," the intertwined relationship of social media and public space is explored through Internet activism. Maintaining social media's legacy of participatory practices, this chapter showcases how digital spaces are not irrelevant to nondigital politics, but rather are increasingly interwoven and often the impetus to political and social action. Nonetheless, problematic tendencies remain. While new technologies offer increased affordances, governments are seeking to intervene through internal surveillance measures and international treaties. Conflicts regarding Internet governance and digital censorship could dramatically impact the global picture over the next few years.

Chapter Two, "Assembling the Publics," begins by asking what are the conditions that produce publicness? The theoretical inquiry is organized into three streams: In the first stream, a *spatial public* is examined to determine how historical conceptions were shaped by material space. In the second stream, a *media public* is traced through communication technologies, beginning with print media and television. In the third stream, a dispersed *networked public* is explored to see how networked relations became entangled with physical arrangement in space. At the conclusion, the three streams are brought together into a reconsideration of contemporary publicness.

In Chapter Three, "Origins of Networked Publics," a place-based geneal-ogy of social media is organized chronologically and thematically, tracing its origins from pre-Internet bulletin board systems (BBSes) to contemporary mobile technologies. That historical account describes a series of indepen-dent processes related to the economic restructuring of the market economy and information technology during the 1970s, contributing to a society or-ganized on a diverse cultural base due to increased access to information. Particular attention is paid to Silicon Valley and San Francisco, Califor-nia. The altruistic motivations of early BBSes enthusiasts are discussed and compared with later entrepreneurial objectives, framing a discussion on the knowledge commons, participatory culture, and market objectives.

Chapter Four, "Networked Identity Making," begins with a taxonomy of networked publics. The most prominent social media platform, Facebook, is closely analyzed, serving as one example of a range of social interactions available online. Online identity formation is critically examined within the media arts. There is further discussion on the significance of the cultural imaginary and its role in prefiguring the actual production of space. That relationship complicates the relationship between online space and physical space, such that there is consideration of how online participatory practices map onto social practices in the physical world.

Chapter Five, "Surveying Social Media," acknowledges that there is a lack of appropriate methods and frameworks for studying social media. The chapter, therefore, proposes Internet ethnography as one possible approach. The results of a mixed-methods study completed between 2008 and 2012 are presented. The findings are analyzed and interpreted, along with some unexpected results, including how networked publics provide opportunities for marginalized groups to create tactical communities where they prosper through everyday practices, finding modes of survival by using and subvert-ing the media infrastructure of the dominant culture. These spaces tran-scend temporality and locality by bridging seemingly paradoxical categories of spatial identification.

The concluding chapter, "Technological Innovation," considers the po-tential implications on the urban public realm. Just as earlier technological revolutions transformed the way that cities were imagined and configured, so too the Internet and mobile technologies have the potential to reconfigure our cities and social practices. Paying particular attention to these historical and theoretical linkages allows us to better trace, understand, and re-imagine the sociospatial-political issues affecting the public realm today and, thus, critically prepares us to modify technologies and infrastructure to suit di-verse needs. However, this is not a one-way street where only one side is impacting the other; instead, it is a dialectic, where we use media technolo-gies and, from what we generate, then impact society and the environment.

Over the past ten years, communication technologies have grown into an economic and cultural phenomenon. Coupled with wireless sensor

Figure 0.0   Zuccotti Park, New York City, New York. One year after Occupy Wall Street, metal barricades block access to the park (9/17/2012).
Credit: Clay Shirky

networks (WSN) and the contextual web, this Internet of Things is becoming increasingly pervasive within everyday spaces. Yet I contend that this is not just a multiplication of devices and applications, but rather a deep structural change regarding the natures of community, borders, and the global economy. If the city, as many have argued, is a type of organizing principal for a series of smaller networks (e.g., the ethno, techno, finance, media, and ideoscopes that comprise what Kevin Lynch calls the social imaginary), then networked publics have become their own organizing principle of space.

OBJECTIVES

In this book, an online morphology—social media—is examined as a means to obtain a richer understanding of contemporary cultural and spatial dynamics. Part of my aim is to describe the formative historical and cultural processes that participated in the emergence of social media. That effort has two principal objectives: first, to situate the phenomena within a specific locational context, and second, to explore the possible ramifications on public space. To fully understand the potential of social media, it is also necessary to understand the nature of everyday social relations, the quality of the interactions and communication, which includes the exchange of information, knowledge, identity formation, and the creation of bonds. That generalized knowledge (the cognitive tasks, socioemotional aspects, and social context of groups) is necessary to create social spaces in the physical world. Therefore, it is critical to view social media in tandem with the broader urban context. The research in this book contributes to contemporary discussions on publicness, in the sense that it questions the basis of previous theories of mediated social interaction while suggesting that their histories may be intertwined.

1   Reappropriating Social Media

Positive changes in the life of the country, including pro-democratic regime change, follow, rather than proceed, the development of a strong public sphere.

—Clay Shirky, "The Political Power of Social Media," *Foreign Affairs Journal*, Jan/Feb 2011

In late 2010 global events began to demonstrate that social media could support and empower marginalized groups. As has occurred with previous revolutions, associated technologies were championed as the impetus for social change, reflecting a technological determinist standpoint on the liberatory potential of Western technology, a position that sets up critical cultural binaries, such as modernity/tradition or the West/Middle East. These binaries presuppose a colonialist perspective harkening back to fictional narratives regarding the gifts of the West, building on such tropes as equating Christianity to progress, or in this case, technology to progress. While technology is clearly instrumental in Internet activism, the core issues are social, not technical.[1] For example, setting up a blog in Burma is helpful only if people dare to post, despite fears of arrest. Technological innovation tends to overcast the actions of the people on the ground who are protesting, as well as enables new methods of surveillance to emerge. While media outlets cover hot topics relating to the prowess and impact of technology, their attention to the long-term efforts and painstakingly slow progress of reform usually wanes quickly after a revolutionary moment.

What might be the motivations for playing up the role of technology in the recent Arab uprisings and in other revolutions? One answer *Foreign Affairs* editor Evgeny Morozov provides is that "by emphasizing the liberating role of the tools and downplaying the role of human agency, such accounts make Americans feel proud of their own contribution to events in the Middle East."[2] The very label of social media overestimates technology's importance and ignores the contribution of offline social networks.[3] This question has then arisen among academic and popular media: To what extent do social media influence political activism and change?

Some cultural commentators credit social media with catalyzing the North African and Middle East uprisings, proposing that together the social media constitute an open forum. In one camp, media theorist Clay Shirky credits social media. He argues that the unique affordances of social media—the ease and speed combined with many-to-many communication—allows for a more efficient method of disseminating information than before.[4] His claim suggests that social media have now expanded the democratic public sphere.

Others disagree, arguing that social media is not democratic. The moral suasion generated by the coming together of protesters in physical spaces triggered change, they say. Morozov falls into this camp, along with journalist Malcolm Gladwell. They both downplay the role of social media in the outbreak and organization of the uprisings. Morozov contends that underlying social and economic conditions, coupled with rising prices and unemployment, political repression, lack of political freedoms, and corruption prompted the uprisings.[5] Gladwell argues that strong local bonds were the primary determinant of political activism: The closer one was with those who were critical of the regime, the more likely one would be committed to the protest.[6] Strong bonds, whether created and strengthened through soccer clubs or other affiliations, were instrumental in creating solidarity between diverse groups.[7]

By analyzing the nature and function of social media in relation to the Arab uprisings and Internet activism more generally, we see that the two positions advanced by those camps are not totally antithetical; indeed, they complement each other. Spatial publics and networked publics are neither separate nor competing spheres. They are bound into a complex assemblage of human actants, media platforms, and transmission devices. Consequently, an explication of the positions held by both camps could produce

Figure 1.1 Mohandiseen, Cairo. Internet and mobile services had been effectively terminated as tens of thousands of Egyptians took to the streets calling for the resignation of Mubarak (1/28/2011).
Credit: Gigi Ibrahim with a RIM BlackBerry 9700

new insights that might begin to contribute to a more robust theory of publicness. Understanding both viewpoints can be useful in articulating some of the complex ways social media recasts public space into new, performative configurations. That transition from digital to nondigital political participation presents a significant intervention and sociospatial formation in an era where online and offline possession of space and spatial presence are increasingly critical.

While the main focus of the chapter is Arab online activism, I have included similar concerns raised by Internet activists from other parts of the world, such as China, New York, Thailand, and Iran.

BACKGROUND

In the Middle East, social media is promoting new social, cultural, and political agendas. In authoritarian countries with government censorship (e.g., China, Russia, Iran, and more recently Tunisia, Egypt, and Syria)[8] social media—particularly Facebook and Twitter—have been increasingly enlisted as counterpublic forums, defined as "as an explicitly articulated alternative to wider publics that exclude the interests of potential participants."[9] The ease of uploading real-time information enables organization and ad-hoc reporting of events. While most scholars accept that social media can address political inequalities and injustices by uniting a given population, is this phenomenon something new? Not if one considers that the use of the Internet for activism goes back more than two decades. In 1989 Tiananmen Square was one of the first demonstrations to use electronic technologies to organize and mobilize large groups of people in physical space; the information was transmitted by simple e-mail.[10] In 1999 the Seattle World Trade Organization demonstrations were organized through a website maintained by the Independent Media Center (Indymedia or IMC), an Internet news/events bulletin board system (BBS) with 150 individual and autonomous centers globally. Simple text messages were effectively used to coordinate the French and Algerian diaspora during their protests in 2005.[11]

Recent protests used Facebook, Twitter, and Short Message Service (SMS or text messages) to oppose government corruption, voter intimidation, and electoral fraud. The public demonstrations were not only purposeful in their respective localities, but they also brought national media attention to political causes vis-à-vis the Internet.[12] Events continue to suggest that it is no longer possible to understand the notion of public space without concurrently understanding its entanglement with social media and ubiquitous computing. Social networking sites have been used to facilitate social and sexual freedom in conservative societies. In 2007 the Revolutionary Association of Women's Rights (RAWA) in Afghanistan posted photos of Taliban oppression that were later accessed and instrumentalized by the U.S. army during their occupation.[13] Later that year, Burmese protest images and videos were posted on the Facebook group *Support the Monks Protest in Burma*. A highly coordinated use of social media occurred during the 2008–9 Israel-Gaza conflict, whereby amateur journalists reported developments over Facebook, YouTube and Twitter. To disseminate warnings, residents also tagged online satellite maps of the Gaza district via a social software application.[14] In Palestine, Twitter was used along with a new software platform, Ushahidi, to report protests and rocket attacks in real time by linking Twitter's application to Facebook and Google Maps.[15] Even simple technology can still be effective, as when the fax machine was enlisted in 2011 in response to the Egyptian government's clampdown on Internet services.[16] In such examples, where the free press is limited or nonexistent, everyday social media, as networked publics, served as effective methods to organize groups in order to redress political inequalities and injustices.[17]

Furthermore, information and communication tools can be used to develop new methods of distributed grassroots decision making. By enabling practices of assembly, alternative online publics can organize as if their constituents are gathered in virtual public spaces. Open-source protest (or in Egyptian nomenclature, *wiki-revolution*) was operative within Internet groups, leading to direct action in Tunisia (2011), Egypt (2011), Syria (2011), and New York (Occupy Wall Street, 2011).

The debate surrounding social media has been pushed to the forefront as the potential for a media-enabled democratic space intensifies.[18] It is disconcerting, however, that media pundits rely on anecdotal evidence, while the critical implications of recent historical events remain understudied.[19] Nearly three years before the demonstrations, the *New York Times* identified the *El-Facebook* group "6 April Youth Movement" as having dynamic debates among its 70,000 members. Their uncensored Facebook page, along with Twitter and Flickr, was used for ad-hoc organization and to disseminate information after workers' strikes on April 6, 2008, in the Mahalla-al-Kubra textile mills that resulted in rioting and police repression.[20] The group was predominantly young and educated, although most had not been politically active before.[21] Discussions focused on broad cultural topics, including religious and sexual freedom, nepotism in government, and the country's stagnant economy, but not revolution.[22] In 2010 another influential Facebook group, "We Are All Khaled Said," moderated by Google marketing manager Wael Ghonim, brought attention to a young Egyptian's death by police torture. Thus, well before the January 2011 demonstrations, an influential portion of the Egyptian population had already established a strong, vocal, and close-knit online community around heated political issues. Moreover, the new technological affordances of social media have changed the context of activism. Their ease of use makes for a more egalitarian method of information distribution—anyone with access to an Internet connection can freely post or upload images—which is significant.[23] These Internet communication tools designed to organize everyday mundane lives have been repurposed and appropriated for political causes. Thus, online communications *and* strong personal bonds, in addition to socioeconomic injustices, foster political activism.[24]

This debate is a continual reminder of one of the difficulties of cross-disciplinary discussions. What we can take from this is that social media practices have changed the context of publicness—and thereby its meaning. Social media supports populist dispersion of information through simultaneous many-to-many communication. Mobile devices in particular are rapidly modifying and transforming practices and protocols. Social media emerges as an individually accessible platform for the distribution of speech and images, while concurrently allowing one to observe the participation of others, resulting in a semivisible public space of assembly.[25] The networked structure of social media and mobile technologies create an expanded public by connecting members and thus inspiring political agency vis-à-vis shared knowledge.

There is another important aspect to the debate that was brought to the fore during the Occupy Wall Street movement. On September 17, 2011, several hundred people marched to Zuccotti Park in Lower Manhattan. Their online conversations included concerns about the increasing economic inequality in the United States and the undue influence of the financial services sector and corporations on government policies.[26] Further, there were more general aims framed around social justice. When the same social technologies were applied in both cases, why was there political change in some countries and not in others? As was discussed with the case of Egypt, one theory advanced was that Egyptian society is formed around strong bonds, in other words, offline social networks, that allowed diverse groups and allegiances to put aside individual differences and collectively work together toward a common objective, the removal of Hosni Mubarak.[27] While it is clear that Occupy Wall Street (OWS) was comprised of highly committed individuals, the national broadcast media trivialized the objectives of the movement. Further, as a nondemand movement, the OWS goals were less easily achieved. In spite of its limitations, however, national surveys confirmed that the majority of Americans agreed that governance should represent the 99 percent rather than business interests.[28] Perhaps for OWS, their significance was in their internal organization, specifically, the way the movements experimented with new democratic practices and instigated a *multitude form*, characterized by frequent assemblies and participatory decision-making structures.

Whether mundane or revolutionary, social media creates a distributed community, not in its material culture, but in the creative practices of knowledge sharing and the acknowledgement of that collective awareness. Cognitive scientist Steven Pinker describes it this way: In isolation, individuals may know something (e.g., that a government is corrupt), but they do not know that others know it too. In public assembly, however, everyone knows that everyone knows.[29] Direct speech, whether face-to face or electronically transmitted, is an explicit language that leads to the acquisition of knowledge. That mutual awareness, according to Pinker, produces new shared knowledge along with an ideological amplification. It provides

Figure 1.2   Chicago, IL. Occupy Chicago protestors wearing Guy Fawkes masks (10/14/2011).
Credit: Michael Kappel

a collective mandate to challenge the authority of the status quo. Similar to direct speech and public assembly, social media information sharing within a distributed community creates a call for agency.

Social media, however, is not simply about connections between individuals in physical space, but also about maintaining a virtual connection to a larger community, both local and international. For example, the OWS movement's conversation about economic inequality extended beyond the confines of Wall Street.

That generative process of publicness is inhibited when the dominant media is owned or controlled by authoritarian governments or multinational conglomerates as a one-way transmission. Whether through culture jamming, brandalism,[30] or Twitter, networked publics reinforce a conviction that free speech is important, that people are not isolated, that their voices are heard, and that they come together as a community—a dispersed *and* expanded public.

DISTRIBUTED KNOWLEDGE COMMUNITY

The networking of individuals over the Internet, whether local or international, can empower minority or marginalized groups by providing a forum in which to voice their objectives. By repurposing the quotidian *El-Facebook*,

Egyptians created an information distribution system for ad hoc mobiliza-
tion. Even though many Western Europeans listened to news reports on
events leading up to the Arab uprisings, few were aware of the conference
Internet at Liberty: The Promise and Peril of Online Expression (September
20–22, 2010), held just prior to the protests, and the direct impact it had
on both the protests and continued Internet activism. The conference was
integral to the play of events because it effectively connected activists in geographically isolated communities and from all walks of life. An alternative
community emerged from the conference among diverse bloggers, nongov-
ernmental organizations (NGOs), and human rights activists on the basis of
a common interest.[31]

Google has been hosting private and public conferences on the topics
of cyberactivism and censorship since 2010. The annual Internet at Liberty conference, cosponsored by Central European University[32] in Budapest,
Hungry, addressed issues of freedom on the web.[33] The three-day, invitation-
only conference attracted over 400 government officials, bloggers, web activists, media corporations, nonprofits, and NGOsfrom all over the world.
Its sessions covered topics ranging from net neutrality and security to the
role of the Internet in propagating rights-based freedoms and the boundaries of online expression. Noting the increased sophistication with which
governments were reappropriating technologies for censorship, security,
and surveillance on the web, Robert Boorstin, Google's director of public
policy, highlighted the conference's critical timing.[34] Although it was not
the first conference that Google had held on these topics, the conference in
Budapest was one of the first to be streamed online, and was, thus, more
transparent than those convened in the past.

At the conference, those advocating individual freedom of expression for
political or social organizing were in conflict with those representing private
corporate interests, such as Google or Facebook. Issues of privacy and individual freedoms dominated the conversations. The *Huffington Post* writer
and founder of *Hotspot Digital*, David Nassar asked, "How do we determine
and who determines when national security or group rights trump individual
ones? Who owns your personal data, both your identifying information and
your usage information?"[35] Nassar continued by addressing issues of national
security and the relatively new shifts of borders—not just in the physical sense
but also in the digital. Since many people were endangering their lives to attend this conference and be a part of these conversations, these concerns were
shared by many in attendance.[36] Digital advocate Mark Belinsky, founder of
the human rights group *Digital Democracy*, was cautious about the tenuous
relationship between governments and digital media. "It's important to be
mindful of the fact that governments are starting to increasingly clamp down
on the crucial tools that protect and preserve individual freedoms because
they don't have examples to the contrary to work with," he noted.

Since 2011, Internet governance has become a contested issue nationally
and internationally as countries attempt to control its effects. The Human

RightS Initiative (HRSI), an NGO working for the right to information as well as police and prison reform, reported that Google's newly launched transparency reports increase governmental accountability. Users can now see government requests to remove or censor content, thus making information that was previously confidential about users accessible.[37] Not only does this report create more government accountability, but the HRSI also noted how the data will be tremendously useful for researchers in the social sciences.

These observations and comments foreshadowed what was about to occur within a matter of months, first in Tunisia and then Egypt. The Budapest conference, along with others that took place in cities such as Beirut and Dubai, provided private meeting space and workshops for bloggers and techies who exchanged practical guidance on how to engage in grassroots advocacy and circumvent censorship.[38] Over a period of years, conferences and workshops held in physical space worked to collectivize and strengthen opinions later dispersed geographically in virtual space.[39] By providing discrete locations for dialogue and cross-community conversation among individuals and human rights groups, those discussions were conceivably more influential in the formation of activist coalitions across country borders.

SOCIAL SURVEILLANCE

While I have addressed the primarily positive accounts of social media's engagement with political activism, now I'd like to shift my direction to investigate the less visible and controversial aspects that compromise online public spheres. We have just discussed how social media can contribute to a new form of publicness, one that is partially invisible and distributed. However, what kind of public is this exactly? Proprietary (commercial) social networks (e.g., Facebook, Twitter, Google+) effectively create a privatized public.[40] While membership is potentially open and accessible to all, social media sites require registration, thereby limiting the conversation to other members. As theorist Michael Gardiner explains, "The forming of new publics, as a process of collectivization, can only take place against the background of a new form of privatization . . . that of self and subjectivity."[41] While the criticism of psychological privatization could be just as well levied at print media, social media is compounded with a technologically supported interface. On the one hand, social media creates a space that mediates and extends discourse beyond face-to-face interaction; on the other hand, it is not universally accessible.[42] The number of Egyptians participating in *El Face* was a minority of the population. For example, about one in nine Egyptians had Internet access in 2009, and only approximately 9 percent of those with access were on Facebook.[43] "Reaching working class Egyptians was not going to happen through the Internet and Facebook," Google executive Wael Ghonim acknowledged.[44] Printed flyers, mass text messaging, and telephone landlines turned out to be more effective.[45] Although access has increased dramatically since then, Internet accessibility in Egypt, as in the rest of the world, is limited to those who are literate and can afford it.[46] As envisioned, a truly democratic public is inclusive of all publics and all people. The Internet is a democratic public sphere only if the agents make it so, which is to say that they useopen standards for messaging and create software that constructs the context of communication (visible to all), *and* if computers or other handheld transmission devices are freely and universally available and secure. At present, these conditions are improving, but universal access is far from being realized.

We are all aware of hidden issues: Various websites and online services track each correspondence and purchase in order to better understand, analyze, and market each member's consumptive practices. Through data mining, aggregating, and selling, online forums are increasingly compromised.[47] While numerous media theorists accept the structural analytics, the market colonization of the Internet leaves many ethical issues unresolved. Due to this programmed default, we must question the ability for a privately held commercial space, whether online or off, to function as a true public space.[48] If a public space is privately owned, it is no longer public. For example, the owner of a privately demarcated sidewalk or shopping mall may prohibit political discussions or solicitation on that property at all times. Privately owned social media sites may remove content at will, as was the case when Hossam el-Hamalawy, an Egyptian blogger and rights activist, uploaded photos of Egypt's security police; Flickr subsequently removed the photos (*New York Times*, March 27, 2011). An image-sharing platform for amateur and professional photographers, Flickr is among the social media networks, along with Facebook, Twitter, and YouTube, that activist forces in the Middle East and North Africa have increasingly enlisted. In November 2007, YouTube had to negotiate controversial content posted by a human rights advocate that conflicted with its terms of service. The video-sharing website removed videos flagged as "inappropriate" by a community member that showed the Egyptian police torturing someone. Wael Abbas, an Egyptian journalist, was responsible for the original posting, along with many others. YouTube staff members later restored the videos after public resistance to their censureship.[49] (The company, owned by Google, now has a process in place to deal with such questions.)

Furthermore, Facebook group profiles in Britain were being deleted without warning or explanation. In May 2011 Facebook removed over fifty sites in twelve hours.[50] It may well be that these groups were in violation of Facebook's terms of agreement, which state that users must not create sites with fictional names. It is also possible that the action could be linked to a wider investigation of protest groups in Great Britain by the British Home Office. This new role for social media has put private companies in a difficult position: how to accommodate the reappropriation of these technologies and services while also appearing neutral.

As long as a social media platform is privately held, the platform is compromised. Government pressure may cause Facebook and other social media sites to suspend activist accounts and group pages for vague reasons.[51] This is an ever-present possibility, particularly in Egypt, Iran, and China, during times of social unrest.[52] These countries have contracts with Internet service providers that allow the government to discontinue the Internet's infrastructure or, when service providers are state owned, to make life difficult for Internet-based organizers. Such actions may be as simple as blocking the Twitter feed of Chinese artist-activist Ai Weiwei, or more serious as the Egyptian security forces arresting Wael Ghonim on January 28, 2011, for his involvement with the "We Are All Khaled Said" Facebook page. Regimes can also use social media for their own purposes, spreading disinformation on their own blogs, Facebook pages, and Twitter accounts.[53]

As social media platforms find increasingly sophisticated ways to engage with mobile technologies, those with access find a proliferation of opportunities for political action and social justice. Marginalized groups forming parallel discursive arenas, termed counterpublics, are often invisible. The ephemerality of a surreptitious counterpublic, hidden within Facebook, is successful partly by its very ubiquity. Nevertheless, the subterfuge, similar to a Trojan horse, will work only once. While many online sites have thrived because of their ability to fly under the radar, governments are now becoming more adept at blocking or filtering Internet minority forums and counterpublics. New agreements between proprietary platforms and state agencies sanctioning monitoring were initiated immediately after the Arab uprisings.[54] Events have outpaced the legal response, and at the time of printing, legal authority remains unclear in this area.

As social justice movements challenge previously constructed notions of publicness online and offline, a critical tension exists between the rights for open free speech and the proponents of closed surveillance. The irony is that the same network structure that enables many-to-many communication also allows for tracing every communication back to its original source. National governments have not been far behind in using the same technology to locate dissenters for arrest and imprisonment, or to paralyze opposition. It was not coincidental that artist and outspoken Twitter activist Ai Weiwei disappeared (along with many other Chinese dissidents) shortly after the Arab uprisings. As long as a social media platform is held privately, it is subject to government coercion and surveillance, although organizations may attempt to keep this information away from its members in the fear that they might delete their profiles or join a different networked public.

Just as some employers may use social media sites to monitor employees, nations may watch their citizens' political activities. The structural configurations of networked publics do, by default, record everything in the process of transmission across the network. This structural capacity makes it possible for intelligence organizations to trace members of online groups and their e-correspondence. Conventional cellular phones can be used to locate individuals through a method known as pinging.[55] Factory-embedded global positioning systems (GPS) and sensors automatically provide location information for smartphones, enabling state authorities to track and monitor physical movements of people, including activists, without due process.

Relevant to our discussion here, worldwide news coverage during the Arab uprisings further illuminated the tensions between cherished Western tropes of democracy and Arab activity. Just as the U.S. government promotes social media for Middle Eastern activism,[56] its own relationship to social media is highly contentious. "US interests (and their surveillance tactics) now make the Internet a more dangerous place for the Arab bloggers [who] used to experience it as a free space devoid of political meaning," said *Global Voices* blogger Ben Gharbia.[57] U.S. foreign policy, advanced by military as well as corporate interests, aggressively seeks to control online free speech and the use of technology for social and political change, thereby making any dissident a potential target.

While authoritarian states have long seen cyberspace as a possible threat and are increasingly vulnerable to direct political action through social media, political regimes in the Middle East are not the only entities to experience sweeping change in terms of censorship across governments and borders. Around the globe, governments are ushering in legislative changes to surveillance policies with minimal public discussion of such actions.[58] Some of these changes have been proactively resisted with some success, although the results have rarely been guaranteed for long periods of time. Social media corporations have not been exempt from international pressures and have also modified their censorship laws to placate local and national governments. In June 2010 the U.S. government, as well as private companies such as Google and Twitter, imposed new censorship rules.[59]

The crucial issue is that there are no legal restrictions in place as yet that protect individual online privacy. Monitoring can take place without legal permission. Case in point: On Thursday, June 14, 2012, the British government proposed a draft communications bill that would produce an overall collection and retention system of all online data to prevent terrorism and disrupt major crime. The nonprofit organization Privacy International, which opposed the bill, pointed out in parliament that "the technology that is being proposed is only currently deployed in Kazakhstan, China, and Iran, . . . subjecting citizens to the near certainty of ongoing and unremitting interference in their private lives."[60]

The bill remains on the table. In December 2012 the International Telecommunications Union (ITU), a United Nations (UN) organization that counts 193 countries as its members, sought to add regulating the Internet to its existing regulatory roles. New policies were discussed at a summit held in Dubai, where the strongest supporters included regimes such as China, Russia, Iran, Tajikistan, and Uzbekistan. Those countries submitted a proposal to the UN General Assembly for an international code of conduct for information security. The proposal's goal is to establish government-led international norms and rules standardizing countries' behavior concerning information and cyberspace. These countries' goals for the summit included an assertion of national sovereignty over cyber communication; a clamp-down on anonymity and encryption; and a change in global governance by enacting a country-by-country policy.[61] While the ITU describes itself as a "multistakeholder" organization, decision making is typically reserved for government agencies, and thus human rights groups were not allowed to participate in the discussions.[62] Although England, the United States, and Canada opposed the new policies by refusing to sign the treaty, what is certain is that multinational legislative changes are still pending. Further-more, the decisions made will, eventually, become a permanent part of the Internet's operations.

Increased accessibility to networked publics has proceeded in lockstep with an equivalent loss of privacy. For many activist groups, new modifi-cations of internal (company) censorship laws for Twitter and Google ap-pear more dangerous than international surveillance legislation. During late January 2012, Twitter announced it would begin censoring tweets based on local laws due to requests from multiple governments.[63] The company stated that the new changes would actually encourage participation from governments that previously had banned Twitter, thus allowing for more transparency. While Twitter users perceive themselves as a global commu-nity, at the same time, each country has its specific concerns. This action, Twitter officials explained, will help with global accountability issues: for the United States it is copyright laws, for Britain it is libel laws, in France and Germany it is pro-Nazi expressions, and in China it is antigovernment sentiments.[64] "How [do] you respect all the laws or follow all the laws to the extent you think they should be followed while still allowing people to get the content elsewhere?" noted Google's chief legal officer, David Drum-mond, on the complex ethical issues at stake.[65]

Critics were quick to highlight the potential economic factors influencing the decision. Some claimed that by modifying its censorship laws, Twitter was trying to appease China and participate in its social market.[66] "Should [Twitter] be more of a free speech tool that can be used in defiance of gov-ernments, as happened during the Arab Spring protests, or a commercial venture that necessarily must obey the laws of the lands where it seeks to attract customers and eventually make money?" people have asked.[67] This complicated question will have to wait for its controversial answer.

What's at stake here? The majority opposing Twitter's new policy claim that if these policies had been enacted in 2010, the Arab uprisings would have never occurred. "This decision is really worrying," said Larbi Hilali, a prode-mocracy blogger and tweeter from Morocco. "There will be [one] Twitter for democratic countries and [a censored] Twitter for the others." These new policies are more restrictive. In Cuba, opposition blogger Yoani Sanchez said, "Twitter will remove messages at the request of governments." She tweeted,

"It is we citizens who will end up losing with these new rules."[68] Compounding these fears is Google's decision to follow in the footsteps of Twitter by adopting a per country censorship policy.[69] Google's blog service, blogger, will now be monitored for unlawful and illegal postings based on local and national laws. Like Twitter, Google announced this would help increase transparency around the world as well as encourage more people to promote freedom of expression. However, the British newspaper the *Daily Mail* commented, "The similarity to Twitter's policy is not coincidental." They share the same legal counsel and recognize that proprietary platforms are not above the law.[70]

Social media supports rapid political organizing, but it also allows for state surveillance. And the game of cat and mouse continues. For example, as proprietary outlets for information sharing and organizing are shut down, Syrian protestors are constantly creating new outlets. Furthermore, dissidents are using certain web proxies (e.g., instant messaging programs, old-school word of mouth), which some argue are more difficult to track. In other countries, dissidents are using mobile devices to capture video and disseminate it; certain governments, however, are tapping mobile phones, claiming they are public. Moreover, users of phones requiring a Subscriber Identity Module (SIM card) must provide information that governments can also use to track phone users.[71] Furthermore, the structural affordances of GPS-enabled mobile devices will continue to reinsert themselves. Twitter allows for amateur reporting during journalistic blackouts, but the platform can be used for reconnaissance of spatial movements. This puts protestors in a precarious position as social media becomes the primary space in which to organize.

Online transmissions can be traced, so they are not secure. The digital trail of information that is left behind suggests that in the near future every action will be trackable, not just by the state, but by anyone able to pay for that information. As a result, many counterpublic sites, most recently in the Middle East, have responded by becoming mobile within the Internet. They have done so by changing their IP addresses and only disclosing the new addresses to their members—face-to-face. As new developments in social media practices and national legislative changes continue to reconfigure the public, historical definitions of publicness are rapidly becoming obsolete.

The year 2011 was documented by historians as a year of social and digital unrest with its impacts and influences only beginning to produce immediate and long-term changes.[72] Social media platforms play an important part in the process of building consensus, providing a sense of community, recruiting a critical mass, and mobilizing action beyond the virtual and into the physical realm.

PUBLIC SPACE AS SITE OF PERFORMANCE

Facebook pages, such as the previously mentioned "April 6th" and "We Are All Khaled Said," have demonstrated their important role in constructing consensus, establishing community, and mobilizing action beyond the on-line discursive world into the physical space of the streets. In nondemocratic societies lacking a free press, sites such as Facebook provide platforms to launch new ideas, debate issues, and disseminate information about current events. In essence, these platforms give individuals agency to use social media *as if it is*, in fact, a public space. This is only possible because there are technological properties specific to the Internet and social media that earlier forms of media do not share. These affordances—such as speed; ease of transmitting text, images, and video; mainstream as well as subaltern access; and distribution of news and information—make crackdown difficult in the long term since certain industries are dependent on Internet transactions and exchange.[73] Thus, social media platforms, despite their compromise and contamination, are still more accessible, and arguably more democratic, and more difficult to censure than what was previously available to these populations.

Spatial publics and networked publics can no longer be understood as discrete operational spheres because the two are increasingly entangled. What marked the Arab uprisings, however, as both a case study and discursive turn in the so-called digital revolution, was not necessarily what occurred online, but rather what happened when the government of Egypt terminated Internet access for four days in January 2011. Working under the assumption that terminating Internet and mobile phone access would curtail political unrest and riots, the Egyptian government (as well as the U.S. government) was unprepared for what actually occurred: Residents left the digital public sphere, walked their neighborhoods, knocked on doors, posted flyers, and spread the word face-to-face. When looked at closely, the media blackout served to mobilize the uprising and, in turn, to reconnect the city. In sum, it was a combination of Internet tactics, along with street tactics, that enabled the revolution to play out as it did.[74] This transition from digital to nondigital political participation presented a significant sociospatial development in an era where online and offline possessions of space are increasingly critical. The innate response when online activism is hindered—as evidenced in Tehran, Cairo, New York, and indeed throughout much of history—is to gather and collectively demonstrate in the physical space of the streets.

That brings the discussion to the main point: Networked publics and physical publics are not separate or competing spheres; they are completing spheres. Social media is seen as a mutual process where structural media and human actions coproduce each other—a chain of circumstance connects both. A Facebook page may emerge as a simple discussion forum, but as members begin to discuss events and their implications, as opinions are voiced and heard, a consensus of thought develops online. Plans and organizational efforts follow. People leave the confines of their screens, offices, schools, and homes and move into the streets to make their voices heard and presence known. The crucial point here is that once a demonstration has moved into the streets—to a physical public space—it is videotaped by individuals, as well as national and international news sources. An important circularity of imaging connects the active practices of a local networked public to the global media public, swaying world opinion. This point is hardly lost on organizers. Imaging is captured and distributed throughout other media channels. Whether mainstream, online, or mobile, media feeds raise awareness and nurture the ongoing cycle of events. A circularity of imaging is critical to understanding the intertwined relationship between media publics and physical publics. The two cannot be separated for they exist in an equivalent reciprocal relationship, registering cause and effect almost simultaneously. Events have demonstrated that public space and social media are part of a cycle of performance, and as such, they are utterly enmeshed and interconnected.

CONCLUSION

Questions about the efficacy of the public sphere continue to arise. As social justice movements challenge previously held notions concerning the construction of public space online and offline, a tension between Habermasian ideals of democratic publics and a Foucauldian observation of biopolitics and surveillance is emerging.[75] Unlike a unitary public, however, today's networked publics are compromised and contingent, flickering between visibility and invisibility.[76] Not only is this sphere relative and variable, but the term *public* is now conceptually bound within its opposite, *private*. As a media audience, it is technologically dependent and thereby unstable. "A public sphere depends on the opening up of a social space for a particular kind of repeated and open-ended interaction," according to theorist James Bohman, "and as such, requires technologies and institutions to secure its continued existence and regularize opportunities and access to it."[77] As long as there is a possibility that these sites may be taken offline for any reason (e.g., due to state interference or corporate censorship) there is the possibility of a substantial loss of a public sphere.

At the time of this writing, the unprecedented hubris about the undisputed role played by technology in overthrowing nondemocratic regimes requires further discussion and analysis. Critical media artist Laurier Rochon contends that geopolitical decisions are being made based on "projections of our own ideals onto the technology itself."[78] The ways in which we construe publicness are not merely theories; rather, our interpretations underlie how our institutions are organized and the degrees of freedoms bestowed. This is why it is crucial to investigate issues in relation to the formative sociospatial processes underway prior to the Arab uprising and to think critically of claims such as "if you want to liberate a society, just give them the Internet."[79] The creation of a civil society is a long-term venture.

Even though the play of social media in the public sphere and in the occurrence of revolutionary change can be contradictory, there is no guarantee that rights will be permanently instituted in the face of continual social and technical challenges. Online social networks can be used just as easily to limit as to liberate. As long as there is a chance that these sites can be monitored and conversations tracked, there is also a chance that free public discourse will be compromised. As evidenced with social media, technology has multiple dimensions and may be repurposed for different objectives. Social media, thereby, can be instrumentalized to lead democratic initiatives as well as hamper them.

2   Assembling the Publics

In the debate on public space, references are still being made to traditional examples: coffeehouses in which politics were discussed, boulevards where vagrants warily eye the bourgeoisie, old city squares used by a diverse public. But are these public spaces still the spaces of the contemporary city? Has the public not become so diverse that a space with which everyone identifies no longer exists?
—Jonathan Budd, *World Architecture*, 2008

As everyday practices increasingly include social media, our notions of public space and the public sphere are altering. For the purposes of this discussion, the term *public sphere* refers to a set of physical or mediated spaces where people can gather and share information, debate opinions, and tease out their political interests and social needs with other participants. While some scholars argue that social media (and the Internet more broadly) dislocates local knowledge and politics to perpetuate a placeless, homogenous global space, others highlight the interdependent relationship of online spaces and offline activities. Either way, divisions between digital and nondigital public spaces are becoming less distinct, resulting in an entanglement of media platforms and practices, formations and allegiances across space and time. As a result, a critical tension between historicized views of *spatial publics* and more recent observations of *networked publics* is emerging. These spaces began on independent trajectories, evolved through mutually dependent relations, and emerge as complex assemblages. Even as new forms, they are still conflicted by the presence of unique sociopolitical histories.

Political unrest and revolution demand a close examination of social media's operative agencies in physical space. The condition of publicness is not a singular, stable entity, but rather a provisional phenomena, historically complex and variable. It is necessary, therefore, to begin with a brief disambiguation of the term *public*, followed by a theoretical and chronological analysis of the *spatial public*, the *media public*, and the *networked public*. While each is at once separate and interwoven, for clarity they will be explored one at a time. Finally, the three streams will be brought together to advance a theory of *alternative publics*, describing a reflexive relationship between social media, governance, and actions of the everyday. While this history is still being written, social media activism is subverting boundaries, laws, and policies—thereby creating new conditions necessitating renegotiation.

SPATIAL PUBLICS (THE URBAN)

The concept of *publicness* is part of a complex and slippery genealogy. The term *public* is heavily contested, having multiple meanings, and is used across disciplines to signify different concepts. If we are to understand the imbrications of social media with public space, we must deconstruct what the term *public* has meant historically. By examining definitions over time, it is possible to see how inherited notions are provisional, at once socially constructed and context bound.

In one of the earliest accounts of the term, *public* meant "of the people" in Old French (1311); yet even then the word had been altered. It was derived from the Latin *pubes*, meaning "adult population," combined with *poplicus* and/or *populus*, meaning "pertaining to the people." Thus, the concept of an adult (or exclusive) public came into being.[1] By 1470 the term *public* referred to "the common good in society."[2] A related term, the *commons*, was then a portion of shared open ground where livestock could collectively graze. Later, the term *public* took on the connotation of "visible or open to the community."[3] In contrast, the term *private* referred to anything considered privileged, at a high governmental level, and related to class position. It can be argued that the term *private* emerged out of aristocratic privilege.[4] The majority of the medieval populace was economically and socially bonded to a local entity, and consequently, they were not perceived as individuals, at least not as defined by the political structures of the time.

If the term *public* originally referred to any space belonging to and shared by the community, then the discourse and performance that took place within that space were also considered public. According to medieval practices, the tripartite of actant/space/rituals could be openly transmitted only in designated places, whether plaza, market, or sanctified square[5]— places accessible to all and where information was exchanged face-to-face. Practices, ideologies, and space were bundled into one assemblage of publicness. In premodern times, it was inconceivable to individuate sociocultural practices from their space of performance; the two, space and sphere, were effectively equivalent.

By the seventeenth century, definitions of terms *public* and *private* had moved closer to present definitions. Due to economic shifts, including the emergence of an increasingly large merchant class, the term *private* came to be defined as a sheltered region of life comprised of family and friends.[6] The term *public* was used when designating theaters, libraries, museums, and schools—institutions that had been constructed for the public benefit by the state.[7] Questions still arise regarding whether or not these institutions were truly public in the egalitarian sense. Public spaces in the seventeenth century may have been construed as public by the bourgeoisie, but they operated under their own prescriptive codes.[8] Dress codes, price of tickets, and cultural education determined access to theaters, libraries, and museums and acted as social filters. While these institutions extended formerly aristocratic cultural privileges and practices to the bourgeoisie, participation was circumscribed.

Acknowledging that the history of public space is a separate subject, my intention is not to present an exhaustive genealogy of publics, but merely to demonstrate that numerous, contextualized understandings can inform the word *public*.

Considering past definitions and comparing them to the modern urban sphere has been a common source of critique since the 1950s when the postwar city came under scrutiny by designers, planners, and social scientists. While the focus of this chapter does not allow for consideration of all of the influential thinking during the postwar period, one important position discusses how spatial theories recast the urban context.[9] This line of thought explores the everyday by conceptualizing a relational and dynamic model of spatial production.[10]

Figure 2.1   Hyde Park, London
Since the mid-1800s, Speaker's Corner has been designated as a public area where
people can speak freely on any topic (6/26/2011)
Credit: Keyphotos

During the postwar period, the urban public realm became one of the defining themes of cultural thought. Notions of a collective vision for a socially just society emerged through a discourse on spatial practice, or the space produced in everyday life.[11] Spatial publics are defined as physical publics that are open, accessible to or shared by all members of the community (for example, public space, streets, water supply, or parks); supported by or for the benefit of people as a whole, as in *common*. Spatial publics may also refer to the provision of services to the people under some degree of state or civic control (for example, railroads, Internet, or Wi-Fi).

Contained within the cultural and political ferment of the 1960s, Situationist International—a group of artists, architects, and philosophers—criticized the dehumanizing effects of modernism and emergent consumer culture on the urban environment.[12] Spatial production, as philosopher Henri Lefebvre argued, is a series of negotiations between the ordering objectives of governments and its economic interests, and the personal trajectory of its inhabitants—their histories, memories, and symbolic interpretations of space.[13] The production of space, then, cannot be separated from more extensive organizing forces, and thus, it is highly specific and culturally active. Individuals act as social agents and produce space in the process of everyday actions; however, their actions are influenced by psychological, sociocultural, economic, and technological factors. Hence, space is the outcome of internal perceptions and external actions. At the same time, spaces constrain and enable actions, so space and action are interconnected. This system, nonetheless, is not deterministic. Cultural adaptation and misuse between elements can occur.[14] Reflexive actions between actants, conditions, and technologies can reverse a predefined spatial hierarchy, a topic we will return to later.[15]

The rapid rate of technological change characteristic of postindustrial societies called for new methods of organizing space that could facilitate the smooth, integrated flow of objects and information. At the 1958 Delos Summit, the field of *Ekistics* (a complex term signifying settlement within ecological balance) was launched by the Greek architect and planner C. A. Doxiadis. Along with the architect Buckminster Fuller and cultural theorist Marshall McLuhan, they proposed the "invisible extension of the physical."[16] Inspired by systems theory, they believed that spatial patterns would follow from detecting patterns in the flow of information. These visionary proposals initiated urban planning within a grid of networks and special interest communities[17]—all predating the Internet.

The 1960s was marked by a philosophical transition away from understanding urban space as a neutral container toward an understanding of it as a conductive medium for the movements and exchanges of people, information, and objects. Some spatial theorists envisioned relational structures as applied topologies that could be projected onto physical social space. In particular, urban planner Melvin Webber's notion of "city as a communication system"[18] and architectural critic Reynar Banham's "autopia"[19] contributed to an increased understanding of the urban condition as a dynamic social space. A vigorous discussion emerged from the University of California–Berkeley College of Environmental Design, where planners theorized that communication technologies would begin to define an urban realm that "is neither urban settlement nor territory, but heterogeneous groups of people communicating with each other through space" and where "communities of associates are no longer synonymous with the communities of place."[20] Urban planners contrasted the physical characteristics of a place with the ongoing intellectual and cultural interconnections. Indeed, a community is comprised of the social relations and informational exchanges that bind it together.[21]

An inherited materialist perspective—one that describes an urban entity bounded by buildings—fails to capture the complexity of social patterns and actions today. An idealized bounded concept of the city excludes overlapping expressions, expressions that are in many ways as imprecise as the words *public* and *private*. Consider two people in private conversation on a bench in a public park, for example. As an alternative, there is a line of thought that proposes that urban areas are not simply defined by architectural artifacts or even population density patterns, but rather by the interdependent interactions between urban agents. What we construe as the *spatial public* is actually the way space adapts to the everyday actions of habitants in lived space. A city, then, is the spatial adaptation to social practices and information exchange.[22] To borrow Webber's phrase, the contemporary city can be understood as an "information system," and it can be conceptualized at a second-order abstraction, whereby the forces behind the form play a role in producing the form. Whereas technological determinists perceived change as originating from modern advances in technology, spatial theorists, in contrast, probed further to inquire into the specific economic and geographic driving forces for those very occurrences. These traditions positioned space as inherently caught up in social relations, thus producing and consuming them.

Cultural theorist Frederic Jameson describes this development as a *spatial turn*, one that defined a historical shift from modernism proper to the postmodern.[23] Moreover, the spatial turn acknowledges geographical specificity; in other words, space is culturally specific and appropriated differently within different cultures.[24] The complex relationships adhering between objects, people, and places are considered the spatial culture.[25] Consequently, what is most urban is not necessarily population density or agglomeration but specialization, the concomitant interdependence and human relations by which interdependencies are satisfied.[26] Adhering to postmodern perspectives, a relational model accepts the distinctiveness of local knowledge resources for the production of heterogeneous places. By understanding the development of a city through demographics, communication, and transportation, spatial theorists and urban planners not only acknowledge the dynamic interactions comprising a city, but more importantly, also conceptualize how migration and economic dispersal can become formative urban factors. Thus, it is impossible to understand space without understanding how people use and move through it.

While the definition of a city envisioned as an information system is compelling, it leaves unaddressed many other important factors at work in the late twentieth century. Market forces expressed through new means of accumulation and distribution were concurrently placing pressure on the historical centralized city and thereby reshaping its borders and diffusing it boundaries. During the early 1970s, independent processes related to the economic restructuring of the market economy and advances with information technology combined to create an emerging order with the characteristics of complexity and diversity. That emerging order describes a society organized on a broadly shared cultural base due to increased access to information (e.g., radio, television, the Internet). The information age, what Manuel Castells calls the "network society,"[27] is organized around new forms of time and space. It links up distant locales around shared functions and meanings, and thereby "reconceptualizes spatial arrangements under a new technological paradigm,"[28] a type of space allowing for distant, synchronous, and real-time interaction. Unlike those living in the historically bounded city, we live in cities today that are conditioned by cultural networks that fall across a spectrum from centralized to distributed.

Thus, the postmodern, postindustrial urban environment is ripe for reconsideration, but it is hindered by idealized conceptions of the spatial public—a romanticized Western European version described by classical canons, preconceived visual attributes, hierarchical centers, and clear boundary separations.[29] The postmodern urban condition can be described as a disparate spatial dispersion, a pattern reflective of increasing diversity in the economy, politics, and cultural life. It is the counterpart to a series of technological developments that allow for spatial separation between closely connected individuals and groups. What is termed *splintered urbanism* documents the uneven economic and technological development through hard infrastructures—transportation systems, electrical grids, and fiber optic networks—that are significantly and permanently altering the relationship between time and space.[30] Today, soft infrastructure—wireless technologies, the Internet, and social media—have equal potential to produce new kinds of space outside of inherited systems.

The contemporary city is based on a pattern of dispersal where individuals construct their sense of place from a series of physically disconnected locations or nodes connected by transport and communication channels. As such, the contemporary city has evolved into a nonhierarchy of places and networks. This does not ignore the problems associated with distance and dispersal, however. The norm of physical space is being displaced by a norm of connectivity, argues Castells.[31] One conclusion is that, at a deep fundamental level, place might not matter anymore.[32] Unlike a notion of community that is grounded in a particular location, a new pattern of social relationships can be created that spans international borders.

In that example, communities of associates are not necessarily synonymous with the communities of place to which previous generations held fast.[33] Communication and transportation systems move information and objects across space, making it easier for individuals to form bonds with others based on shared interests. These special-interest communities may be professional, intellectual, political, religious, fan oriented, hobbyist, or social in nature. Furthermore, spatial proximity or concentration may not be necessary to sustain close bonds beyond the formative stages of development.[34] This is an increasingly important feature of contemporary urbanization: – communication and transportation improvements have made it possible for anyone (not just urbanites) to participate in a more expansive cultural life.

Returning to an earlier point, to say that place might not matter anymore is at once provocative and not entirely true. If urban formations adapt to everyday social practices, it seems inevitable that there will always be cultural or economic specificities. As urban theorist Richard Florida argues, location represents a locus of intellectual and cultural capital where professional or cultural interests and market conditions promote more intensive concentrations.[35] Even with present-day advances in communication technology, commerce still clusters geographically. Silicon Valley, where an infusion of academic and military research, as well as venture capital, fosters entrepreneurial interests, is an example of this. Without an exchange of ideas and capital, cities would cease to exist. Due to this exchange, wealth tends to accumulate wherever human intelligence clusters evolve.[36] Like-minded individuals tend to coalesce, whether online or offline.[37]

Granted that affinities attract, a distributed network offers a very different model of social organization than centralized or decentralized (i.e., suburban) models, which still dominate the hierarchical structure of the contemporary city. A distributed network is dispersed and nonhierarchical; however, it is not self-organizing. Mostly invisible, new kinds of communities are emerging by way of wireless technologies, social media, sensors, and robotics in physical space. The *Telegarten* project by the University of California–Berkeley media artist and industrial engineer Ken Goldberg is an example of this. It enables a community of dispersed individuals to tend an actual garden online.[38] Through use of the Internet, these individuals plant seeds, water, and share responsibility for the garden by controlling a place-based robotic arm. The convergence of social media, wireless sensor networks, and robotic technologies in physical space is becoming increasingly prevalent. It is clear today that we are deeply embedded in cultures partly formed by new information technologies and partly entrenched within older spatial models; both play a role in the formation of contemporary subjectivities.

MEDIA PUBLICS (THE MEDIA)

While much of today's research in new media focuses on technology, it is important to remember that all media were once new.[39] When they were developed, writing, the printing press, and the radio, for example, were unlike any previous modes of communication. In this respect, new media research is situated within a more extensive history related to science, technology, and society. Each of the aforementioned inventions eventually led to subsequent social and cultural disruptions that were unpredictable at the outset. Technology, then, is never neutral, because new technology changes the context in which a task is performed, and that change can then also change the content.[40] While said change is inevitable, it is not purely deterministic. Studies confirm that technology develops differently in different contexts; for example, mobile banking practices differ in Mumbai and Minneapolis.[41]

During the fifteenth century, the invention of the printing press contributed to the first information revolution. The mass dissemination of texts led to the emergence of a collective discourse that was cultural, scientific, and political. In addition, the invention of the printing press was credited with larger social transformations, including the increased cultural exchange during the Renaissance, the Protestant Reformation, the establishment of scientific journals and scientific inquiry, and the dissemination of populist notions shaping the American and French Revolutions.[42] The printing press, in particular, demonstrates how widespread and unpredictable technology's effects can be. Just as the agricultural and industrial revolutions transformed the way that cities were imagined and configured, so too the Internet and new media platforms have the potential to reconfigure our cities and social practices.

Popular journalists optimistically claim that the Internet offers new possibilities for political participation and that it has the potential to replace earlier mass media models of democracy. Most scholars, however, are still undecided about how and to what degree the Internet will contribute to a new public realm. One view takes the position that institutions, such as voting and parliamentary assemblies, are fixed and unchanging—and the Internet will eventually evolve into a conventional broadcast model. A contrasting position upholds that any new technology also includes new possibilities. Both positions presume a kind of technological determinism that is devoid of cultural context.[43]

The structural properties of mediation, as well as the asynchronicity of social relations in time and space change social environments and, thus, influence people and their behaviors.[44] The vast transmission range of broadcast media displaced the stability of place. "Electronic media," according to communication theorist Joshua Meyrowitz, "affects us not through [its] content, but by changing the 'situational geography' of social life."[45] Distancing of audiences reconfigures publics in scale, complicates the boundaries between public and private, and collapses distinct social contexts, all of which challenge the authority of physical place to circumscribe public agency.[46] All of these effects of mediation have the potential to change the social and cultural environment of publics.

Architecture, as a cultural organizer, structures social relations, but now it can be argued that the Internet produces similar effects. The existence of a meaningful public sphere today depends not only on physical space but also on accessible communication technologies and institutions that create an intermediate space to extend the discourse beyond face-to-face interaction. According to sociologist James Bohman, writing, as a new media, opened up an "indefinite social space for possibilities with spatial extension of the audience and temporal extension of both uptake and response."[47] The printed word also resulted in a new form of interaction; it extended the one-to-many form of communication to an indeterminate mass audience, as did radio and television.

In *The Structural Transformation of the Public Sphere* (1963), Jürgen Habermas discussed the roles of print culture and public opinion in eighteenth-century Europe. While Habermas's idealized forum consisted of people physically present for face-to-face interaction, he also recognized the importance of the print industry—newspapers, pamphlets, and books. Printed publications exerted a powerful influence on political life, separate from the traditional ruling agency exerted by the king, aristocracy, and parliament. It was not simply the growth of publishing that created the public sphere, "it was the simultaneous dawn of a kind of consciousness that the public could be systematically addressed through a pamphlet as if a group of strangers were gathered together in a giant auditorium."[48] For Habermas, public space designates less a particular space than a particular form of interaction that cuts across a variety of institutions and spaces. Consequently, the conflation of public space with public sphere misses an important point about a disembodied arena of argumentation. Habermas visualized this public sphere as a potential democratic utopia where individuals could discuss national issues and come to common consent. Subsequently, he described the loss of this democratic sphere during the nineteenth and early twentieth century, when publishing media became consolidated in the hands of a few. The press media was decreasingly a voice of a democratic public (if there ever was one); instead, it evolved into an instrument of hegemonic forces.[49]

Print-based media, nevertheless, can participate in the construction of an active public sphere, which means it can enable a distributed discourse. But is this sphere egalitarian? Comparing the transmission structure of print-based media with the Internet, we find that, while both are forms of media transmission, their organizational structure is very different. Print-based media is typically a *one-to-many* transmission, whereas online-networked publics are *many to many*. Along similar lines, the Habermasian public sphere is presented as a rationalized conceptual order: monolithic, overarching, and operating as a clearly defined entity. Unlike the historical public sphere, postmodernism reflects a division of the social sphere into diverse specificities that defy the possibility of a unified or coherent overview. Those spaces of difference, as alternative publics, serve a justified purpose. For example, Michel Foucault calls for a society with many heterotopias, emphasizing that society is not only a space with several places for the affirmation of difference, but it is also a means of escape from authoritarianism and repression.[50] This view warns that a society without any kind of cultural plurality, without dissent and new ideas, has the potential to become an inherently repressive one, as demonstrated in countries currently limiting Internet access and legislating censorship. Counterpublic opinion, that which counters the dominant discourse, addresses this irregularity and represents a subaltern constituency. The discourse on counterpublics, as cultural theorist Michael Gardiner argues, emphasizes "the heterodox and pluralistic nature of such spheres, which are often in opposition to the procedures of the dominant public sphere, as well as to sensitize us to the wide variety of normative ideals that regulate interaction in different areas of socio-cultural life."[51]

Unlike McLuhan's utilitarian definition of media as an "extension of human sensing" designed to enable communication beyond face-to-face interactions, media theorist Henry Jenkins conceptualizes media as a transformative threshold for a participatory community.[52] An opposing view has been advanced by political scientist Robert Putnam, claiming that a mediated public is a self-absorbed public. He describes an aggregate loss of participation in many civic organizations during the 1950s and 1960s by examining the practice of bowling. Although the number of people who bowl increased during that time, the number of people who bowl in leagues decreased. If people bowl alone or with friends and family, they do not participate in social interaction and civic discussions that might occur in a league environment, where conversations can occur on multiple levels and bridge differences. Television, as a new media, made people leave communal space and retreat into a private sphere, according to Putnam. Critics argue that in the 1950s, however, people watched television together and discussed content, in a manner that was similar to radio before.[53] Even today, we find instances of participatory television with competitive singing shows, such as *American Idol* or through programs that televise twitter feeds.

In this sense, even a one-way transmission of visual and voice information, such as by television,[54] can serve as a gathering place and site of meaning for society. The notion of media as *place* is typically refuted by architects; nonetheless, I borrow a definition of place from the geographer Paul Adams, where "place refers to firstly, a bounded system in which symbolic interaction occurs (a social context). Secondly, a nucleus around which ideas, values, and shared experiences are constructed (a center of meaning)."[55] Here, media is conceptualized beyond the transmission device; instead, it is conceived as a tool that incubates a social network and community. Media can also serve as a location marker, performing the way an architectural monument, library, or temple did in the past, orienting our perceptions of the world and providing a sense of knowing. "Media are really environments, with all the effects geographers (and) biologists associate with environments. We live inside our media."[56] This notion more closely equates with McLuhan's global village, where media is defined within an intrinsic social context; in that sense, it stands at the center of our experience. Social life is founded on shared meanings, and meanings are created through social life—they are mutually defining.[57]

NETWORKED PUBLICS (THE INTERNET)

Social media inspires reflection on the formative aspects of communication media in shaping culture and developing political structures. Research across different disciplines suggests that these patterns are tied to broader trends in the changing structures of sociability, where there is evidence of a move toward more individualized and flexible forms of engagement with media environments. Castells has described this as a turn toward "networked society" (1996), Wellman and Hogan as "networked individualism" (2004), and Matsuda as "selective sociality" (2005). Each of these texts provides analysis on how Internet practices have been an influential part of the drive toward more culturally specific, individualized, and diversified forms of social engagement. For our discussion, *networked publics* refers to a community that forms among some set of members of a social media site. They are defined as publics that are restructured by networked technologies as spaces and audiences bound together through technological networks.

Can we extend an individualized model to networked publics? Reflecting on the intertwined relationship between individual and community, the political economist Harold Innis argued that a balance between oral and written forms of communication contributed to the flourishing of fifth-century BC Greek civitas, defined as citizenship, especially as imparting shared responsibility, a common purpose, and sense of community.[58] His thesis revolved around the notion of bias and how the form of a communication technology shapes the social organization of a culture.[59] McLuhan furthered Innis's concept of bias by emphasizing that the formal characteristics of a media were more important than the content. He ultimately concluded that media organizes people, not civic plazas. While McLuhan's statement was intended to be provocative, it is important to examine his claim more closely in light of Internet activism.

McLuhan linked the notion of a media-enabled civitas to communication advances that occurred much earlier in history. He posited that it was the practice of writing, in addition to the affordances of the printing press, which subsequently contributed to the formation of an individual private persona. The printed book enables a redefinition of individual identity and affects the way a person perceives society.[60] Unlike orally transmitted information that requires simultaneous time and space relations, print is a technology that promotes individualism through asynchronous time and space (as does the Internet).

McLuhan, however, could not imagine a media-pervasive environment enabled by wireless communication and mobile technologies, nor wearable devices with information available on the go. When considering the potential for a diverse networked public sphere, earlier theories adhering to a one-way, one-to-many transmission model lacked a framework for interactivity between agents and artifacts. Consequently, McLuhan's theories now suffer from methodological problems since they fail to explain how context and participatory practices can shape a space.[61] If social media is associated with information sharing, collaboration, and user-centered design,[62] then a space of relations is being actively produced, online and offline. Ongoing discussions are formative to the creation of a space of deliberation and organization. The shift from Web 1.0 to Web 2.0 resulted in a concurrent shift from a one-to-many model involving passive consumers to a many-to-many model involving active participants who play a constitutive role in shaping the discourse. Furthermore, the notion of a mutually constituted field of relations emphasizes not only the tenuousness of any absolute boundary, but also the mutual dependency of entities. Online users, through their spatial practices of reappropriation, complicate the normative definition of space.

The relationship between social media and everyday life in the physical world, however, is not merely one of communication.[63] Online social space is actively constitutive of everyday life, and by extension, our everyday spatial environment. Online interaction not only records and reflects the actions of everyday life, but it also has a role in producing everyday life for a media-enabled public. Social media, along with symmetrical participation, creates the life of a social group, neighborhood, or metropolis. Writing *and* online interaction produce a social space for a media-using public. In turn, a mutually defining circularity of representations and practices influences what is "real" in the everyday and consequently frames our expectations of the real.[64] This view complicates earlier media debates that failed to capture the entangled, mutually productive, and therefore dependent interactions between social media and public space. Rather than entering into an existing public space, the Internet is public only through the actions of its agents, who engage in reflexive, spontaneous, and potentially democratic activity. "The question whether we belong to a larger community," offers philosopher George Herbert Mead, "is answered in terms of whether our own actions call out a response in this wider community, and whether its response is reflected back into our own conduct."[65] Community, for Mead, is defined by reciprocal participation.

What must be emphasized is that as social media is appropriated by human actants, new social practices alter our everyday environment, politically and culturally, which is not a small matter. People look to the Internet instead of a newspaper for information regarding world events. Social media, by default, is where the public discussion actually occurs today. Microblogging *is* the space of debate and deliberation. Twitter feeds represent an interactive diagram of an emerging public conversation where users not only can ascertain the cause of a debate, but also learn what others are thinking about it. Syria's amateur reportings posted on Flickr in 2012 demonstrated how smartphones became media-processing devices by displaying both mundane and classified content: text, images, and videos are shared across borders in real time. Just as the definition, expression, and organization of the public has changed over time, so too have social practices evolved (and continue to do so), creating new kinds of publics with new spatial expressions.

All space, however, is not equal. In societies structured by inequalities, dominant groups have advantages since they create the rules for public speech and behavior. As cultural theorist Catherine Squires explains, "Even if access to public arenas is theoretically guaranteed to all, all will not necessarily be equal within those spaces."[66] In this way, a dominant or mainstream culture participates in a public sphere, while marginalized groups may seek expression through invisible publics. From a global perspective, this is not insignificant. Each historical period has its own invisible populations, those typically excluded from the public sphere. In the nineteenth century, when social protocols excluded women from public discourse, these same protocols implicitly conferred a belief that the subaltern's voice had little value.[67] By denying women access to a public place or forum, social protocols acted as an effective form of censorship. And without access to a public forum, there is no means for injustices to be addressed and righted.[68] Civic plazas or market squares already exist in our cities, as do numerous modes of mass media in the form of newspapers, magazines, and television. The critical question is, can social media provide a voice for those traditionally excluded, such as marginalized social groups who use the Internet to organize themselves as publics with agency?

In this respect, Jenkins's concept of civic media is crucial in the sense that it moves out of electronic media and into the physical world. "We must occupy real and virtual spaces," tweeted Reuters' journalist Anthony De Rosa, who was quoting an occupier at the second Washington Square Park General Assembly in early November 2011. In this way, the virtual and the physical are mutually constitutive. "A Tumblr of user-submitted handwritten signs with bleak personal testimonies first captured the Internet's attention," writes *Rhizome* editor Joanne McNeil. "Presented are the lives of real people, unmistakable hardships, ready to reblog and retweet. But implied—by the faces, the faces, the faces—is that to sympathize, you must show up. This time, a Facebook 'like' is not enough . . . To properly commiserate with the enormity of this curated series of individual misfortunes, one must in person participate."[69] The actions of a civic media cycle find realization through our screens, tabs, and mobile phones in several ways: first, through shared production of user-generated content, which allows users to easily upload, organize, modify, share and access digital content; second, by coalescing a dispersed public in physical space; and third, by national and international media televising these events, prompting further social media debate and participation.

In this respect, while counterpublics tend to fall within the category of special-interest or affinity-based groups, they are more closely defined as "parallel discursive arenas where members of subordinated social groups invent and circulate counter discourses to formulate oppositional interpretations of their identities, interests and needs."[70] Within a historic context, hegemonic ideologies frame the meaning of the public in order to refer solely to its own values.[71] Unlike the hegemonic public, counterpublics provide a venue for alternate voices. In this respect, counterpublics share the discursive nature of publics, although their discourse is, in general, different or in opposition to what the mainstream public believes.[72] Amateur journalism via Twitter, Tumblr, or Facebook, though not a counterpublic in the strict definition, allows for alternative voices to be represented, a requisite for democratic discourse.

Due to open messaging protocols and an easily accessible interface, a networked public has the potential to be structured as a nonhierarchical system of social relationships, an assemblage where auteur, amateur, and professional have equal space for creative acts. In this respect, networked publics can be conceived as multiple publics endowed with diverse rationalities and modes of interaction and expression. The wide-scale adoption of the Internet and social media may mean that we are moving away from the heroic public of early modernity and more toward the existential and everyday concerns of life politics.[73] Although this philosophical territory is in continual negotiation and flux, postmodern publics have the potential to be heterogeneous, nonexclusive, and open to all types of media and topics of discussion.

Critics argue that with the current trend of individualized, anonymous, and fragmented communication (due to limited access and filter bubbles), audiences on the Internet could eliminate or hinder the possibility of an online public sphere. These considerations are worth noting, as the structure of online-networked publics could just as easily close off possibilities as it creates new ones. Thus, we may have determined that social media can provide a deliberative space for subaltern constituencies; however, the market objectives of proprietary platforms are increasingly troubling, as is their network morphology that allows for surveillance. The formation of a flexible market economy, as well as the globalization of capital, labor, and culture, is critical to understanding the problematic tendencies of network culture. Knowledge, as information, becomes a key commodity to be produced (as in data mining) and sold (as in retail-tracking mechanisms). The Internet, vis-à-vis social media, thus becomes a new territory to be colonized. "Knowledge labor," according to media scholar Christian Fuchs, "is labor that produces and distributes information, communication, social relationships, affects, and (their attendant) technologies."[74] Ideally, through this labor, knowledge becomes a productive force to educate and engage citizens across a variety of platforms. In actuality, however, knowledge labor is being appropriated by capital and is reflecting traditional market exchange values. In other words, user-generated content produces new knowledge, but capital appropriates and takes hold of this knowledge for profit.[75] Not surprisingly, the top websites are founded on user-generated content, although users' knowledge resources do not remain within the commons.[76] "With the rise of informational capitalism, the exploitation of the commons and the commodification of human creativity has become a central process of capital accumulation."[77] Unlike print- and broadcast-based models, visible

advertising is only a small part of the market quotient with networked publics, which is a high-yielding info-business where members are cultivated as
economic resources and their use value extracted for commercial profit.[78]

Thus, members of networked publics are not only producers of content
but also the producers of attention. Power relations gradually and algorithmically become actualized through a logic of data aggregation. Attention
is a mechanism to both predict and inhibit future access to information by
measuring, calculating, and accumulating bits of information into larger
patterns or tendencies. Algorithms expropriate user-generated content, predict future network behavior, and ultimately refine the network in ways that
might advance proprietary interests and limit the agency of media publics.[79]
In other words, the algorithmic logic is a direct response to user actions; it
gives the user more of what he or she has already paid attention to, at the
expense of difference.[80] Algorithmic filtering, then, not only results in the
loss/acquisition of personal information, but, more significantly, in the loss
of diverse voices.

While many champion the benefits of the Internet and the so-called commons that it produces, skeptics are not alone in questioning these ideas,
primarily the platitude that communication equals democratic process.[81] On
the one hand, the distribution of networking capabilities within everyday
spaces and contexts is frequently associated with new forms of collaboration, political economy, and public activism. On the other hand, "it is
increasingly clear that these networks are also aligned with new economic
frameworks and powerful forms of governance that thrive on decentralisa-
tion, monitoring behaviors, extracting surplus value from user-generated
content and otherwise surveying, exhausting and constraining online cultural
activities," explains theorist Rachel O'Dwyer. "The reality is not a dialectic."[82] All of these issues—data mining, filtering, surveillance—compromise
a public space of discourse and deliberation.

Indeed, these are not neutral platforms. Yet how do we reconcile social
media's visible affordances with its invisible mechanisms? What kind of a
public are we left with? If in the past public space was defined as a coffee
house, a market, or a freely accessible commons, what has now emerged by
way of social media is less definable, unstable, and as complex and conflicting as the everyday material world we live in.

CONCLUSION

In this chapter, the variable, value-laden word *public* was examined through
three streams: the spatial public, the media public, and the networked public. First, we looked at how a spatial public is constructed through face-
to-face communication within a performative space. Next, we examined
how media complicates historical notions of publicness and, consequently,
redefines an individualized distributed space of reception. The introduction

of the printing press in the fifteenth century allowed for the mass dissemination of texts, which led to the emergence of a collective discourse and knowledge sharing—cultural, scientific, and political. Finally, we explored how contemporary advances in networked technologies have replaced the one-to-many model with a many-to-many network, where communities of associates might not necessarily be synonymous with communities of place. Rather than one unitary public, there are now many diverse publics. Finally, an ensemble of networked relations and commercial mechanisms discloses the structural discontinuities embedded within networked publics.

Speech and space have an intertwined history. Social spaces are produced through the everyday social practices of human beings, yet the unique affordances of networked communication problematize the public sphere in complex and unintended ways. The Internet changes the fixed connection between information and place, just as flexible accumulation decouples capital and goods, supporting a distributed global economic system. Openness and visibility, which were so crucial to the historically grounded commons, are nonetheless lacking with social media. In contrast, the very lack of visibility can be an asset for counterpublics, where social media can serve as an enclave or safe space for congregation, discussion, and forming consensus.[83] There are other theoretical difficulties acknowledged within social media—unequal accessibility, monitoring, and the commercializing influence of the market economy—and all of these compromise today's networked publics.

Nonetheless, social media is where public discussion occurs today. It is conceptualized beyond the transmission device and conceived of as both (1) a social network of significance and (2) an environment, with all the effects geographers and ecologists associate with environments. While social life is founded on shared meanings, and meanings are created through social life, they are mutually defining.[84]

Thus, the three theoretical streams of public—the spatial, the media, and the networked—can be brought together in a reconsideration of contemporary publicness. Because of this shared aspect of production, social media cannot be understood as something separate from everyday physical space. Online publics are mutually constituted as an embedded feature of everyday social practices in the physical world. Just as theories of publicness are provisional, space itself is neither permanent nor fixed. If space is reflexive and relational, then human operations are not limited but always have the potential to recreate and redefine a preexisting spatial order.[85]

What I am emphasizing here is that physical face-to-face communication imposes severe spatial and temporal restrictions, so interaction is limited. If it is agreed that the necessary condition for public communication space is face-to-face interaction, then online-networked publics fail in this regard. If, on the other hand, public communication means to address an indefinite audience, then all public spaces fall short.[86] Any kind of social exclusion undermines the public sphere. A conversation is not simply public because it can be heard and overheard by others, but also because *it could be directed at anyone*; hence, the publicness. This audience also comes with the expectation of a response and, therefore, relies on the opening up of a space for increased opportunities of engagement.

Intermittent, compromised, and contaminated—however flawed as today's public is, in authoritarian countries without a free press or the right of assembly, where spatial movement is limited by gender, ethnicity, or political persuasion, this imperfect public is still better than what was previously available. Heterogeneous publics require spaces where disadvantaged groups can deliberate in safety.[87] Thus, publicness is not an abstract concept, but it requires active engagement in legislative efforts to protect Internet freedoms and individual privacy, as well as to develop non-proprietary platforms, regularize access, and opportunities. While the tasks to secure a free public space of discourse and deliberation may seem immense, it is imperative that we, the network public, attempt to realize them.

3   Origins of Networked Publics

What's exciting is that it harnessed the same kind of irrepressible, irreverent, geeky originality that characterized the years . . . before the Web arrived. . . . Events in Egypt make one realize how badly this kind of innovation is needed. The way in which the Mubarak regime was able to shut down the net provided a sobering reminder of the power of governments that are prepared to take extreme measures. As the country disappeared from cyberspace, I was suddenly struck . . . that if PCs still came with steam-age built-in dial-up modems, Egyptians could have logged on to servers abroad and stayed connected. The only way of stopping that would be to shut down the entire phone system. And even Mubarak might have balked at that.
                            —John Naughton, *Observer*, February 5, 2011[1]

As we have seen thus far, mediation, and more specifically, social media and the Internet, has contributed to a slippery public, evading a fixed description, flickering between visibility and invisibility. These ambiguities and contradictions are even more evident now as the term *public* is applied to new forms of media, new contexts, and new social practices.[2] Events leading up to the Arab uprisings suggest a paradigmatic shift away from the Habermasian public space toward one that is complex, conflicted, and increasingly contaminated by state controls and private infiltrations. Granting that social media lacks many of the constituent conditions for earlier definitions of publicness, was this conflict inherent from its developmental beginnings? This chapter allows us an opportunity to consider the origins of social media and reflect on its formative influences.

In tracing the development of networked publics from 1970 to the present time, attention is drawn to specific geospatial regions involving not only the historicization but also the spatialization of analytical categories. Underlying this analysis is the understanding that social media culture is located in historically and geographically specific amateur and entrepreneurial contexts that originally structured both content and access. By tracing pre-Internet social networks, a pattern emerges whereby early volunteer activities encompassing diverse peoples, politics, and influences, shift as commercial practices gain dominance and seek to capitalize on subscribers' social practices. This important aspect has been underplayed in previous historical accounts, with commercial practices being accepted simply as analytics of the software. Whereas social media develops over time into a complex assemblage of personal and proprietary practices, the use value of these practices remains consistent, with its members as social capital.

Throughout this recent history, I intertwine two levels of abstraction: (1) a chronological narrative beginning with early modem-based communication systems and (2) a more general (but less explicit) organizing concept of actor network theory. An actor network consists of and links together both technical and nontechnical elements, granting equal amount of agency to human actants and nonhuman artifacts. Hence, the concept of a sociotechnical system describes the interrelated historical, economic, and social processes that shaped social media, as well as how they instantiated a cycle of production and reproduction, not only of technologies, but also between programmers, their products, and a geographically fixed community of users. This chronological account analyzes the history of social media by first documenting avant-garde print networks; second, neoliberal economic networks; third, electronic (computer-to-computer) networks; and fourth, mobile networks.

Prior to the rise of the Internet, print-based media, as a network of subscribers, evolved into one of the earliest social networks by way of modem-based communication known as a computer bulletin board system (BBS). An early forerunner to today's social media, BBSes represent a series of spatial nodal points in the development of communicative media as technology and cultural practices, and as processes that both construct publics and are constructed by them. As with many inventions, bulletin board technologies developed in parallel in different geographic locations. While the scope of the book does not for allow a discussion of all the influential trajectories, specific sites of emergence are discussed: the CBBS in Chicago, FidoNet in San Francisco and a more detailed history of the WELL in the San Francisco Bay Area.[3] These projects were authored by electrical engineers, computer programmers (some self-taught), and hobbyists. However, the terms *hobbyist* or *amateur* are misleading; they are used only in the sense that technically proficient individuals volunteered hundreds of thousands of hours of unpaid labor designing, developing, and maintaining computer-to-computer networks. The inventors of early bulletin board systems, Ward Christensen, Randy Suess, Tom Jennings, and others, are examples of actor-network theory (ANT) in action.[4] I will argue that the microagency of shared objects, that is, text and/or print-based publications and later electronic bulletin board systems, was used to maintain a social reality. Together, the subscribers and the BBS communication technology formed a sociotechnical system, with the widespread acceptance of the Internet leading to social media today. Here, the complex assemblage of actant and media artifacts has the potential to create a third new thing—an individualized, networked, and alternative public space.

LOCALIZED NETWORKS

From the perspective of someone who is connected to the Internet twenty-four hours a day through a mobile device, it is difficult to imagine a time when the Internet did not exist. And yet clearly there was. For our purposes, a working definition of the Internet is a "worldwide computer network of networks that use the TCP/IP protocols to facilitate data transmission and exchange."[5] At its most basic formal level, the Internet's function is to encode and transmit data from sender to receiver. Transmitting data or information over long distances cannot be considered novel, however. Indigenous cultures developed tonal and/or optical coding systems to connect distant spheres; similar methods were employed by the ancient Greeks. In 1793 Claude Chappe invented the semaphore telegraph, and in 1839 the Great Western Railway established the electric telegraph network. Public circuit-switched telephone networks have been around for nearly a hundred years, in addition to more specialized networks, telexes, and/or wire services for photographs.

How then were bulletin board systems, which emerged in the late 1970s, prior to the Internet, different from the telegraph or telephone? One answer that Clay Shirky provides is that social media tools, lightweight though most of them are, have an ease of accessibility and use.[6] Prior to the Internet, there was almost nothing that supported conversation among many people at once. While telephones could also be said to decouple individuals from space, the radical change with social software was the decoupling of groups of people in space and time. For example, to enable a conversation around a campfire or conference table, first the participants must all be gathered in the same place at the same moment. By undoing those restrictions, the Internet allows for a host of new social patterns, from mailing lists to chat rooms to blogs.[7]

Within popular perception, Mark Zuckerberg may be credited with inventing social media in 2004 at Harvard University, yet that contradicts earlier histories dating to 1997 with the launching of SixDegrees.com.[8] Unlike proprietary outlets, however, computer bulletin board systems appeared fifteen years earlier in the 1970s. At that time, BBSes were underground phenomena, accessed predominantly by scientists, engineers, and professionals working at military sites, research labs, and universities—places where computers were integrated into work life far earlier than they were introduced to the general populace. Local computer clubs also played an instrumental role; clubs represented a do-it-yourself subculture, an eclectic mix of self-taught programmers; electronics enthusiasts; and technically minded hobbyists, iconoclasts, and artists. Within an incubator environment, specific historical moments make visible a particularly salient relationship between information, technology, and a localized community. By tracing the place-based connections between traditional print media, social groups, and the emergence of online social networks, a shared public space was created (both physical and media supported) where individuals came to see themselves as members of a unified social network.[9]

PRINT NETWORKS

Geographic placeness figures more prominently in the account of the *Whole Earth 'Lectronic Link* than does a person. The story takes place in Santa Clara County, a region thirty-two miles south of San Francisco, where the integrated circuit, microprocessor, microcomputer, and other key technologies were developed and sustained by about a quarter of a million information technology workers. The popular term, Silicon Valley, describes a zone where new technological knowledge was generated by a group of skilled engineers and scientists from major universities. There was also generous funding from the Department of Defense and an efficient network of venture capital firms—and, in the early stages, Stanford University.[10]

What other factors contributed to the emergence of a space for social and environmental consciousness? Silicon Valley has been credited with many social and intellectual innovations. While Stewart Brand's connection to this region began with his undergraduate studies at Stanford University in 1956, it was not until 1966 that he began to realize many of his projects, principally creating and maintaining a dispersed social network supported by diverse media outlets.

As a student at Stanford, Brand was already committed to reconfiguring modern American industrial society along more ecological and socially equitable lines. He followed the activities of the Free Speech Movement (FSM), a student protest that took place at the University of California–Berkeley during the 1964–5 academic year. This shaped much of his thinking. After receiving a small inheritance, he was able to move forward with many of his projects.[11] His background in biology framed a perspective that NASA's satellite photograph of the entire Earth as seen from space would allow people to visualize their world as a whole and closed system, as well as advance an ecological approach to the allocation and distribution of the world's finite resources. That same year, Brand was also introduced to the architect and inventor Buckminster Fuller, and the two began a long collaboration.[12] Even more important, Brand established the Whole Earth Truck Store, a mobile store conceived of as the first phase of his Whole Earth idea. It was "an alternative library"[13] and an abbreviated version of Brand's earlier plan to tour the country with educational festivals. The truck was a store, but at the same time it was also a lending library and mobile microeducation fair.[14] It was installed in his 1963 Dodge truck, and five years later, Brand and his wife, Lois, went "on a commune road trip" across the country. The Truck Store finally settled in its permanent location in Menlo Park, California, the same site that also served as the offices of the *Whole Earth Catalog*.[15] It was at that location that Brand, along with his friends and colleagues, used basic analogue typesetting and page layout tools (including an X-acto knife and Scotch Tape) to create issue number 1 of *The Whole Earth Catalog*, published by the Portola Institute in 1968.

That first oversize catalog, and its successors into the 1970s and 1980s, presented many useful tools: books, maps, garden tools, specialized clothing, carpenter's and mason's tools, forestry gear, tents, welding equipment, professional journals, early synthesizers, and personal computers. The catalog published where these objects could be located or bought. Most surprising is that the catalog did not offer any products to sell, nor did it include any advertising. Unconventional in concept and format, it nevertheless earned the 1972 National Book Award, the first time a catalog had ever won such an award.[16]

As Gareth Branwyn put it, "The *Whole Earth Catalog* changed my life. It was my doorway to Bucky Fuller, Gregory Bateson, whole systems, communes and lots of things that formed a foundation to a world model I've been building ever since."[17] It is significant that the *Catalog*, as print-based media, depicted both the products of an emerging counterculture *and* linked the members of that culture to one another. More importantly, as a dispersed public forum, it served as an early example of *participatory culture*, the current term for user-generated content, as Brand invited reviews from academic experts on many of the items listed. Additional comments, updates, and recommendations from readers further contributed to a print version comparable to today's social media and blogs.[18] Rebuttals were intelligently argued, sparking further debate that continued in subsequent issues. The ensuing discussions were as important to the subscribers as the items featured; the *Whole Earth Catalog* encouraged a do-it-yourself ideology that explicitly critiqued the consumer culture. Brand's literary *weltanschauung* emphasized that the solution to people's needs was not to promote purchasing things, but instead to encourage people to take technologies into their own hands. The *Catalog* also disseminated many environmental ideas now associated with the 1960s and 1970s.

> For this new countercultural movement, information was a precious commodity. In the '60s, there was no Internet; no 500 cable channels. . . . (The Whole Earth Catalog) was a great example of user-generated content, without advertising, before the Internet. Basically, Brand invented the blogosphere long before there was any such thing as a blog. . . . No topic was too esoteric, no degree of enthusiasm too ardent, no amateur expertise too uncertified to be included. . . . This I am sure about: it is no coincidence that the *Whole Earth Catalogs* disappeared as soon as the web and blogs arrived. (Kevin Kelly, cofounder and editor of *Wired* magazine, 2008)

Although scholars have credited the influence of the *Whole Earth Catalog* to the rural, back-to-the-land movement of the 1970s and the urban communities movement (whereby substandard housing in the inner cities was purchased and restored) in which it played a vital role, Brand's approach was more of a generalist's response to the technology available at the time. The *Catalog* promoted computers as enthusiastically as it promoted alternative energy production. By late 1968, Brand assisted Douglas Engelbart, an electrical engineer at Xerox PARC (Palo Alto Research Center) with "The Mother of All Demos," a now-famous presentation of many revolutionary computer technologies (including the mouse) at the fall Joint Computer Conference in San Francisco.

By 1971, when the term *Silicon Valley* was coined,[19] strong counterculture politics were mixing with high-tech military research, and not all of the players were antithetical to each other. According to one programmer, marijuana use was not unknown at NASA's Ames Research in Moffett Field, and at the same time, computer geeks were leaving to join communes.[20] Amid a context of multiplicity, Steve Jobs returned to his adopted birthplace in Mountain View (after dropping out of Oregon State University) and began attending meetings of the Homebrew Computer Club with Steve Wozniak in 1974. The word "homebrew" accurately captures the DIY (do-it-yourself) hands-on aesthetic of the time. At nineteen, Jobs took a position as a technician at Atari, a video game manufacturer, with the primary intent of saving money for a spiritual retreat to India.[21] Jobs, similar to many others during the 1970s, was interested in Eastern spirituality, although his interest was tempered with a strong streak of libertarian individualism and Richard Alpert mysticism (the Harvard psychologist and colleague of Timothy Leary).[22] They stayed a year, before Jobs returned to California as a Buddhist and working with Wozniak on Apple I.

By this time, Brand had another publishing scheme ready to develop: in 1974, he began the *CoEvolution Quarterly* (*CQ*) as a means of carrying on the objectives of the *Whole Earth Catalog*. It would publish full-length articles on specific topics in natural sciences and invention, on numerous areas of arts and social sciences, and on the contemporary scene in general. With the Vietnam War covered daily by mainstream broadcast news programs, it seemed that Brand's solution to "building a better society required stepping outside politics and turning towards small-scale technologies (particularly architecture, alternative energy, and information technologies) as the primary tools by which consciousness could be changed."[23] Fueled by a social and environmental vision and embracing a do-it-yourself ethos, *CQ* would inspire individuals to create independent communities outside of market-driven agendas. In addition to theoretical essays,[24] the content of *CQ* included profiles on the San Francisco industrial designer J. Baldwin, who collaborated with Buckminster Fuller; sustainable architects Peter Calthorpe and Sim Van der Ryn; and the architectural writer Witold Rybczynski.

A series of new publications were released within a two-year period. By 1983 the *Whole Earth Software Catalog* by John Brockman was proposed as a magazine that "would do for computing what the original (*Whole*

Earth Catalog) had done for the counterculture: identify and recommend the best tools as they emerged."[25] Other publications advancing alternative design approaches to the Internet, such as Xanadu in *Computer Lib/Dream Space*, were released.[26] They advocated the then-radical notion of computers as personal devices to create new literary and artistic works.[27] Within one year, Brand followed up with the *Whole Earth Software Review* (a supplement to *The Whole Earth Software Catalog*), which then merged with *CQ* in 1985 to form the *Whole Earth Review*. The parallel development of alternative print media and DIY computer clubs is significant to this history because this development represents thriving knowledge communities that laid the foundations for a new kind of public—one concurrently local and dispersed—poised for implementation with the advancement of networked communication.

ECONOMIC NETWORKS

As both amateur and research-based computing cultures were taking off in Santa Clara Country in the late 1970s and early1980s, what was the larger economic context? According to sociologist Manuel Castells, scholars of regional development typically treat Silicon Valley as a "classic example of the external economies that are derived from industrial localization. They are seen as cumulatively self-reinforcing agglomerations of technical skill, venture capital, specialized input suppliers and services, infrastructure, and spillovers of knowledge associated with proximity to universities and informal information flows."[28] The economic forces that contributed to the development of electronics and the computing industry were driven by a mixture of U.S. Department of Defense spending, academic funding, and venture capitalism.

This economic period also signaled a "flexible regime of accumulation," according to social geographer David Harvey. During the 1980s, corporations became more internationally mobile, due in part to a globally connected telephone network and a financial system with floating exchange rates; corporations, in turn, used this mobility to untether the state-labor contract of the postwar Fordist economy. Along with increased mobility, corporations gained more flexibility with regard to employment practices.[29] In order to lower production costs (and increase profits), corporations downsized the number of permanent employees with full benefits and increased the number of subcontracted or temporary project-based workers, whose jobs are typified by low wages and few benefits.[30]

The degree to which computing practices contributed to corporate flexibility is still debated by scholars.[31] Boundaries between previously distinct financial institutions (e.g., banking, insurance, stocks, loans, consumer credit) became increasingly porous. "Banking is rapidly becoming indifferent to the constraints of time, place and currency" (*Financial Times*, 1987).

Corporations used this mobility to relocate manufacturing in developing countries while concurrently dismantling the labor contracts of the Fordist economy. In Silicon Valley, however, the existence of firms with permeable boundaries and strong interpersonal networks substantially predated the rise of computer networks.[32] In addition to increased financial mobility, corporations gained flexibility in the work force. More influential though, would have been the increase in subcontracted positions in lieu of permanent employees, creating a climate of instability. Perceived economic vulnerability is one of the primary reasons for collective organization. Recent studies on collective behavior in the natural world conclude that collective organization serves two purposes: superior sourcing and protection,[33] in other words, jobs and job security. Another reason for collective organization is shared professional interests and/or knowledge sharing; for example, the medieval craft guilds. Bulletin board systems, as social networks, would become beneficial collective infrastructures that supported and protected an increasingly mobile and impermanent workforce of computer programmers. As Harvey puts it, "To the degree that collective action was thereby made more difficult—and it was indeed a central aim of the drive for enhanced labor control to render it thus—so rampant individualism fits into a necessary, though not sufficient, condition for the transition from Fordism to flexible accumulation. It was, after all, mainly through the burst of new business formation, innovation, and entrepreneurialism that many of the new systems of production were put into place."[34] Within the early history of electronics there were pragmatic reasons for a shared communication platform. Individuals throughout history have collectively banded together to increase protection, knowledge acquisition, or sourcing; computer programmers did the same thing as they began to respond to a highly fluid and impermanent job environment.[35]

COMPUTER-TO-COMPUTER NETWORKS

A print-based media such as the *Whole Earth Catalogue* could shape a dispersed public through a network of subscribers. At the same time in history, neoliberalism was reconfiguring economic practices towards global dispersal. It was within this context of economic flexibility and experimental media that I would like to discuss in greater detail the emergence of bulletin board systems in North America.

In the early1970s, most computers were fixed mainframes that cost tens of thousands of dollars with controlled access by military, academic, or commercial researchers. As with most innovations, there was a zone of slippage between targeting the problem, developing the technology (or having the technology developed by others), and conducting the experimentation before eventually arriving at a solution. The military had strong and sustained interest in developing computer-to-computer communication,

Figure 3.1 Berkeley, CA. Berkeley Community Memory Project 1972–4. ASR-33 teletype at the entrance to Leopold's Records connected by a 110-baud line to an XDS-940 host in San Francisco. It was designed for public access: anyone could *Add* a message, attach keywords to it, and *Find* messages.
Credit: Lee Felsenstein and Mark Szpakowski

as did universities and private companies, such as Bell Laboratories, that performed military research. At the same time, there were also grassroots examples, including the Berkeley Community Memory Project, established in 1972 as an electronic message and information board inside Leopold's Records as shown in Figure 3.1. and later located at the Whole Earth Access Store in Berkeley.

The Berkeley Community Memory Project was created by Efrem Lipkin, Mark Szpakowski, and Lee Felsenstein. Lee devised the hardware, Efrem the software, and Mark the user interface and information management. It was initially an experimental super bulletin board, where users could send and collect messages quickly, although a subsequent version aimed at nothing short of inventing a global information network. Their manifesto stated that "strong, free, non-hierarchical channels of communication—whether by computer and modem, pen and ink, telephone, or face-to-face—are the front line of reclaiming and revitalizing our communities."[36] Berkeley Community Memory was closely followed by the educational Programmed Logic for Automated Teaching Operations (PLATO) project implemented in 1973 at the University of Illinois at Urbana-Champaign, which gave rise to the first electronic message board software, PLATO Notes, the first multi-user chat system.

In the decade prior to the release of Apple II in 1984, there were scores of avid computer hobbyists interested in the potentials of computer-to-computer communication. Filled with curiosity and excitement that often accompanies the prospect of inventing something that did not exist before, most worked within the concept of open-source software.[37] Many were also motivated by the opportunity to overcome social, cultural, or intellectual isolation by strengthening geographically dispersed communities.

One of the most promising directions for computer-to-computer communication involved the use of telephone connections. In 1968 Bell Telephone released *Bell 103*, a modem that was designed to transfer data over phone lines. By 1977 Bell had improved the modem so that it would operate inside a microcomputer. Not surprisingly, file sharing was the primary impetus behind the project because there was no way outside of floppy disks to exchange independently derived software through various computing platforms. No unified standards had been established. A software program written with others would be listed in ASCII format (American Standard Code for Information Interchange) in a message; the receiver would have to either write it down, retype it, or if he or she had the expertise, code a program that would convert the message directly into the computer's language.[38]

Just as Steve Jobs and Steve Wozniack participated in the Homebrew Computer Club in Menlo Park, others in computer clubs throughout the country were contributing to the informal advancement of technological knowledge. In many ways similar to the *Whole Earth Catalogue*, these clubs functioned as sites of knowledge sharing and as learning communities. Computers were expensive, and in lieu of commercial outlets (Apple Stores and online outlets were nonexistent then), individuals assembled electronic components at home. "There was a time when cobbled-together technology and underground culture converged to form digital communities that felt genuine, even revolutionary," according to early programmer Joe Nickell. "The remains of that heady time largely lie scattered on dusty 5¼-inch floppy disks and tape backups."[39] Working with computers in the 1970s meant that you had to be able to improvise, and the clubs were where ideas, procedures, software, and equipment were shared or traded.

With the iniquitousness of today's Internet, it is difficult to imagine that someone in the 1970s would exclaim, "Wow, you can talk to someone through your computer!"[40] It is even more difficult to imagine the extent of relative cultural or geographical isolation that existed at the time. Inclement weather played a significant role in the development of the first dial-up computer BBS in Chicago. A heavy snow (dubbed "the Blizzard of 1978") prevented programmer Ward Christensen from driving to work. Reflecting on the upcoming Chicago Area Computer Hobbyist Exchange (CACHE) newsletter, he called fellow member Randy Suess to explore the possibility of sending the newsletter directly from computer to computer, rather than by mail. During the phone call, the two men agreed to undertake the project: Christensen would write the software, and Suess would assemble the hardware, as illustrated in Figure 3.2.

It took the pair less than a month to get the computerized BBS working.[41]

A bulletin board system is a simple computer system with software installed that allows users to login and connect to the system by way of a

Figure 3.2   Chicago, IL. Chicago bulletin board system (1978).
Credit: Jason Scott Sadofsky, courtesy of Ward Christensen

modem and telephone line. Once a member logged in, he or she could perform functions such as exchanging messages with other computer enthusiasts (topics were usually limited to computer-related subjects), downloading
or uploading software and data, or reading news. Other BBSes offered
online games in which users could interact with one another; some were
organized around ANSI and ASCII art (such as found on Aperture), pornography, and music. If there were multiple phone lines, BBSes also offered chat
rooms that allowed users to meet and interact with each other.

By 1980 BBSes had a loyal, but primarily underground, following.
Among Andover Cnode members, there were discussions about the possibility of BBSes transferring messages to each other laterally, neighbor to neighbor, and avoiding dialup charges, however, nothing came of the idea. Tom
Jennings, a creative programmer specializing in device drivers and system
software for new computer hardware, had been part of those discussions.
At the time, Jennings was an experienced user of BBSes, primarily CBBS, but
also Andover Cnode, BCCS, and even DIAL-A-MATCH. Having relocated
to San Francisco in 1983, Jennings came up with a highly innovative BBS
design called Fido. A year later, Jennings rewrote the Fido BBS program to
network with other Fidos and called it FidoNet. It was the first message
and file networking system for BBSes, initially used to distribute a FidoNet
newsletter. Jennings' important contribution was not only in authoring the
code, but also in conceptualizing intercomputer communication as "a network plus a node list," defined logically as the way data pass through the

```
The World's First    /‾‾\
  BBS Network       /|oo \
  * FidoNet *      (_| /_)
                    _@/_ \    _
                   |    | \   \\
                   | (*) |  \_ ))
                   |_U__| /  \//
  ‾‾‾‾‾‾‾          _//||_\  /
 / FIDO \         (_/(_|(___/ (jm)
(_____)
```

Welcome to Grotto de Blotto!
Your sysop is Michael Dispater

Supporting 300/1200/2400 baud, Open 24 hours/day

Figure 3.3   San Francisco, CA. Initial logon screen for FidoNet. BBSing at that time was serial, character-based communication; the dog is an example of an ASCII (American Standard Code for Information Interchange) image creation (1984). *Credit: Tom Jennings*

network from one device to the next. In other words, it was an alternate Internet before the Internet.[42]

As FidoNet gained popularity, other BBS software was independently adapted to support the relevant FidoNet protocols. The reliability of the system allowed it to achieve cult status, and it continued to expand to become the largest international intercomputer network, (Figure 3.3). At its peak, FidoNet handled over 30,000 nodes. Until 1994, with the arrival of commercial Internet, FidoNet was the only noncommercial means for most of the world's population to send e-mail to and from the Milnet, Arpanet, or Minitel networks.[43] To visualize the extent and size of this network, consider that if each of those Fido nodes had only 50 users (and they had many more), that approximates to over 1.5 million users, the largest social network system of the time.

As such, BBSes were an experimental, alternative media.[44] They were the only medium that supported interactive communication in real time and with file sharing, especially software sharing, which was crucial from their earliest inception. Telephone numbers for BBSes were available in all of the popular computer-related magazines and, similar to short-wave radio, were usually accessed at night. Programmers also accessed them from the work place; while they were supposed to be working at their terminals, they were really posting to BBSes.[45] As the popularity of BBSes spread, the demographic widened extensively beyond engineers and programmers to include amateurs, students, counterculture types, musicians and anarchists; many different subcultures were involved in the phenomenon. The concept and culture spread quickly as a hobbyist phenomenon; during the 1970s, there were approximately 150,000 computer bulletin board systems throughout North America and other countries. The height of the BBS scene peaked just before the mid-1990s when the Internet became popularized.

Technologies of social media have differed over time, but the urge to connect over distance with others of similar affinities remains consistent. Messaging creates a community through routine social practices and activity. Or as theorist Michel de Certeau describes it, "space is a practiced place."[46] BBSes were created around specialized interests where the ensuing conversations led to the formation of close knit communities. Messaging defines a "space of enunciation . . . as actions, their intertwined paths give shape to spaces. They weave places together."[47] The boundaries of communities as well as electronics were expanding, and over time, users of bulletin board systems formed a strong sense of attachment to one another as well as to the group as a whole.

Whole Earth 'Lectronic Link (The WELL)

The narrative now moves north of Silicon Valley to Marin County. The year was 1985, which saw the furthest extension of Brand's print media, the *Whole Earth Review*. At the time, Brand was also the director of the Point Foundation, a nonprofit environmental organization in Sausalito, California. An important meeting was about to take place. The epidemiologist Larry Brilliant of Networking Technologies International (NETI) approached Brand with a business offer.[48] Brilliant's team had developed a new communication technology, a computer conferencing system. But a network is a sociotechnical system, meaning one can have the technology, but without individual human members, there is no social media. To get the system up and running, Brilliant required a membership list, so he contacted Brand to see if he could recruit users or readers from the *Whole Earth Review* subscribers' list.[49] The two agreed on the financial terms, and in 1985 the *Whole Earth 'Lectronic Link* (WELL) was launched. The WELL was one of the original dial-up BBSes and later evolved into a user-owned online forum as the Internet and web technology continued to develop.

The WELL's original management team—Matthew McClure, soon joined by Cliff Figallo and John Coate—collaborated with its early users to foster a sense of community.[50] Their organization relied on decentralization, resilience, and autonomy. The members' activities, online and off, included job sourcing, knowledge sharing, decision making, and collaboration—especially in the shared production of new software. Their activities also included other diversionary pursuits, games, and music. Over time, membership extended beyond the immediate geographic area. Such a contingent, relational viewpoint between technological systems and social worlds has been advanced through actor-network theory (ANT) by sociologist Bruno Latour, who argues that technological networks are inseparable from actual space and place. Latour calls these "skeins of networks"; therefore, a networked public is an assemblage formed around the production and distribution of online culture.[51] The assemblage includes the producers and consumers of content; the content in question, comprising text, voice, or rich media; and the underlying technical structure that facilitates its trans-mission. In addition to the human actants, this sociotechnical system is com-prised of contingent logical and physical strata; the higher level protocols and services implemented in software; and the lower substrate network, comprising tangible hardware such as user devices, transmission technolo-gies, and the available physical resources such as spectrum, bandwidth, real estate, labor, and energy.[52] It is clear, therefore, that the *networked public* is a complex assemblage comprising not only human relationships but a whole range of logical and physical resources.

As a sociotechnical experiment, the history of social media, and of BBSes specifically, exemplifies the appropriation of technology for individual-ized objectives, similar to spatial theorist Michel de Certeau's individual-ized method of navigating the city and intervening in a creative way. Social media creates a framework for individual adaptation and personal expres-sion. That history illustrates how particular social situations and human actors enroll pieces of technology, machinery, media, and money into actor networks, configured across space and time. By connecting a dispersed com-munity, social media is increasingly linking the personal to the public realm, vis-à-vis formal and informal, spatial and nonspatial relationships—the clear division between public and private realms is being superseded by a complex layering of actors, platforms, and technologies.[53]

Economic pragmatism and social innovation drove the BBS model; in geographically or socially isolating circumstances, this model was less ex-pensive and less time consuming than individual telephone calls or sending paper newsletters to each member of a social network or club. In that sense, BBSes constituted one of the earliest examples of concurrently spatial and mediated publics—at once a place and a nonplace realm. Nevertheless, it is a misnomer that BBSes were referred to as virtual communities because the historical data suggest that most BBSs were connected to specific locales and geographical areas. Fee-paying BBSs such as the WELL (San Francisco/Stanford/University of California–Berkeley) and Echo NYC (New York) had close-knit communities and scholarly discussion forums.[54] Most had annual or biannual events where users would meet face-to-face with their online friends, as well as informal meetings or group projects as shown in Figure 3.4, parties, chili cook-offs, or trips to the circus.

Even with lesser-known BBSes, relationships were clearly interwoven with events in physical space.[55]

BBSes possessed the characteristics that sociologist Barry Wellman calls sociability, social support, and social capital. Due to high level of technical expertise in the San Francisco Bay Area, however, the nature and value of the information exchanged on the WELL was qualitatively different from that of many BBSes. More kinship than communication system, BBSes tended to operate within a gift economy, also known in anthropology as a gift cul-ture, or altruistic exchange without expectation of immediate reward.[56] As it was explained, "People do things for one another out of a spirit of building

Figure 3.4 Sausalito, CA. Merrill Peterson and other WELL members replanting the roadside with wildflowers near the WELL office (August 1992).
Credit: Matisse Enzer

something between them, rather than a spreadsheet-calculated quid pro quo."[57] Systems operators who donated their time and resources explained it this way: "It was a service [to the community]" while others offered, "It enriched my life."[58] Communities of practice, in this case computer enthusiasts, political activists, journalists, educators, and others, are more concerned with the processes of enculturation, information sharing, and knowledge development. As a community, it was also an incubator for other communities; an example can be gleaned from the Electronic Frontier Foundation (EFF), a nonprofit public interest group formed in 1990 to protect online free speech and privacy as well as advocate for open source and innovation.

As the use of the Internet became more widespread in the mid- to late 1990s, traditional BBSes rapidly faded in popularity. Today Internet forums and social network sites occupy much of the same social and technological space previously occupied by BBSes. Although many of the early BBS adopters express that the vast size of Facebook in relation to their pre-Internet communities has resulted in a proportional loss of primary physical connection,[59] we will have to wait to examine empirical evidence before that belief can be either validated or discounted. In any case, an experimental culture was instrumental to the formation of BBSes, and the subsequent mainstreaming of social media could easily dilute the focus of their interests.

The development of social media, as a sociotechnical system, emerged from specific historical and locational forces. Our history traced the connections between the *Whole Earth Catalog*, a print-based architectural DIY network, the *Whole Earth Software Catalogue*, and the *Whole Earth 'Lectronic Link*, a modem-based bulletin board system. It wasn't until 1997 that SixDegrees.com, the first online social networking site, appeared on the Internet, replacing the features and functionalities of BBSs. My intention by presenting a historical narrative was not to document all examples, nor to establish an exact date of social media's origins, but rather to advance the point of view that (1) networked public spheres preexisted the Internet and (2) social media's history originally emerged from strong local bonds in physical space. In this origin narrative, social media, whether BBSes or today's social networking sites, does not stand in opposition to physical networks. Rather, it is entirely enmeshed within them.

The social protocols that structured the WELL contained many of Habermas's criteria for public space: free discourse, equality, and social codes. Here, media, whether print or electronic, functions as an attractor for independent empowerment and community building. In the case studies of the bulletin board system in Chicago and the WELL, it was demonstrated how media connects special interests, affinities, and place-based relationships. Furthermore, the ad hoc structure of BBSes, including the WELL, supported largely participatory practices and knowledge sharing, which created a sense of coownership among its members.

Was the WELL entirely virtual? In a word, no. Brand provided the names of his subscribers; these people were friends and colleagues he had known, visited, or worked with for many years.[60] They belonged to a fairly specific demographic: college-educated, liberal-leaning, and technologically literate men and women between the ages of eighteen and fifty (although some were older). However, it can also be argued that Habermas's public sphere was not truly public either. It was bourgeois, Western European, and predominately male; thus, similar social filters existed in the nineteenth century.[61] Were the Chicago BBS or the WELL virtual communities? If the descriptor, virtual, means exclusively online interactions, then no. Brand's friendships extended throughout the Bay Area as well as across the United States. Many of the members worked together, lived near each other and hiked together.[62] Some of those friendships began in Palo Alto; others were fostered in New York and extended nationally via the *Whole Earth Catalog*, Truck Store library, and other activities. Rather than defining the WELL as a virtual community, it may be more accurate to conceptualize it as a special-interest or affinity-based community, established mostly through previously connected relationships in locational space. In this respect, the history of networked publics is interwoven with physical publics, to the extent that relationships are often (but not exclusively) intertwined with location.

Economic pragmatics necessitate that mobility is implicit within flexible accumulation, and in this case study, the San Francisco Bay Area is no exception. The WELL, as a complex sociotechnical system, brought together collective organization (providing superior sourcing and protection) coupled with altruistic and utopianist motivations. But it also created a third new thing—an individualized mediated public sphere.

As we reflect on the fact that there were hundreds of BBSes a few decades ago, we also recognize that today the social media landscape is increasingly dominated by a few platforms. To recite all of the developments is beyond the book's scope; nevertheless, it is important to note that we have witnessed a significant philosophical and technological shift. From 1970 to 2000, social media transitioned from its origins in academic research and amateur experimentation to responding primarily to market driven forces. Unlike hobbyists and systems operators who freely donated their time and equipment in the early stages of the social web, venture capitalists and other investors turned Internet platform development into a multibillion dollar industry by 2005. "Thus there is tension at the core of the social web," Felix Stadler points out, "created by an uneasy (mis)match of commercial interests that rule the back-end and community interests advanced at the front-end."[63] We will discuss this problematic relationship in greater detail with Facebook in the next chapter.

MOBILE NETWORKS

As long as the manufacturing requirements of computing, for example a desktop monitor and tower, fixed the human-technological interface to a permanent place in a research institute (defined solely as a computer), then formal and spatial distinctions were clear: computing was done at work; socializing was done at home. By the 1990s, however, the computer had transformed from a calculator to a communicating and media-processing device. The hardware continued to shrink, and wireless technology made it mobile, severing the technological object from its context. This portability made it possible for the computer to migrate and miniaturize, first to offices, then to homes, and finally to the pocket. Through an alteration in context, the two oppositional spheres, spatial and mediated, became much less distinct. When the computer remained fixed to a desk, the relationship between user and content could be framed within previous media conventions and potentials, such as radio and television. What has changed, and this is significant, is that the computer, as a miniaturized, portable processing and wireless communication device (e.g., BlackBerry, iPhone), became seamlessly integrated into everyday social practices in physical space.[64]

The chapter will conclude with the development of applications in 1997 for mobile communication devices that leverage locational awareness through global positioning systems (GPS). What happens when mobile computing, social media, and urban context collide? Information begins to permeate the built environment as ambient content, accessible on demand.[65]

As social media became widely adopted, people began experimenting with proprietary platforms through the practice of misuse, while hackathons spawned user-generated applications. In 2006, a mobile messaging system, Twitter, was tested first in New York and San Francisco. Twitter combined the ease and immediacy of instant messaging with roving entities (in other words, people), and thus mobility is central to Twitter's conceptual foundations. Its origins describe a dynamic and complex image of the city delineated by user status in real time. How did social media commute from the fixed location of a desktop computer to an ambient sea of sociocultural information?

Again, San Francisco and Silicon Valley proved prominent in the development of Twitter—the availability of venture capitalists, entrepreneurs, skilled programmers, and early adopters all contributed to it. Yet in contrast to BBSes, where print media in the form of newsletters or catalogues offered preexisting membership lists, Twitter, hasn't followed this pattern. Unlike a newsletter or catalogue, Twitter was conceptualized as a dynamic model from its earliest inception. It is important to see what the designer's intentions were and how social practices change over time. To a generation that grew up with *SimCity*, open-ended city-building simulation, and *Grand Theft Auto*, an action-adventure open-world video game, such a dynamic urban context organized around time and motion needs no explanation. Within such a perspective, physical space exists as a foil for social practices, that is, the actions of agents otherwise known as actants, and implicitly assumes a socially constructed position of the city. And yet this is not originally what president and CEO Evan Williams set out to achieve.

Twitter began as a small start-up called Odeo in San Francisco, cofounded by Evan Williams, Biz Stone, and Noah Glass, along with angel investors. Prior to Odeo, Williams had already created a successful website, Blogger, which Google purchased for several million dollars. Odeo was functioning out of William's apartment where programmers Florian Webber and Jack Dorsey were working. Their task was to design a podcasting platform—no one had yet done it successfully. As can happen with technology development, Apple beat Odeo to the goal and launched iTunes with podcasting capabilities. As a result, Williams changed objectives and asked his team of highly skilled programmers for other projects to pursue.

Programmer Jack Dorsey first suggested the idea for a microblogging application, according to an interview in the *Los Angeles Times* (February 18, 2009). Dorsey was fascinated by Instant Messaging and LiveJournal, a hybrid social networking and blogging platform: "What if you have LiveJournal, but you could just make it more live?" Dorsey had already designed a delivery messaging system in 2001; the inspiration and architecture was developed as a mobile platform exclusively for cell phones. He authored a simple e-mail program that could be used on the RIM 850, a predecessor to the BlackBerry—it had four lines of text and the keyboard—that could send and receive messages. The software problem had been solved, but the hardware problem remained. Technology had not advanced to where most individuals could afford a mobile communication device with messaging capabilities. The unspoken assumption was that a blogging community requires an audience, and each audience member requires a device.

By late 2005 cell phones and short message service (SMS or texting) were in higher use. Text messaging had introduced and normalized a 160 character constraint. Following existing protocol, Twitter then allocated 20 characters to the username and 140 charters to the text body. The message could be sent over e-mail, Jabber, or SMS.[66] Finding people meant finding their username e-mails or typing in their names.

Twitter had its conceptual foundations in vehicle dispatch—automobiles, trucks, and bicycles—and their speed, locations, and task status. What is significant is that Dorsey saw that this system through the filter of social media. "[Twitter] . . . started with a fascination with cities and how they work, and what's going on in them right now . . . a visualization . . . to create software that allowed me to see how this was all moving in a city."[67] Twitter was conceived as a kind of mobile instant messenger for roving entities. Yet, for Dorsey, the vision was incomplete without including the urban inhabitants. The public conversation was missing—the objective was to know, in a moment, where friends are and what they are up to. A circle of friends could read each person's status in real time from any location. First-generation names for the microblogging platform included Status and Twitch (because a cell phone vibrates), and then Noah Glass came up with Twitter—defined as "a short burst of inconsequential information," "chirps from birds," "twitterpated."[68]

Dorsey posted an early hand-drawn sketch of the Twitter application to the photo-sharing site Flickr. The original design included a significantly large pair of eyes, which were supposed to be watching. The notion of tracking was implicit from the beginning. Again from the *Los Angeles Times*, "Later (watching) was changed to following" Dorsey explained. "The important consideration was that on Twitter, you're not watching the person, you're watching what they produce." (February 18, 2009). As a test, the application was released to a small group of early adopters in two cities: New York and San Francisco. As the medium evolved, it became less a social network and more of a conversation among interesting, like-minded individuals.[69] "That as the mobile phone and other ICTs become established, the frontiers between the 'public self' and the 'private space' will become blurred and less solid. Or at least, the differentiation between our public and private aspects will no longer be governed by the architectonic structure of the city, but rather by the type of person with whom we are interaction at that moment, in person or virtually."[70] Unlike Facebook, there is no need to "friend" someone since Twitter cultivates virtual relationships based on content published over mobile devices. (The irony is that as Twitter has gained more members, it is increasingly accessed through nonmobile hardware, laptop, and desktop computers.)

Mobile microblogging documents the tangential and conditional aspects of the everyday, even as these conditions overlap with similar operations of print culture. Twitter is an example of a roving urban conversation; navigating the everyday environment allows for adjacent connections between disparate individuals in real time, both mundane to profound. Twitter's documentary status was tested in Tunisia, Occupy Wall Street (OWS). Hurricane Sandy and the Boston marathon bombing. Its immediacy enabled organizational and logistical coordination of activities, as well as amateur news reporting. In combination with Instagram, a mobile social media image application developed by former Odeon employees and friends of Dorsey, Kevin Systrom and Michel Krieger, Twitter opened further access and participation in the sharing of local and worldwide conversations.

CONCLUSION

What is most salient from these histories is that social interaction preceded technical development. Or as Gilles Deleuze explains, "Tools always presuppose a machine, and the machine is always social before it is technical. There is always a social machine which assigns the technical elements used."[71] Local computer clubs combined a knowledge-sharing ethos with an ad hoc approach, offering social interaction whereby technological ideas were tested and implemented. Media deterministic accounts tend to focus on the development of the software while ignoring or downplaying the importance of human actants. Unlike those histories, the emphasis here is that electronic media forms only one part of this sociotechnical system. Analyzing the relationships critical to social media as a networked public reveals that the inherent value of a network is not in the system, but in its actants as social capital. Whether as a BBS, community Wi-Fi, or microblogging platform, all effectively demonstrate that without the human actants, there is no communication. Furthermore, shared interests and affinities of the members was a crucial factor to these platforms' initial adoption and subsequent rapid dissemination.

It is also important to recognize that a major site of conflict with social media's history is user-generated content. In the example of Berkeley Community Memory, the inventors foresaw that public access and ownership were crucial for full-knowledge participation. Yet what happens to user-generated knowledge? Media theorist Christian Fuchs argues that user-generated knowledge (i.e., knowledge labor) such as found on the Internet, as well as social media outlets, is changing the ways audiences are being construed as commodities.[72] That aspect critically changes the way social networking sites are being employed as a social practice. Just as Twitter reflects an expanded public for discourse exchange, it also presents a space for extended commercialism and capitalism where the audience can be purchased and commodified. The critical understanding of social media sites, as they progressed from early examples of volunteerism to information markets, significantly alters the meaning of user-generated technology and content.

The operations of capital, vis-à-vis Facebook, Twitter, and others are in contradistinction to our understanding of a commons, defined as commonly held resources that are reserved for the use of the entire community. Today, social media performs as a community on the front end, while active data mining is engaged on the back end, shifting our definitions of what is publicly owned.

Although this history is still developing, we have, for the purposes of discussion, mapped the origins of networked publics, situated their histories in space, and explored the significant relationships between users and how they perceive themselves in relation to technologies. While pre-Internet forms of social media appear to more closely conform to idealized notions of the commons, Web 2.0 presents many sociospatial problems affecting its ability to act as such. Scholars are challenging claims of technologically limitless and utopian notions of the commons and instead are promoting cautious and critical consumption, production, usage, and treatment of an expanded digital public.

Understanding that technology is culturally and socially specific in terms of its use, deployment, sociability, comprehension, and so forth, this narrative does not represent a comprehensive documentation of historical events. My aim is to trace a trajectory identifying important trends and linkages among users. By paying particular attention to these linkages, we can better imagine and solve the sociospatial-political issues affecting public space and the public sphere, and thus critically prepare ourselves to modify and alter social media technologies to suit our diverse needs. However, this is not a unidirectional narrative, where only one side impacts the other; instead, this is a cyclical process where users adopt social media, and then what is generated impacts society. By maintaining social media's legacy of participatory practices, this history describes how digital spaces are not irrelevant to nondigital politics, but are rather increasingly interwoven and are often the impetus to action.

In the next chapter we will look more closely at the less visible aspects of social media. Through the creation of identity by way of a profile page, advanced over time, the social life of an active public space now competes with media technologies by turning interaction inward. This review will allow us to see how these new networked publics are simultaneously searching for a private sphere.

4 Networked Identity Making

See you on Facebook!
     —Hailed one student to another, passing by the Campanile,
               University of California–Berkeley, April 7, 2010.

Nearly 1,000 social networking sites were up and running on the Internet in 2013, with new startups launching daily—and billions of registered users.[1] Over 66 percent of the North American population actively uses these sites, integrating them into their everyday practices.[2] These sites represent a vast and varied cultural milieu based on interaction among users and user-generated content. Some social networking sites are commercially owned and charge fees; others allow access by invitation only; most, however, are free of charge and open to new members, although their platforms are licensed, patented, and controlled by privately held corporations.

The high rate of use, as well as the extensive global reach of social networking sites, demonstrates that there is a public for every type of online culture. Public sites span the gamut from politics to gaming, from slashdot to bird-watching, and every type of fan or music culture across the entire spectrum. In this chapter, my analysis will center on how social media can be understood as publics that are simultaneously spaces constructed through networked technologies and imagined communities that emerge as a result of the imbrication of diverse people, technologies, and practices.

Due to its recent and rapid growth in membership and usage, social media remains understudied.[3] danah boyd's 2008 ethnographic study contributed to a greater understanding of young people's practices and motivations with regard to social media use, but the study was confined to users under eighteen years of age.[4] Other studies have explored topics related to social media users and content producers in cross-platformed media ecologies, but not all were substantiated by empirical research.[5] Still others focused on the debilitating effects of mediated relationships.[6] There is also a growing body of research on identity formation in terms of ethnicity, religion, and gender within online communities. However, scholars still have only a limited understanding of the complex relationship between online practices and their translation into physical space, which has significant implications for designers and urban planners today.

Framing complex interactions between social media and public space has proved to be something of a challenge. On the one hand, social media is often perceived as merely a passing trend and, thus, not worthy of serious study. On the other hand, recognized media theorists have regarded social media as something exclusive of or in opposition to the physical world.[7] A theoretical framework based on isolation or opposition, however, does not accurately capture what is currently occurring in the field. Internet ethnographic studies have shown many quantifiable indices of intersection between online space and physical space within many demographics. Furthermore, the convergence of mobile devices integrated with global positioning systems (GPS) and application programming interfaces (API) connects users to environmental contexts. Because location-based media are digital media applied to geographic places, they trigger social interactions in physical space, such as participatory mapping, checking in, and amateur news reporting, among other uses.[8] As mobile technologies are increasingly adopted as the primary source for Internet connection in developing countries, mobile practices are becoming an increasingly important research area.

DEFINING NETWORKED PUBLICS

In this book, the terms *social media site* or *social networking site* refer to Internet platforms that encourage user-generated content and exchange. The term *networked public* refers to communities that form among users of a social media site. This is an adaptation of researchers danah boyd and Nicole Ellison's definition of networked publics, which describes social networking sites as a category of website housing personal profiles that are a combination of self-expression and others' reactions to that expression. This includes a traversable, publicly articulated social network displayed in connection with profiles in which users designate other user profiles as *friends, acquaintances, contacts*, or an equivalent.[9] This generates a social network graph that may be undirected (as in the *attention network* variety, in which friendship does not have to be confirmed, as with Twitter) or directed (in which the other person must accept friendship, as with Facebook). The articulated social network graph is displayed on a user's profile for all other users to view. Thus, each user profile contains a link to the profiles of others, so users can traverse the network through the profiles of friends, friends of friends, and so on. Online social networking sites, then, allow individuals (1) to construct profiles within a bounded system and (2) to interact with other members. Particular characteristics or applications vary between different sites.[10]

SOCIAL NETWORKING VOCABULARY

Includes mobile platforms, functionalities, and applications (apps).

Semi-persistent public comments: Comments (e.g., testimonials, guestbook messages) that users can leave on other users' profiles for all viewers to see. These comments are semi-persistent in that they are not ephemeral but may disappear over a period of time or through user removal. They are typically displayed in reverse chronological order. Because of these comments, profiles are a combination of a user's self-expression and what others say about that individual.[11]

Peers: Users who are part of a lateral network of social relations, either acquaintances or colleagues, who are more or less socially equal. These relationships encompass affiliation, competition, disaffiliation, and distancing.[12]

Friend: Refers to relations that people self-identify as such, a subset of the peer group with which individuals have close affiliations. The term *friendship* refers even more narrowly to those shared practices that grow out of close relations in given, local social worlds.[13]

Wall: A message board where members might update their statuses or post other information. The origin of the *message board* dates back to early bulletin board systems.

Checking in: Location-based social networking sites allow users to post their location at venues or check in using mobile devices. At each check, the user is allotted points and/or badges. Location is determined by a GPS hardware device in the mobile device (e.g., tablets, pads, phones) or network location provided by the application.

Within each type of social site, varying levels of representation and engagement exist, from text-based interaction to immersive worlds. Our discussion must also consider social media sites in combination with mobile technologies. Now that mobile technologies (generically known as smartphones, tablets, or laptops) access the web and encourage the use of participatory media, they have enabled new social practices. Furthermore, mobile devices in tandem with social media applications are creating unique developments in personal relationships. Mobile and digital technologies are bringing people together both incidentally and by design with location-aware applications. Moreover, there are multiple ways in which people employ mobile texting and online instant messaging to talk to their partners, thus transforming traditional practices in intimate relationships.[14] The ubiquitous presence of computing technology, by way of mobile technology, allows for the joining of previously discrete spheres of life. Online users tend to leverage social networking sites to engage in common offline practices, incorporating social media into their everyday lives and complicating some practices while reinforcing others.

The participatory features integrated into most sites enable users to readily appropriate the technology for their own creative objectives. This open structure, at least under current conditions, allows for diverse practices that are dependent on culture and context. As unexpected applications and mashups emerge, a technologically enabled, participatory culture engenders a new sociotechnical relationship between subjects and objects. That is, users are influenced by the technology, and the technology is further shaped by users. Contrary to the commentary on social media sites, a growing number of qualitative studies find users of networked publics to be actively constructing their social and cultural worlds, not acting as innocent victims or passive recipients of media messages.[15]

Furthermore, the participatory element of social networking sites has spread beyond the sites' original profile-based interfaces and has been integrated into many other online and offline destinations. The ubiquitous social media logos, along with the *Like* or *Follow* buttons that now appear at the top or bottom of most published online articles, come to mind. These graphics are also included in many offline advertisements such as billboards, posters, and others. Thus, social media is no longer a singular platform or device that connects one person to another through linear actions in a set online environment. Rather, social media is comprised of increasingly complex and dynamic technologies that connect us to many users and audiences in multiple ways across virtual and physical space.[16]

IDENTITY AND NARRATIVE CONSTRUCTION

While postmodernist theory examines the operations of narrative construction in social practices, the fields of psychology and cognitive studies are also invested in this concern. With that in mind, a Facebook page may be construed as a personal or autobiographical narrative or profile, a visual construction of the self. Psychological research, particularly in the realm of ethnopsychology (a comparative psychology of social groups) has examined narrative construction as the process by which the self creates itself. For psychologists Don Bannister and Joyce Agnew, not only do people construe, or interpret, their own personas, but they also construe others and the experiential world around them.[17] This interpretation concludes that everything is seen in relation to the self; the self is a datum or reference for measuring all other selves or relationships. In other words, our sense of self is mutually constituted with our environment; we are the director, actor, and audience, incorporating wider systems of subcultural meaning within the community. In this sense, ethnopsychology conceptualizes the process of creating an online autobiographical narrative, or profile, as a process of self-construction.

Today's assemblage of self-construction is now technologically mediated. One way of addressing the technological interface is to consider actor-network theory (ANT). According to social scientist Bruno Latour, subjects and objects (technological objects, such as social media sites) are *actants* that engage in networks of interaction.[18] The relationship between a subject and a technological object is both iterative (adapted and refined through use) and responsive. In other words, the design of technology evolves in response to social values. The design of a bicycle is one example of this: Social concerns about speed, safety, and gender issues (including the social fact that nineteenth-century women wore long dresses) all informed the final design, including its size, mechanics, and formal configuration.[19] The physical design, hardware, and meaning of a technological object are socially constructed. Hence, technologies are not merely tools with fixed meanings; on the contrary, they are imbued with intentionality. Social values and objectives are embedded into the technological devices that humans create and thus are woven into the fabric of society.

Postmodern critical theorist Jean Baudrillard used the term *mutual constitution* to describe a condition of "self-referentiality where culture keeps imitating and duplicating itself in a pervasive game of mirrors."[20] When this was written, Baudrillard was referring to the effects of media and simulated experiences; if he were alive today, Baudrillard might suggest that social media both produces the cultural images of a society and mirrors those images back to its users in a process of self-referentiality, creating an endless circularity of images. From a Baudrillardian perspective, entities that are mutually constituted both draw from and reflect back upon each other. From a Latourian perspective, interactions between a human actant and technological object are a mutual process whereby structural media and human actions coproduce each other. From a psychological perspective, images serve as memories, cognitive maps, and creative projections with the potential to reconfigure reality, and vice versa.[21] In the case of social media, the functional operations of an interactive profile or wall become a performative space wherein subject and audience are mutually constituted and the differentiation between representation and the real is blurred. This indistinctness occurs because user-generated content can influence events (or perception of events) in physical space. Due to those reflexive operations between images and the real, urban scholar and historian Nezar AlSayyad contends that boundaries between the real and its representation are no longer useful to maintain.[22] That is, the division between the happenings of the physical world and the representation of those happenings in online user profiles is indistinct, as the real and the representation have effectively merged.

The cultural imaginary as advanced by urban planner Kevin Lynch (and a related concept, collective intentionality) serves as a theoretical framework for our analysis, and the term is applied here in its broader sense rather than in a strict Lacanian definition. I use the term to refer to the intersections of images and discursive forms in which cultural communities articulate and mirror themselves and act as points of reference for their collective identity formations. Cultural theorist Graham Dawson defines the cultural imaginary as "those vast networks of interlinking discursive themes, images, motifs and narrative forms that are publicly available within a culture at any one time, and articulate its psychic and social dimensions."[23] The intersection of the social, the psychic, and the visual expression is an important aspect of this assemblage. According to Dawson, "cultural imaginaries furnish public forms which organize knowledge of the social world."[24]

ORGANIZING THE FIELD

The complexity of networked publics makes it difficult to arrive at a highly accurate and stable taxonomy for all such platforms. While the structural framework is fairly consistent, the trending of social media has already witnessed Facebook's ascendance over Myspace, as well as the rise of Twitter, Tumblr, and Instagram, among others. Accepting this limitation, it may be more useful to conceptualize networked publics as dynamic sociotechnological systems rather than as fixed types. Observation and analysis of the diverse array of practices within networked publics suggests that they can be clustered based on the type and quality of interactions (the interactions exemplify the representational models) within the sites. The primary distinctions that can be made within networked publics are among sites that (1) enable *local social relations*, (2) support *shared interests*, (3) allow *mobile engagement*, and (4) provide *alternative immersive worlds*. These correspond to different genres of online culture and social network structures.

In the first category, I use the phrase *enabling social relations* to refer to the dominant mainstream practices of people undertaking everyday online interactions with friends and peers. These interactions occur with peers whom users encounter in physical space on a daily basis, but they might also include friends and peers whom users have met through work, school, sports affiliations, and other forms of local activity. For most people, these local groups are their primary sources of friendship, and their online lives mirror this local network. Facebook is the paradigmatic online example of this category of social networking site.

In contrast to friendship-based groups, *shared-interest groups* are those in which specialized activities, interests, or career aspirations—forms of identity—drive social relations. In these cases, however, the interests come first and structure the peer network rather than vice versa. These sites provide opportunities for individuals to connect with others with whom they share interests that might not be well represented within their local communities.[25] SoundCloud, a music-sharing platform, is an example of this category of social networking site.

Sites that allow *mobile engagement* are known as location-based social networks (LBSN), in which the Internet is accessed through mobile devices, meaning information is pervasive. Net locality implies the ubiquity of networked information; it is a cultural approach to the web of information that is intimately connected to the perceptual and experiential realities of everyday life. It instills locations with data resources, making physical location part of the web. User locations are associated with longitude and latitude coordinates, as well as with streets, buildings, landmarks, and others. This information transmitted via satellite or radio tower can be sorted not only by who, what, when, but also *where* activities take place. Thus, together—people, places, and things—create a nearly comprehensive map of where each is in relation to everything else.[26] Foursquare, a site that allows users to check in at certain locations, is an example of this category of social networking site.

Immersive worlds are, for the most part, interactive online gaming environments that enable players to cooperate often as teams and compete with each other on a global scale. Even though their players may form strong social alliances over extended periods of time, these online gaming environments (Multi User Domains or MUDs and Massively Multiplayer Online Role-Playing Games or MMORGs) are not addressed in this book due to differences in structure and intent—gamers usually do not participate in these sites for social networking ends. Final Fantasy and World of Warcraft are examples of this category of social networking site.[27]

SOCIAL SEGMENTATION

In *Cinematic Urbanism*, urban theorist and historian Nezar AlSayyad describes the reflexive relationship between media and the life of the city. He argues that the public's imaginary of the city and the physical city "reference each other in an act of mutual representation and definition."[28] If this notion is extended to the Internet, the latter can be viewed as an online metropolis. Clusters of networked publics can be conceptualized as constituting multinucleated patterns. Just as a metropolis is a complex system of spatial divisions—financial, entertainment, or ethnic neighborhoods and districts—so networked publics have different characteristics and functionalities.[29]

From a utopian perspective, social media would form an egalitarian space. Recent studies have invalidated this notion, however. Socioeconomic segmentation in urban neighborhoods has the effect of reproducing preexisting economic or cultural divisions online, such that even when content has a wider audience, it may not cross sociopolitical divisions.[30] Although social media supports mass communication, the dynamics of memes and media contagion demonstrate that what spreads online and to whom usually depends on the underlying socioeconomic structure of the sharing user base.[31]

Acknowledging a socially segmented model of social media assumes that equal access already exists. Not surprisingly, the acquisition and implementation of digital technologies is often limited to those in higher income levels, reinforcing a preexisting economic and social divide—a phenomenon that has come to be known as digital difference.[32] This term denotes the gap between populations with effective access to digital and information technology and those with very limited or no access.[33] It connotes imbalances in both physical access to technology and in the knowledge and skills needed to effectively participate as digital citizens. The uneven access to information and knowledge is typically influenced by gender, income, race, ethnicity, and location. Such digital exclusion is part of a broader divide contributing to social and economic exclusion. The demographic reality has serious implications—while the digital divide is traditionally defined in terms of access to computers and the Internet, it is concurrently bound up with a knowledge divide.

The data on the digital/knowledge divide suggests that many of the consistencies of the physical world map onto online worlds. Just as residential neighborhoods in the physical world tend to self-organize by attracting individuals with similar economic, social, or cultural identifiers, those economic distinctions also exist among networked publics. Socioeconomic patterns not only reveal themselves in choice of sites and creation of profiles, but also broadcast their presence in the physical world through friends of friends or places to frequent. Social scientist Eszter Hargittai's study of Facebook and Myspace users revealed that a person's gender, ethnicity, and parental educational background are all associated with membership in particular social sites.[34] In another study, users emphasized how website aesthetics influenced their browsing choices.[35] Unfortunately, networked publics appear to reproduce many of the biases that exist in physical publics. Furthermore, search algorithms are designed to reflect personalized interests, so each Internet user views a different Google search results page even when the same term is searched. Ads are algorithmically curated according to each user's social markers or interests.[36] Thus, political beliefs, religious views, and social signifiers based on income, race, gender, sexuality, and age are reproduced online.[37] Hargittai observed that "people are segmenting themselves in networked publics and this correlates to the way in which they are segmented in everyday life."[38] Even online, there are economic markers and ideological domains that map onto the everyday.

Unlike those who use general social networking sites, members of shared interest or fan culture sites tend to be more spatially dispersed. Their sites are designed and configured so that diverse and unconnected individuals can connect based on affinities or other activities.[39] Even so, special interests may reveal social markers related to social or economic status. Some sites may be structured to allow the exchange or sharing of an underrepresented language or culture, while others support shared racial, religious, or diaspora-based identities that extend beyond national borders.

For example, queer youth in rural America are destabilizing expectations for practices surrounding queerness, space, and the politics of visibility in their participation in social media outlets.[40] Queer youth in rural spaces are engaging these various topics within online spaces and propagating dialogi-cal exchange between differing perspectives. Rural spaces operate in unique ways not necessarily valued or understood by urban populations. In ac-cessing chat rooms, these youth do not use digital media to escape the con-fines of their communities but rather to "expand their local belonging."[41] As identities become sociotechnical, Internet and mobile technologies are fostering tools that challenge hegemonic ideas regarding community, space, and belonging. According to Mary Gray, author of *Out in the Country: Youth, Media, and Queer Visibility in Rural America*, some "young people confound clear boundaries between online and offline worlds by integrat-ing their uses of media and public space in everyday processes of identity negotiation and articulation." Many use digital spaces "not to hide but to be seen," she writes.[42] From frequenting chat rooms in order to better un-derstand queer sexualities to finding other queer youth in other local areas, rural youth are transcending the boundaries of previously defined identities through the use of digital media. And by blurring the boundaries of physical and digital spaces, similar special-interest groups, whether gendered, reli-gious, or political, are becoming increasingly significant social actors that challenge the status quo.[43]

EXPLICATION OF SOCIAL NETWORK SITES

The study of new media, in particular, poses a daunting challenge due to a lack of disciplinary constraint and institutional tradition. There is no cur-rent orthodoxy outlining a step-by-step methodology, thus my method has been to borrow methods from other disciplines, even if only to critique them or use them as sites of departure. Any humanities study attempting to theo-rize communal social practices relies on a heuristic model, which involves the interpretation of data. That imperative is heightened when studying new media, which typically exhibit an exclusively visual mode of interaction. New media researchers studying graphical artifacts such as online platforms must continually ask, as did David Bailey, the London photographer in Mi-chelangelo Antonioni's film *Blowup* (1966), "What is the meaning of an image?" Here, methods drawn from visual and cultural criticism can assist with interpretation.

Analysis of interaction, especially in regard to how online activities re-produce everyday social practices in the physical world, is also a key com-ponent in the hermeneutics. In that respect, networked publics are part of a circularity of self-representation and replication in the cultural imaginary and physical world.[44] Unlike a mass-produced commodity or a one-way broadcast model, however, a networked public is successful because of the creative content that the user brings to it. The psychological mechanisms at work bind the sociospatial self to the media platform by forging an iterative relation between the two.

CASE STUDY: FACEBOOK PROFILE

The Facebook page reproduced in Figure 4.1 is not very different in appearance from many other web pages or blogs on the Internet. The graphics are familiar, presenting an HTML-designed, interactive web document with various images and boxes highlighting personal information. The page is a portrait of an individual and her friends within a bounded, gridded, two-dimensional space. Across the top of the frame is the ubiquitous blue Facebook menu with its various drop-down selections: Home, Profile, Friends, and Inbox. The name and settings are personalized. The compositional format is subtle and restrained, with a white background and sans serif font in a web-safe blue, a style that was launched and refined by industrial designer

Figure 4.1   Facebook timeline.
Credit: Maria Julia Escalona

Jonathan Ive at Apple Computers. There are various temporal and spatial layers with which Facebook users interact. In the foreground is the current page, displaying the user's wall of interactions, including text and image exchanges. Backgrounded (but accessible by hyperlink) is an information page that displays this user's personal narrative: education and travel history, likes and dislikes, favorite quotations, and more. This information can be changed at any time although the framework remains fairly stable. What continually changes are the updates, photos, and messages posted to the user's wall.

As documented in Chapter Three, this volume, social media is constructed through specific historical processes in which both textual *and* visual language play an important, but not constitutive, role. As shown in Figure 4.2, each page is invisibly guided by a grid, which lends coherence to the composition, acting as both organization and vehicle. The structure of the two-dimensional graphical interface constrains interactive possibilities.

Yet the visible profile page belies the immense invisible infrastructure of the larger Facebook social network. One aspect thereof is the sheer immensity of its population (over a billion as of May 2013)—the largest in the social media world, indicative of a complex social ecology. A Facebook profile page is but one interior node within a dynamic networked system; each page features a multiplicity of invisible links to profile pages of friends and acquaintances. In this networked public, the subset of user profiles and friends' profiles constitutes a functioning social system.[45] Within this functioning system, users' prior social relationships and life experiences inform their current social practices. Thus Facebook acts as a relay system, organizing a circularity of images and imaging, consumption and production, and

Figure 4.2   Facebook wall.
Credit: Maria Julia Escalona

learned social practices and lived social practices, including those in physical space.

As a vast social sea, the user's active production of a single node provides a composite visual picture of a life at a given moment of time.[46] This interactive journal changes by the minute. Within certain programmatic constraints, the user sorts the ephemera of everyday experience, the user's context as it were, choosing the most meaningful images and artifacts, such as invitations, photos of activities and events, club memberships, interests, and videos. The profile page serves as a medium through which users can express feelings and make sense of events. Therefore, the subjective content contained within the profile is hardly neutral. Images, online and off, shape our cultural imaginary and psychological expectations and so prefigure reality.

Facebook can be further analyzed as a visual grammar, a temporal photobricolage of possibilities.[47] While the technique of bricolage is easily translatable into digital media, it was identified before digital media came into being. Recognized by anthropologist Claude Lévi-Strauss, as well as cultural theorists in art, theater, and music, bricolage is a technique that incorporates existing everyday materials into the construction of new works (its original meaning is close "to tinker"). The artist Kurt Schwitters's mixed-media work *Merzbild* (or *Merz*) is an example of bricolage as an attempt at psychological integration of the artist's immediate personal environment, including test prints of graphic designs, bus tickets, found objects, and ephemera given to him by friends. While the technique is often associated with twentieth-century modernism, the use of borrowed or fragmented pieces of the everyday has also come to be associated with postmodern literature and architecture, with sampling in music and, most recently, with Facebook or Pinterest's Protopop aesthetic, a precursor to Pop Art that contained pop culture imagery such as mundane objects culled from American commercial products and advertising imaging.[48]

In the bricolage of a profile, is the Facebook user simply a consumer of media, appropriating and lifting images to use as fragments of an evolving visual script? Or is it possible that bricolage and sampling are instrumental in a reflexive relationship between user and environment? I would like to suggest that Facebook profiles extend bricolage well beyond an aesthetic surface treatment. Unlike with television content, the viewer is also the user and is actively engaged in producing the work. The process of active production suggests that the bricolage profile as a genre is more closely aligned with autobiography than with a pattern of consumption.

Bricolage and autobiography have been paired successfully in modern American literature, as in William Burroughs's *Naked Lunch* and Theresa Cha Hung's multimedia autobiography *Dictee*. Each of these works draws on fragments of the writer's life in a dynamic, nonlinear narrative form. Autobiographical work has historically been a popular genre in the United States, owing in part to Americans' high geographical mobility. Unlike in parts of the world where one's identity is preinscribed by one's birth parents and birthplace, in the United States, the so-called lack of strong class or social identity and fixed geographical contexts creates a need for individuals to tell their stories.[49] A Facebook profile, like an early twentieth-century scrapbook, draws on existing material in the user's personal landscape,[50] be it celebrity profiles, reality television, or YouTube videos. Profiles are part of the visual vernacular; at the same time, they entail a compositional decision-making and editing process. This editing process most commonly results in an idealization of the self if only as a means of creating a stronger narrative. When speaking of the *bricoleur*, Lévi-Strauss explains how myths are generated from everyday reality and heroes emerge from the banal.[51] When confronted with sociogeographic fragmentation, individuals tend to respond by seeking stable personal or collective identities.[52] If fragmentation is symptomatic of a postmodern condition, the self-constructed narrative of bricolage lends visual coherence to the user's varied life experiences and serves as a method of production for navigating a changeable postmodern, postindustrial condition.

As a representation, is a Facebook profile a simulation in the Baudrillardian sense? One could argue that it is no more a simulation than is an artist's self-portrait or an autobiographical novel or film because the content is derived from personal engagement with the everyday. Most of the content (75 percent) exchanged over social network sites is digital imagery, and subjects typically construct their identities by availing themselves of digital imaging and photo editing.[53] How people alter content in networked publics varies, but code, text, images, and videos are frequently modified or remixed; issues of authenticity are thus at stake. Furthermore, the underlying open framework seems to encourage modding and performances that include the subversive reappropriation (as with political groups) or bending by culture jammers, artists, or by anyone willing to create a Facebook profile page.[54] Alterations can be functional (when applied to code to make it work in a new environment), aesthetic (when images are altered to remove red eye), political (when famous photos are modified to make political statements),[55] or socially deceptive (when others' textual statements are changed).[56] In determining authenticity, the autobiographical contract between author and audience prohibits fabrication, but where does artistic license end and deception begin? While the remix is economically and politically contested within the entertainment industries, media theorist Lawrence Lessig thinks that it reflects an active and creative engagement with media artifacts while blurring distinctions between consumer and producer.[57]

One could also consider a Facebook profile from Melvin Webber's perspective regarding the nonplace urban realm. As urban planner Webber describes it, "accessibility rather than the propinquity aspect of 'place' is the necessary condition [for community.][58] Accessibility is also embedded within historical notions of the commons. As an accessible common place, Facebook can be conceptualized as a social condenser, in sharp contrast with Sennett's windswept modern urban plazas.[59] This concept of a social condenser is derived from Soviet Constructivist theory and contains the premise that architecture has the capability to influence social behavior. The intention behind a social condenser was to influence the experience of public spaces, with the expressed goal of breaking down perceived social hierarchies in an effort to create socially equitable spaces. Some approaches to creating the built form of a social condenser are not readily translatable to online spaces; for example, intentional overlapping and intersection of architectural programs within a space through circulatory paths. Their organizational strategies, however, can be applied to online spaces. It is possible that member profiles as shared nodes could create an environment wherein the potential exists for otherwise dispersed social communities to interact. Does Facebook succeed at this? Yes and no—we have seen how users tend to aggregate along preexisting social lines; nevertheless, in the 2008 presidential election, for example, Barack Obama was able to unite constituencies of previously unrelated individuals through the medium of social network sites such as Facebook and Twitter. In 2013, after the Boston Marathon bombing, Twitter offered amateur reporting updates during the lockdown.

As much potential as the Internet has to connect dispersed social communities, there is not enough recognition of the structures of power that lie behind the screen. Facebook, as a form of computer-mediated communication for social or financial interactions, extracts data on individuals' lives (both public and private) and packages it to external sources.[60] Corporations use these same methods to centralize and concentrate their global marketing efforts and financial networks. Data mining (and the selling of that data) is the primary economic objective for commercially owned networked publics, with advertising secondary (note selective advertising based on data mining). With mobile technologies, users' movement patterns are now also tracked and analyzed. On one level, Facebook members are engaged in strengthening their social networks; on another level, their social actions are being monitored, analyzed, packaged, and sold to marketing companies.

The question remains, then: Is Facebook a public space? While Facebook *is* an online social space, a networked public, it is not wholly public. Legally, Facebook is a semipublic forum. Due to its ubiquity, however, many perceive it to be a public venue or forum. This view disregards the obvious pragmatic and economic requirements of a computer and Internet connection, in addition to the requirement that Facebook members must be registered due to safety and data mining purposes. danah boyd's social network research on teenagers, the most extensive to date, concluded that for most users, social networks were equivalent to hanging out at the mall. Moreover, boyd's teenagers expressed strong desires to occupy a space apart from adults. There are various motivations that contribute to this line of thinking, many of which are outside the scope of my research (it goes without saying that teenagers in many societies seek differentiation).[61] For teenagers seeking differentiation, networked publics largely meet the need for a discrete public space. We will discuss in the next chapter how that pattern continues into college.

Social media has become embedded in many North American adults' quotidian social practices.[62] As media scholar Michal Daliot-Bul puts it, "The popularity of . . . the mobile internet evolved through its colonization of the in-between moments of everyday life."[63] Social media operates as a relay point between activities in physical space, such that, flexibility, adaptability, and mobility are influential in the adoption pattern of social media. Even before the emergence of the Internet, relocation and change were givens in postmodern, postindustrial culture, especially in the United States, with most relocations occurring during college age and continuing throughout the working years.[64] Yet mobility creates an equally valid need for a constant, which is one reason why people belong to social networks. Similar to physicist Leon Foucault's pendulum, networked publics can provide the subject with a fixed point in a changing world. More importantly, most networked publics are grounded in actual relationships and tied to everyday activities and spaces in the physical world. Although they are dynamic in form and content, web designers assert that "the successful online social networks are the ones which most closely map onto the physical world."[65]

IDEOSCOPES AND CULTURAL IMAGINARIES

We have explored how social media is engaged with everyday culture, describing a permeable boundary between online and offline practices. Although some social critics say that mediated relationships are contributing to confused sense of self among adolescents, others say that experimentation with identities is an intrinsic part of adolescence.[66] Social geographer David Harvey suggests that individuals will explore all of the divergent possibilities and will cultivate "a whole series of simulacra as a milieu of escape, fantasy, and distraction."[67] Creative expressions of postmodern sensibilities are mimetic of everyday cultural fragmentation, ephemerality, and collage. Harvey, however, identifies an equal but opposite tendency of those faced with fragmentation and ephemerality. He says that individuals reach out for a "personal or collective identity . . . for secure moorings in a shifting world."[68] In other words, people experience a concurrent grounding impetus. Harvey's theory emphasizes the connection between place and social identity, and at the same time, it identifies intensified fragmentation as people seek to attach themselves to particular places, perhaps at the expense of more universal identifications, a topic we will return to in the next chapter.

Facebook exemplifies Harvey's grounding impetus, while the online immersive environment, World of Warcraft, more closely resembles his notional milieu of escape and fantasy. The two sites also differ in terms of authenticity. Social networking sites, based on physical world relationships, rely on the photographic image as a referent (whether a still image or video), evoking cultural theorist Roland Barthes's notion of the transcendent possibilities of photography to inspire subjective affect. Photography, as a first-order referent—reality once removed—pulls a previous moment from the past into present time. For Facebook members, it is clear that the observable relation between the profile image and the user is quite close because, for many, their social relationships are preexisting in physical space. Even the autobiographical model presumes an element of truth—otherwise a profile is fictional.[69] While one is potentially free to create a new identity, adult Facebook users generally do not—preeexisting relationships and the autobiographical contract between author and reader preclude it.[70]

When networked publics ignite the cultural imaginary, new allegiances and participatory practices are formed. One example is The Berg social media site, which effectively lives in the public imagination. It was initiated by architect Jakob Tigges, who designed a 1,000-foot-high artificial mountain (hence the name) on the former Templehof airport site in Berlin, Germany.

The project's presence, as represented in Figure 4.3, has been witnessed through newspapers, magazines, blogs, and subway posters distributed nationally and internationally. Social media has been instrumental to the

Figure 4.3   The Berg, Berlin, is a 3,281-foot urban mountain for public use: hiking, skiing, or relaxing (2012); http://www.the-berg.de/proof.html.
Credit: Jakob Tigges

viral spread of the mountain's image; The Berg even has a Facebook page with thousands of members, a Twitter account, and YouTube videos. Urban kiosks sell postcards and souvenirs documenting its existence, while live-feed webcams monitor earthmoving activities at a simulated construction site. Not only has The Berg become Berlin's most popular attraction with tourists expecting to visit it, but by some accounts, it has surpassed well-established landmarks, such as Mount Rushmore and Niagara Falls, in popularity.[71] What these tourists do not know, however, is that the project makes use of the reflexive power of cultural imaginary—the dimension through which human beings create their ways of living together and their ways of representing their collective urban experience. In reality, The Berg does not exist.

How did such a fiction take hold in the mind of the public? Historically, architecture and urban design propositions are components of larger myths, sometimes founded on the real, but other times, only in the broader cultural imaginary, in other words, they are socially constructed through narratives, myths of origins, symbols, and rituals. Imaginaries, however, are not immaterial. Indeed, scholarship on imaginaries emphasizes "the impossibility of defining clear-cut boundaries between the real and the imagination."[72] For every physical site, including Templehof airport, there are multiple narratives constructing the imagined geography that residents and others associate with a particular location. Thus, the imaginary is intricately linked to the material, explains sociologist Rob Shields, as "these spatial conceptual forms play a significant part in the rationale by which daily lives are lived and by which decisions, policies, and actions are rationalized and legitimized."[73] Urban imaginaries play an important role in understanding place and in influencing the decisions that either enable or limit possible futures for them.

While not constituting an established reality, The Berg's ontological basis exists within a system of meanings that govern a particular social structure. And social media acts as the vehicle that structures a reciprocal relationship between the individual and the physical environment. Within the cultural imaginary, The Berg can be understood as a historical construct (even if fabricated) defined by the interactions of subjects in society. The Berg leaves the spectator somewhere between believing it was there and wishing it were true, according to Tigges.[74]

As with The Berg, social networking sites allow urban residents to reflect on their urban experience and intervene in decision-making processes. They instantiate a public forum where people can attempt to make sense of the world around them in a given time and place. The Berg's social media presence enables a collective conversation and deliberation among urban residents, as a space to envision a different kind of city from what was inherited. Architect Stewart Hicks says that architecture such as this "poses questions, images alternatives, and stages potentials—nudging the public toward a new openness and expanded understanding."[75]

CONCLUSION

As we have discussed, a networked public such as Facebook is a space con-structed simultaneously through networked technologies, as well as by re-ality and the imagined community. Because social media organizes people and practices in the physical world, these platforms and their applications have increasingly critical implications. If we are to understand social media, we also must understand the sociocultural forces operating in the larger environment. Social media is not outside the physical world; on the con-trary, it is designed by, and entangled in, physical world social practices. To such a degree, social media effectively acts as a novel form of architecture, which creates opportunities for social interaction and ultimately, the two are intertwined.

Building on the notion that online social spaces and physical spaces are mutually constituted, it would seem important to observe and critique the existing physical world as a means to envision alternatives and avoid repro-ducing its inequities and inequalities online. "The task before us is not one of prioritizing technological solutions over human solutions," as architect William Mitchell argued, "but rather one of imagining and creating digitally mediated environments for the kind of lives we want to lead and the sorts of communities we want to have."[76] Cultural imaginaries and the collec-tive discussion that emerges from such imaginaries, whether informed by political or design aspirations (and ultimately, all design is political), have significant implications: They enable a process of reflexive interaction with the potential to contribute to transformative change.

5 Surveying Social Media

> Mobility complicated [ethnographic] matters, but mediated technologies changed the rules entirely. In a networked society, we cannot take for granted the idea that culture is about collocated peoples.
> —danah boyd (2008)[1]

Networked publics are produced by specific geographic, material, conceptual, and experiential processes. In the previous chapters, we have discussed theoretical constructs of public space linked to communal identity, civitas and democracy, and self-expression.[2] Now we shift our focus to explore the quotidian practices as well as other complex conditions that influence participation in social media. The findings of an Internet ethnography I completed between 2008 and 2012 will be analyzed; these findings not only represented a test of concepts but also revealed unexpected complexities. The Internet ethnographic data were derived from a multiphase study called "Situated Networks: In Search of the Public" initiated at Dalhousie University in Nova Scotia, Canada. First, a pilot study was conducted from April 29 to May 30, 2008, and a second, primary study was conducted at the University of California–Berkeley from September 24, 2008 to June 1 2009, with an informal follow-up study completed on April 2, 2012. All data was anonymized. In this multiphase study, I collected 210 surveys: 67 surveys from the phase 1 pilot study, 107 surveys from the phase 2 primary study, and 36 surveys from the follow-up study. The studies were not merged.

Out of the total number of participants of the online survey, 80 individuals also agreed to participate in an optional interview: 6 from the pilot study and 74 from the primary study. Note that the quantitative data from the multiple-choice survey questionnaires of both studies were not merged. This is because the pilot study was set up to test the instruments, and as a result, some of the multiple-choice questions changed or were reworded between phase 1 and phase 2 (for additional information, refer to Appendix A: Methodology).

While a number of methods arising out of Science, Technology & Society (STS) have proven useful for the formation of a theory of networked publics, this chapter considers Internet ethnography as another suitable approach. There is ample precedent for applying a social science methodology to learn about social spaces in the physical world, and logic suggests these same methods would apply to social media. Online research has been called by different terms: Internet ethnography, online ethnography, or simply, nethnography. Within the social sciences, online methodologies came into broader usage as classical ethnographic inquiry moved away from defining fields as spatially defined localities and more toward sociopolitical locations, networks, or multi-sited approaches. Notions of fieldwork have also had to contend with digital spaces, and this methodological transformation seems to be necessary. The development of social media and its effects are of immediate relevance to networked urbanism, political economy, public culture, migration and diasporas, transnational communities, mass media, and cultural studies, among others. Anthropologist Maximilian Forte emphasizes the importance of developing "an anthropological perspective on the processes through which grassroots visions . . . are being mobilized to link different countries, regions and localities."[3] That position acknowledges that some of the largest international mobilizations of protest have been coordinated and orchestrated via social media.

As to the question, why survey research? "Surveys are useful for descriptive, explanatory, or exploratory purposes," according to social scientist Earl Babbie. "They are chiefly used in studies that have individual people as the units of analysis. . . . Survey research is probably the best method available to the social scientist interested in collecting original data for purposes of describing a population too large to observe directly."[4] Furthermore, anonymous online interviews may tend to mitigate the so-called Bradley effect (the phenomenon of social desirability bias where interviewees may feel under pressure to provide an answer that is deemed to be publicly acceptable). In this case, net ethnography can be advantageous to direct observation. As anthropologist Annette Markham concludes, "Online or offline, all of us make sense of our experiences and tell the stories of our lives in self-centered and self-understood ways."[5] In summary, an online methodology was evaluated and considered appropriate for studying online cultures, in addition to methods of direct participation and observation.

The sample group was drawn from a North American demographic of early Internet adopters over a two-and-one-half-year period. Social patterns for North Americans are not isolated, however. They often predict patterns that develop subsequently in other regions of the world. I applied a mixed methodology consisting of two phases: (1) an objective phase in which the relations of online social space and the structures of the field were examined; research instruments consisted of online surveys for social media participants; and (2) a subjective analysis of social agents' dispositions to act, as well as their categories of perception and understanding resulting from inhabitation of the field. I employed a range of qualitative analytical research techniques: personal interviews, participant observations, and accounts of individuals.[6]

Out of 107 respondents, most (70 percent) were less than thirty-four years old. They were born after 1987 and for them, digital and mobile technologies are familiar aspects of everyday experience. Their perspectives on how technologies impact social practices may differ significantly from those of someone raised more than thirty years ago. Electronic games and the Internet were thoroughly integrated into their play prior to entry into elementary school. As a result, most have seamlessly assimilated social and other forms of digital media into their everyday experiences, rather than having acquired them at later stages of their lives. While there was a broad spectrum of responses, the study discerned a diverse population with largely heterodox practices spanning mainstream to subaltern. Within the sample group, there existed a gradient from public to private. It should further be noted that that even within proprietary social media platforms, there is no one universally identifiable public.

While the primary objective of the study was to isolate the online social practices of a group of users under the age of thirty-four, the findings directed attention to the larger socioeconomic environment, including effects of increased mobility, economic uncertainty, and potential marginalization. Out of the responses, there emerges a complex and diverse portrait of individuals negotiating a need for connectivity in the face of dislocation—social and/or geographic. From a larger perspective, this trend indicates a disjuncture between the associative aspects of the Internet and the disruptive effects of contemporary social and spatial dispersion. Applying an inductive approach, I argue that forces associated with dislocation and intensification are giving rise to a new norm of connectivity.

BACKGROUND

Over the last decade, a growing body of Internet research has contributed to knowledge about networked cultures. Nonetheless, there is insufficient consolidated empirical research into social media and its formative role in the production of space. While the Pew Research Center provides extensive resources for quantitative information, its studies lack associative analyses with geospatial models and practices. As noted in the previous chapter, danah boyd's mixed-method study (2008) was limited by its narrow sample demographic of 14- to 18-year-olds.[7] While one of boyd's key findings was that oversupervised teens use networked publics as online "hang-out spaces" after school, the combination of limited physical mobility coupled with Internet access (for the ostensible purpose of homework tasks) consequently resulted in virtual "malls for teenagers to hang out in."[8] This prompted me to inquire whether an autonomous, more socially mobile demographic would rely on social media in a similar manner. What happens when high school students graduate and move on? Do they retain the same online practices, or do they change? And what might be the implications of that trend?

While boyd's study made visible the popular perceptions and social practices of a large subculture within the virtual mall of Facebook, a distinct psychological transition takes place between the stage of living at home as a teenager and that of being an autonomous adult. I suspected that this would be an important factor in studying the individual's relation to community (however defined). Thus boyd's study became the launching point for my own research. Since boyd surveyed 14- to 18-year-olds, I chose a demographic of 18- to 35-year-olds. I also wanted to verify two important trends related to online communities: first, the development of social networks based on geographical proximity and close contact (otherwise known as strong bonds), and second, the growth of a smaller percentage of niche or shared-interest groups (based on knowledge acquisition) that extended beyond the physical boundaries of the neighborhood to encompass national or global communities.

Other qualitative background research applicable to this project included an important 2007 study based in New Orleans by Claire Procopio and Steven Procopio that investigated how online social networks were used as search mechanisms to geographically locate neighbors, friends, and relatives for economic and emotional support in the aftermath of Hurricane Katrina.[9] Another study by anthropologist Thomas Schweizer considered how social networks are embedded within physical space, acknowledging the global embeddedness and cultural heterogeneity of the Internet.[10] A study in Jamaica by anthropologists Heather Horst and Daniel Miller surmised that each culture produces *its own* Internet. They concluded that online social practices are culturally reflexive and unique.[11]

As I was organizing the study, mobile technologies (specifically smartphones) came into wider use. Mobile devices are important to this topic because they change the situational context of Internet access and social media content. Mobile devices were also understudied, since they were not included in boyd's research. More than 100 million people currently access Twitter or Facebook through mobile devices, and they are twice as active as nonmobile users.[12] This development is gradually transforming the manner in which we engage and interact with public space. Mobile devices are not only used for personal messaging; they are also being employed in unexpected ways. For example, cell phones support small entrepreneurial enterprises in rural areas of India and Ghana, where fixed infrastructure is lacking.[13] In such developing-world contexts, cell phones may be employed as mobile clinics, data-processing devices, remote sensors, and economic exchange methods—that is, as portable computers with wireless access. Within these contexts, mobile devices are increasingly becoming the primary mode of Internet connection.[14] In North America, smartphones are regularly employed for mobile banking and shopping.

The mobility aspect is becoming increasingly critical within the field of urban informatics, where unanticipated practices and user adaptations of devices and platforms are being integrated into mobile program development.[15] Networked and interactive technologies realize their utility through ecologies that include more than the technical alone; they also include the logic of users, which can diverge significantly from the engineer's logic. Ad hoc experimentation and mobile application development are examples such responses. That divergence can become particularly intense—and especially variable—in the case of urban environments, given the multiple socioeconomic subjectivities that they encompass. This study provides more extensive quantitative and qualitative information about those new conditions and their relation to user appropriation of and engagement with physical space.

Whether mobile or desktop, networked publics are temporally and spatially noncoincidental. A networked public has the advantage of being individually accessible, which was viewed as an important affordance by the participants in this study, who tended to have diverse schedules and often resided in different time zones than did their friends and families. The study demographic, 18- to 34-year-old college-educated Internet users, seems in general to be experiencing dislocation and life change. Most individuals have moved from their birthplaces for college and will probably move again after graduation. Factors related to economic opportunities (or the lack thereof) are also formative conditions for geographic dislocation within advancing economic globalization.

There are significant differences between how people are organized online and the organization of face-to-face relationships. Due to varying levels of accessibility and transparency, social media differs from past forms. While the Habermasian model isolated discursive publics (e.g., cafés, squares, pamphlets), online publics, unlike singular publics, include an entire spectrum of social practices, which was discussed in "Assembling the Publics" (Chapter Two) in this volume. The online spectrum extends from wholly public discussion groups and/or forums (open to all), to semipublic affinity-based groups (shared interests), to semiprivate professional groups (membership requirements), to private networks (private groups), which, it could be argued, no longer constitute *publics* in the discursive sense. Online publics are not meant to substitute for physical publics. Respondents readily admitted the limitations of social media, acknowledging the shortcomings and difficulties involved with maintaining nonproximal relationships, whether personal or professional.

Urban sociologist Manuel Castells has long contended that the norm of physical space is being displaced by a norm of connectivity,[16] and the findings of this study do not dispute this. The terms *online* and *offline* were used repeatedly by participants in the study to describe Internet-based experiences in contrast to experiences in physical space, respectively. For the respondents, the connection, the *line*, is the norm of measurement to which all other experiences are compared. If language or terminology reveals tendencies about people's unconscious assumptions, then society, defined as social actants in physical space, seems to be increasingly modulated by online social practices.[17] In other words, as connectivity becomes the new measure of interaction, social practices exist relative to the line of connection. One conclusion advanced by the respondents, however, is that connectivity alone is insufficient to produce a social space. Production of a social space depends upon its enaction. Participation over time—in the form of content uploading, reflexive commenting, and meme sharing[18]—builds up spatiality vis-à-vis interaction and thus imbues a space with potential for agency.

A critically important finding of this Internet ethnography is that members of networked publics have varied and diverse sets of opinions, just as do those of spatial publics, and they interact online in many diverse ways. Any theoretical model must accept diversity and fragmentation as intrinsic to a contemporary definition of publicness as the condition of a site where differences are assembled. Networked publics consist of heterodox practices; indeed, we find not one Public but many publics. Due to extensive cultural specificities, social media operates as one part of a complex social ecology of relations, devices, filters, and types of activity—some geospatial and some not.

Acknowledging that the phenomenon of social media is highly diverse, it is still possible to ascribe generalizations. First, for many of the respondents (but not all), a geographic dislocation of some form was an influential factor in their initial participation within networked publics. Second, many expressed a need for close personal relationships, which at times competed with other influences in their lives. Third, membership in a social media platform provided an alternative public, a readily accessible mobile community, into which one could escape the demands of life. In general, the interpretation of this data yields a population of individuals trying to create wholeness, stability, and community in their lives at a time when the economic environment was not particularly well suited to support those same objectives. Most of the respondents insisted on maintaining connectivity in spite of increasing financial and work-related stress. The irony is the same technologies used to alleviate dislocation might actually acerbate it.

QUANTITATIVE SURVEY DATA

What Social Networking Site?

For 96 percent of survey respondents, Facebook was the preferred social networking site. Most said that they had "no special loyalty" to Facebook; sharing a platform with their friends was the most important factor. As one respondent said, "A surprising number of my friends belong to it." About half (48 percent) of the respondents had a constant online presence or persona in the form of a personal blog or homepage in addition to a Facebook profile. The vast majority belonged to one or two networked publics (81 percent), with a lesser percentage belonging to three or more (19 percent).

What Are You Doing Online Socially?

Almost all respondents belonged to networked publics primarily for social purposes (98 percent). Other reasons included professional activities and various special interests. While logged onto their home pages, the vast majority of respondents used social media to accept or send invitations for future events (75 percent). Next frequently mentioned were activities related to the planning or organizing of events to be realized in physical space (46 percent). These findings support the notion that online use typically parallels telephone use, where both methods of communication facilitate or enable activities in occurring physical space.

Media sharing was almost as important as invitations, with 70 percent of all respondents sharing videos, photos, or links to online content. Sometimes the content was acquired (freely shared from outside sources online), but more often it was original (user-generated) content. Social media companies have responded to this trend; popular platforms have increased image and video-sharing capabilities (which may explain why Facebook paid $715 million to acquire Instagram, a photo-sharing application). Respondents described these sharing activities as self-expressive, creative, and fun. Videos shared ranged across genres, from fictional to documentary (i.e., documenting events occurring in physical space).

Another common activity within networked publics was that of regularly updating personal pages (65 percent). There were fewer instances of other activities; for example, 20 percent used social networks to meet new people, 9 percent self-advertised and promoted their careers online, and 8 percent arranged for hookups (an ambiguous phrase, usually meaning any form of sexual interaction between two casual acquaintances).[19] A significant group (31 percent) said that they were involved with "other" online activities. This is a large percentage to go unmentioned; such activities may include seeking music, videos, or software; undertaking research; seeking pornography; shopping; and more.

Frequency and Duration

The average user checked his or her Facebook wall once or twice a day (44 percent) and spent about fifteen minutes online each time. A smaller group, only 17 percent of respondents, spent more than an hour a day on Facebook or other networked publics.[20] Another 29 percent of respondents checked the wall two to four times a day, and another 27 percent checked five or more times a day. Similar to the Internet in general, a blog or personal profile page allows for slippage in time and space whether social networks are proximal or nonproximal, depending on how frequently the users access their messages or update their status. Online communication may precede events in physical space (for planning purposes) and/or document events afterward (share photos). For 53 percent of respondents, distance was too great to use a networked public for planning, but the connection allowed them to view their friends' activities from afar.

INTERPRETATION

My ethnographic/participant observations had already documented the privileging of visuality in networked publics, for example, via text- and image-based exchanges occurring in a mediated physical space. Nevertheless, in this part of the study, my question aimed at something beyond representational issues—it could more be accurately stated as this: What is the basis of knowledge that corresponds to a social reality, and how is that knowledge acquired and disseminated? While I will argue that networked publics are less material and less proximal, nonetheless, they *are* experiential. If visual knowledge is foregrounded, are networked publics' representations of the world therefore representations of physical-world public spaces? Or is it possible that they are abstracted and/or internalized by users and therefore more closely aligned with a broader theoretical definition of space, which is to say that public space is created and defined through social action and not only through physical constructs? In summary, is the phenomenon of networked publics competing with physical space, or is it an alternate mode of public interaction?

As an interpretive framework for organizing the responses, the respondents need for connectivity is applied throughout. It expresses itself through four conceptual categories: Distal Relations, Concern to Maintain Intimacy, Life Balance/Control of Communication Style, and New Spaces of Play and Creativity.

1. Distal Relations

Within the sample demographic, the reason most frequently cited (by 61 percent) for engaging in online networks activities involved nonproximal relations. "I am at college away from home, and a number of my older friends have scattered in different areas." In spite of these relocations and the resulting social fragmentation in the respondents' lives, much of the data revealed a desire to maintain strong social networks. (Note: There was also conflicting evidence of an equally strong desire to maintain autonomy and distance.) This tendency was paralleled by the pragmatic desire to make oneself accessible quickly and efficiently.

> My best friend moved away after our freshman year of high school. . . .
> We have stayed in touch, and continue to do so, through our common

hobby of Final Fantasy XI. We have only seen each other for the collective span of several days over the five-year period. When I moved away to college, AIM and MySpace were crucial (or at least they seemed so at the time) to maintaining relationships in my absence, and the all-powerful Top Friends phenomenon [*sic*] gave the experience a much more traumatic flavor.

For some respondents, physical separation was caused by life transitions (e.g., graduation from high school and moving away to college, change of jobs). In other cases, online activity was linked to work-related travel. There were many other cases in which geographical separation was cited as a factor, yet the person in question might have been only a half-mile away or even in the same building. Indeed, within this subjectivity, distance and separation are relative concepts. The subjective notion of accessibility may therefore be more meaningful than that of distance per se. At one pole of the access spectrum, international students described geographical separation on a global scale, with relations in vastly different time zones, complicating contact with human beings who worked and slept in cycles often opposite to their own. At the other pole, friends or relations may have been geographically close, but personal factors, such as shyness or need for control, precluded a meeting in physical space.

For most (but not all) respondents, online friendships were the result of prior friendships in physical space. When asked how extensive their social networks were, 43 percent of respondents indicated 200 or more people, which appears vastly inflated relative to proximal relations. However, almost all respondents said they were at home when they socialized online (98 percent); most said they preferred to access the Internet from a comfortable and private place. Not surprisingly, even applications designed for mobile uses, such as Twitter, are frequently accessed from a desktop computer rather than a roaming device.[21] A very small percentage (1.9 percent) said that, as a result of online socializing, they spent less time with friends at a café or library.

2. Concern to Maintain Intimacy

Overall, most users were fairly cautious about pursuing relationships with unknown persons online. One-fifth said that they would never friend someone that they did not already know in physical space. Half of the respondents (52 percent) decided whether or not to initiate a new friendship based on the presence of mutual friends (similar to physical world behavior). For the other half (46 percent), the decision was based on a combination of factors, including mutual friends, profile information, and photos.

Most respondents (63 percent) had never made an online acquaintance that later developed into a friendship in real life, verifying that for a significant number, online friendships were a close reflection of physical world (offline) relationships. There were a number of explanations, but most were variations on "I only 'friend' people I already know," or "I do not talk to people online whom I have not met in person. The people who try to make friends online are known as 'creepers.'"

As can be surmised, those having online relationships that developed into physical world friendships were in the minority (27 percent). Most reported initially meeting someone online and then, after a while, meeting the contact in physical space. However, there were also a smaller number of respondents who said that they had met individuals online, and that although the friendship had continued (sometimes for many years), they had never met in physical space:

> At what point does an "online relationship" become a "real life" relationship? Is it a function of time? Whether or not the conversation goes from text to telephone? Or is it at the point that two people meet in physical space? If the answer is the third, I was in an on-and-off online relationship from the age of fourteen to nineteen. We have never met. I have many friends I have never met that I have known for the same amount of time or near it. Many of these people have been incredibly monumental figures in my life, equivalent (and in some cases, vastly greater) in influence to people I know in physical space.

The majority of the group who had met someone online said that they were either introduced online or met online through mutual friends. Sometimes this meeting occurred through a networked public, but in other cases it occurred through instant messaging, for example, AIM. Others mentioned meeting through special-interest groups, such as for role-playing games, fan culture, or other common interests. "He was pretty vocal in a chat room conversation and I liked his opinions. We ended up really getting along when we met up . . . and became pretty good friends." One respondent reported meeting a contact through an e-mail introduction from a colleague; they continued to work together online but had never met face to face. Another mentioned using an online dating site. Notably, of the respondents who eventually met contacts in physical space, none reported any negative experiences.

These answers begin to describe varying levels of emotional comfort within online interactions. Individuals belonging to online forums, gaming sites, or other special-interest groups seemed to have a stronger sense of trust, familiarity, and confidence when meeting others online and consequently were more open to establishing new relationships, whether for friendship or knowledge sharing. One possible reason is that special-interest communities tend to be supportive and/or provide mentoring for their members. Many users such as role-players or programmers have been using the Internet from an early age as a resource for problem solving in addition to entertainment and for maintaining friendships.

Finally, during the online interview, respondents were asked, Is physical proximity a requirement for a friendship? Is it a requirement for a partner? For a business relationship? What are the determining factors? There were three position options for this question, and they spanned the spectrum of possible answers. A large percentage (79 percent) of respondents agreed that physical proximity is always very important and/or necessary at some point in the relationship. Some emphasized that physical proximity is *always* very important, in all contexts, at all times. "Otherwise, it's not a relationship," explained one respondent. Respondents cited cases in which the parties knew each other before initiating an online presence or already had a common history rooted in a physical place. In other words, social media was useful for "the maintenance but not the initiation" of relationships. "Physical proximity is not required if you already know the person, but I prefer hanging out, having coffee, going to events, etc. with friends and family to online chatting. I am a touchy-feely person and touch people when I am in close proximity."

Physical and emotional intimacy was not the only area singled out as problematic. Social intimacy was important too. Typically, respondents expressed a strong belief that trust can only be built within a shared proximal space. Others said that physical proximity made their interactions "more real." One respondent indicated that close, long-term relationships, whether familial, friendship, or partner, were often structured on emotional idiosyncrasies that could never be replicated outside of physical proximity—these could include a sympathetic glance, a gentle pat on the back, or a secret shared. Others said that even in business, a handshake was irreplaceable: "Direct eye contact or shaking hands are an important part of business interviews and related activities," and physical proximity is "the only way to get to know someone." Even more effort was required to make romantic partnerships work, and online communication created too many misunderstandings. Online relationships were perceived to lack the open-ended spontaneity that occurs in physical proximity.

At the opposite end of the spectrum, a smaller group (23%) was adamant that physical proximity is not an important factor in relationships at all. However, even among the respondents who agreed in principle that physical proximity is not always necessary or required, many considered online interaction only a temporary solution to maintaining a relationship. "Online relationships just facilitate relationships but do not maintain them"; "There has to be some kind of offline foundation." These responses then seemed to sound a cautionary note that online relationships lack the depth and closeness that can only come from close physical proximity.

Conversely, a minority (2 percent) believed that physical proximity is never necessary in a relationship. Their commonly expressed opinion can be summarized along the lines of good communication is the only requirement for a relationship, although it was unclear whether or not they meant friendship or romantic relationship. A pragmatic group qualified their remarks by emphasizing that online social spaces were not meant to be a replacement for physical relationships; they only make planning and organizing easier. According to most respondents, social media *augments* physical world relationships and activities. Appropriate online behavior was related to levels of emotional familiarity.

3. Life Balance/Control of Communication Style

When asked which communication mode was selected for contacting friends or associates, one respondent answered, "I choose from levels of intimacy and availability. Some people I don't want to have my phone number. Other [friends] never check their Facebook." Networked publics were thus only one option within a broad spectrum of interactive modes. This seems to generally suggest that the respondents were sophisticated media users, readily able to discern and adapt to whatever mode or platform was most appropriate or efficient.

Respondents expressed a strong desire for increased control over their networked communication, for a discrete and low-pressure space of interaction. There were also conflicting responses relating to spontaneity and control. The desire for more control by the respondents seemed to emerge out of a sense of increased public exposure or public accessibility engineered by the very same communication technologies they employed. Respondents sensed that the boundaries between public and private were more porous and less structured than in the past. It is of interest that increased exposure, as a boundary condition in physical space, is something that the field of architecture has articulated and defined throughout history.

Online interaction was viewed as more efficient than any other existing communication method. "I can easily communicate information to thirty friends in much less time than it would take me to tell each of them individually or in small groups." Many respondents stated that they were too busy to socialize in other ways. Online interaction was also cited as a discreet way to ask for advice, suggestions, or opinions from many people in a short time. In short, online communication required less time investment than conventional letter writing or physical meetings. In other cases, the efficiency factor was related to cost, in the sense that online contact was less expensive than a long-distance phone call.

Respondents frequently mentioned a strong desire to keep in touch without a strong need to see the other person in physical space. Many respondents preferred online interaction when they were simply too tired for face-to-face meetings or "when I don't like someone enough to make an effort. The advantage is that I can stay at home; minimal effort with maximum results."

Sometimes efficiency meant the option of multitasking. "The Internet allows you to flit in and out of conversations or wall posts while still taking care of other tasks." Individuals may be in the same city, neighborhood, or even dormitory building, and working at separate computers. Although each individual is physically separated, there is a flurry of online interaction, consisting of conversations, observations, and media sharing, that occurs while each also is engaged in other, work-related activities.[22]

The research suggests that respondents strive to maintain a balance between the exigencies of increased work and personal relationships by attempting to adapt all available social media to everyday protocols. This reflects the respondents' intentions to remain sociable in spite of heavy work demands. At the same time, once such a pattern is established, even convenient relations can be impacted. For example, one may resort to sending an instant message (IM) or posting to a wall when a friend or colleague is actually in the next room.

4. New Spaces of Play and Creativity

A smaller but still significant group (21 percent) of those preferring online activities to interaction in physical space did so because it allows for more socially nuanced interaction. Nuanced communication is especially important in the context of initiating new relationships or in unfamiliar situations. Respondents stated that online interaction allows for a casual, less formal, and less pressured way of getting to know someone. Those users described social media as a more flexible social space, with room for humor, flirtation, or teasing and less risk of rejection because the desired level of intimacy and familiarity can be gauged or tested gradually.

Respondents also cited interactions that involved power differentials or social hierarchy, such as, for example, "if the person intimidates you." These respondents repeatedly stated that "it's easier to say no" or to not respond online than it is with face-to-face interaction. Online interactions also allowed more time for preparing responses, more considered replies, and subtler wording than did face-to-face interaction. "It allows you to respond only when and if you want to rather than the necessity of contact that occurs in physical space." Unlike the middle majority, it must be noted that there were emphatic minority positions at opposite ends of the online social spectrum. A minority (10 percent) advanced the notion that online interaction is "never" preferable to activities in physical space.

An almost equal and strongly voiced minority (8 percent) stated that online interaction is "richer, freer, and more varied," especially given media-sharing practices. Within this group, conversations emerging from media sharing and/or editing were found highly engaging, extremely humorous, and socially meaningful. It is notable that among 18- to 24-year-olds the practice of media sharing is an important part of a collective identity.

New media has changed cultural and creative production, making art more accessible to more people. Desktop production of graphics and videos enables a democratic approach to media production and exchange. Both open-source and proprietary software support DIY computer animation, digital video and film, computer games, and machinima. Some of the most inventive and imaginative work involves editing preexisting media as brico-lage, such as annotating or altering photos and remixing videos or films as a means to create new subversive narratives and meanings. While these re-flexive creative practices do not fit easily within established one-way broad-cast media models, the reappropriation of mainstream content, as a form of culture jamming, capitalizes on new forms of interactivity and is sociality supported by social media.

For the most part, respondents were simply appropriating existing tech-nology creatively for their personal objectives. Unlike face-to-face interac-tion, with its socially prescribed codes, protocols, and inherent obligations, social media can be tailored to individual life patterns. While most respon-dents said that online activities should have the same protocols as in physi-cal space (60 percent), users had quite different expectations in actuality. Some noted lower pressure in online interactions than would be required in face-to-face interactions. The pragmatic reality is that social media creates an indeterminate informal context.[23]

The adoption of social media into everyday social practices is a recent phenomenon; the only certainty is that protocols will continue to change and develop over time. Nonetheless, obvious tensions exist between how we define ourselves as individuals and as members of a community. With online interactions there are far more ways to be anonymous, to gain space and distance from others and their observations, while at the same time keeping track of others and even drawing conclusions about them from the information posted—without anyone knowing. There are those who use their virtual anonymity to uncover the anonymity of others. So it may be these two elements, this layering or in-betweenness, of anonymity *and* con-nection, which allows us to function in both the physical and online worlds. With connections and filters, we learn how to navigate, and to connect, both the virtual and real planes of our social lives.

Navigating physical space, however, contains an element of uncertainty or risk that can be both exciting and harrowing. Unlike the unpredict-able public space of the physical world, online environments offer that in-betweenness as an insulated layer in both time and space. The majority of users said that they felt more comfortable, safer, and *more in control* online than in unmediated public space in the physical world. Based on the data, social media users may prefer to trade some freedom for increased control.

When asked how well their profile pages represented them, respondents (41 percent) replied, "It's only a small part of who I really am." The middle group (37 percent) called it somewhat accurate, and the smallest group (22 percent) stated that it was accurate. Opinions on the presentation of self and identity were thus varied. "I cannot reduce my personality and my being to the contents of one Facebook profile page."

> Online, one has the advantage of being defined solely by one's words, as opposed to the myriad biases that occur in physical space due to physi-cal appearances and social status—online, it is easier for me to be my

true self. Realizing that, I've tried to become less inhibited in person, trying to match or exceed the realness of my online persona. I think, in a large way, I've succeeded. On the other hand, there's a distinct realness of character only existent in person—and we have to call our folk theories of the self into question before we can parse out the nuances of these definitions.

For some respondents, social media acts as a performance space to experiment with self-expression. They enjoyed the visual and auditory richness of online sharing. This group also expressed the opinion that a self-constructed profile or "About Me" summary was not limiting. They maintained that users' likes and dislikes could reveal quite a bit about them. By reading a profile page, it was possible to learn a great deal in a relatively short time, "faster than in regular life." Others enjoyed having alternate personas: "Online, I can be myself, but I can also be someone else!" Some said that they were more chatty with strangers online than in physical space.[24]

Previous theorists have frequently positioned online interaction as in opposition or detrimental to physical-world interactions.[25] To test this position's validity in the eyes of the respondents, the survey queried whether networked publics "detracted from regular life activities." This question had a range of responses, with no one position holding a majority. Over a third (43 percent) reported that networked publics were not a distraction, while a third reported otherwise. A third (37 percent) replied, "Yes! It detracts from work and/or studies," including the comment, "Facebook detracts from my attention in class." In other words, the student scanned e-mail or other messages during lecture.

Many of those who reported negative impacts considered networked publics a distraction; one respondent even referred to them as a "time vacuum." One called Facebook "addictive." Other responses mentioned that social media competed (for time) with sleep. Others responded that onscreen socializing detracted from "living life." Some respondents mentioned that they had initially used Facebook to communicate with distant friends but later came to use it so much that they did not leave the residence hall all day, nor did they drop in and visit nearby friends, even some within the same building or just down the hall. "Sometimes I get so engrossed that I forget that I have friends who are nearby and that I can call and meet with face-to-face."

One of the most emphatic responses came from an individual who replied, "What do you mean, does Facebook detract from regular life activities? It IS regular life!" For the vast majority of respondents, social media is integrated, albeit somewhat awkwardly, with everyday social practices.

It all depends on what one defines as regular life activities. Everyone can attest to having wasted a lot of time on Facebook, but there are also times when participating in an online activity IS part of regular life. . . . My friends are involved with Livejournal, to the point that although we see each other in person (almost) every day, [when we are online], we communicate the most important things, a bit apart from the insecurity that characterizes our face-to-face-interactions.

While networked publics are not substitutes for close physical relations, many respondents perceived them as portable communities or pleasurable distractions. Unlike public spaces of the past, today's networked publics are individualized and highly mobile.

SURPRISING COMPLEXITIES

Social theories attempt to provide constructs that capture the mutual oppositions, disjunctures, and paradoxes that exist within any given phenomenon. During the course of the study, some unexpected complexities surfaced, which were unforeseeable at the outset. These complexities are important to discuss because they point to interesting trends and possibilities for further research.

The initial work of the pilot study conducted at Dalhousie University, Nova Scotia, involved gaining online access to several subaltern groups as a means of increasing the diversity of the sample (see Appendix A. The two populations selected were southwestern Texas border communities and Canada's aboriginal First Nations. In order to increase the rate of distribution and thereby the rate of response, the first step was to find and persuade gatekeepers to allow permission to access online members.[26] Access to the southwestern Texas border community was denied. Bureaucratic issues might not have been the only cause for denial. Due to their members' concerns related to documentation and/or residency status, a suspicion prevailed toward those collecting the data, as well as about the purposes for which the data would be used.

For the second group, a gatekeeper approved my request to distribute the survey to an online social network serving Canada's indigenous populations. One important feature of online surveys is that the analytics are accessible to the principal investigator; thus, I could determine if the questionnaire had been opened, as well as how many questions had been read, but not answered, and more. However, there was not one completed survey response after three weeks of posting online; there were only hundreds of individuals who had read the questionnaire but declined to answer. In follow-up discussions, my research team agreed that (1) distrust with regard to our motives and (2) concerns about inequality with regard to knowledge sharing were factors contributing to the lack of response. As a result, a new announcement was designed and released, with detailed information on the purpose of the survey; more importantly, it included a personal background narrative about the researchers (we were nonnationals). It was hoped that equal knowledge sharing would lead to trust and in some way operate within a potlatch gift economy.[27] Unfortunately, the new announcement had no effect, even though over 300 people had read the questionnaire.

The closed ranks of these two social networks opened up a new conceptualization of the field. Their existence, but lack of response, seemed to verify that online publics can indeed operate as temporary autonomous zones (with the southwestern Texas border community for their nomadic members) or alternative publics (with the First Nations).[28] This appearance of such an invisible public space was indeed a surprising finding versus what had been expected. My assumption was that a diverse sample would contribute to greater understanding of the importance of online community building. Instead, by acknowledging a covert existence, it seemed that I had stumbled upon something very important but outside my original predictions. Various factors—trust, jeopardy, political recognition, and so on—have the potential to form the basis of a separate research project of their own.

Whereas invisible publics, or in this instance, counterpublics, tend to fall within the category of special-interest or affinity-based groups, they are more accurately defined as "parallel discursive arenas where members of subordinated social groups invent and circulate counter discourses to formulate oppositional interpretations of their identities, interests and needs."[29] Marginalized groups that form their own public spheres provide information necessary for members' everyday survival (e.g., information, jobs, meals, transportation, safe houses), so any risk of exposure is rejected. Therefore, many of these communities are opaque to outsiders, and attempts to gain access to an internal *res publica* of these communities are rarely successful.[30] As anthropologists Horst and Miller confirmed, each culture produces *its own* Internet.[31] However, even without participation in the survey, the simple fact that over 300 people registered an online presence by opening and reading the entire questionnaire (even if they did not respond) points to the existence of an invisible counterpublic, knowledgeable and skilled with the tools of social media.

Counterpublics are worth further examination because they enable marginalized groups to find voice through political activism, as described in relation to the Arab uprisings and OWS. Within mainstream media, hegemonic ideologies frame the meaning of a public solely within their own values.[32] Microblogging platforms, such as Twitter, demonstrate that these counterpublic forums are instrumental within nondemocratic societies as a means for generating alternative discourses and disseminating ideas and opinions. The discovery of online counterpublics allows for new questions to emerge: Beyond assisting with the aggregation of information, which tools and platforms will assist collective deliberation and debate? Or to engage in wider spheres of influence? What types of platforms and mechanisms will aid the formation of political identities of dispersed and deterritorialized groups?[33] These questions present cause for future research.

Another important consideration is how borders, boundaries, and deterritorialization affect diaspora populations. In these examples, indigenous peoples and undocumented residents share a significant spatial disconnection. Exclusion as a result of discriminatory practices based on racial, gendered, or religious reasons, as well as the result of being unemployed, represent other examples of ways groups can become deterritorialized. Social media can create a collective presence for marginalized or vulnerable populations who have been, and continue to be, excluded from place-based public discourse.[34] The online sites of subordinated populations (whether border communities, gender-specific, or aboriginal groups) form significant unifying and social support systems within their communities. Although the majority of these sites are inaccessible and invisible (sites are nonproprietary and thus not linked to search engines), the sites may provide vital services to their communities that are typically unavailable within their geographic municipalities.[35] More dramatic are examples of networked counterpublics playing instrumental roles in mobilizing communities; examples include Mexico's 1994 Zapatista uprising[36] and more recently with uprisings in Tunisia, Egypt, and Syria in 2010, 2011, and 2012.

Spaces of difference remain important because of their characteristic expansion into larger discursive arenas. Countries that legislate censorship and/or limit the Internet repress the spread of diverse ideas. According to theorist Michael Gardiner, networked counterpublics emphasize "the heterodox and pluralistic nature of such spheres, which are often in opposition to the procedures of the dominant public sphere, [and] sensitize us to the wide variety of normative ideals that regulate interaction in different areas of socio-cultural life."[37] Unlike the historical public that opposed public and private, state and public, reason and nonreason, such boundaries today are viewed as porous and permeable, suggesting that a unitary framework no longer holds true. The historical public denies a concept of multiplicity, an especially important one for any social media or public space study. Mikhail Bakhtin recognizes "the irreducible complexities that inhere in particular lived contexts . . . [and] to reflect on multiplicities and alterity."[38] Any vibrant public space—for example, the street markets of Asia or the Travestere district in Rome—will see an intermingling of diverse social groups and performance.[39] Facebook's group pages also reveal an extraordinary assortment of interests and affinities, expressive of a renewed awareness of "the hidden and all too often suppressed potentialities that lie within . . . everyday reality."[40]

CONCLUSION

The nethnography began with a question about the actual practices of social media participants, yet over time, the analysis brought to the forefront the larger socioeconomic context, focusing attention on economic recession, relocation, increased work demands, and possible marginalization. A complex social media landscape emerged from the study, populated by a majority of individuals experiencing sociogeographic dislocation, in addition to intensification of competing demands from work, family, and peers.

As a result, we find a portrait of a group of people trying to create stability, wholeness, and community in an economic environment that is not particularly well structured to support those objectives. As sociologist Ulrich Beck observes, "People are forced to seek biographical solutions to systemic contradictions."[41] In spite of those serious concerns in the larger context, social media is generative in its potential. Participatory media enables members to create their *own* publics, with many diverse publics responding to various interests, needs, and concerns. In general, networked publics can support locally based associations that tend to mirror members' physical-world relationships. Yet a significant number also used the online interface to forge global bonds. Such special-interest groups transcend local boundaries to find a distributed solidarity with others across borders through shared interests, politics, or identities. This is one of the contradictory aspects of social media: the same conditions that dilute local alliances, such as anonymity and distance, tend to encourage global solidarity.

Crucial processes such as migration, resource sharing, and collective action are explained by the interrelation of actors pursuing development and community formation. Not surprisingly, among such counterpublic groups, relative anonymity may be crucial for maintaining social bonds. Marginalized groups, as noted by Fraser, are typically excluded from a universal public sphere, and consequently, the potential counterpublic presence in the survey seems to underlie a possible correlation between deterritorialization (as in this case, indigenous peoples and border communities) and participation in networked publics.

If the value of a networked public is in its members, then by default, the most significant platform is the one to which meaningful others (however defined) belong. As theorist Clay Shirky argues, "Historically, we have overestimated the value of access to information, and we have always underestimated the value of access to each other."[42] At the same time, open messaging protocols enable anyone or any group to create a public, so the organizational possibilities span people and autonomous devices, mainstream and subaltern, fixed and mobile.

As social media platforms become increasingly entangled with everyday interactions, it is becoming more difficult to segregate public practices into discretely bounded spheres or space. Today's networked publics may have less spatial definition, less spontaneity, and possibly more social anonymity than in the past, but that does not mean that social media is without agency and effect. As an alternative public, each culture is empowered to adapt social media to its own expressive ends. For most North American users, it serves as a portable community, while for subaltern constituencies, it enables its members to organize and act with agency. Mundane or revolutionary, social media takes many diverse forms depending upon the collective imaginary of its members. That flexibility of adaptation is essential to understanding the critical contribution that social media makes to the production of an alternative public space.

6 Technological Innovations: Public Implications

When Sandy hit New York City, it completely destroyed some neighborhoods just as it completely spared others. While Breezy Point was
under water *and* on fire, for example, the Upper East Side could
still watch Netflix. When news spread of the devastation—and in
particular, when people saw *images* of the devastation—those New
Yorkers who still had power and running water rallied, volunteering
by the thousands to help.

—*Huffington Post*, November 19, 2012[1]

Thirteen-foot waves surged across Battery Park on October 29, 2012, while
the Hudson River flooded its banks. As New York City (NYC) firefighters
climbed into rescue boats to navigate Lower Manhattan, brave (or merely
incautious) citizen journalists ventured into waist-high water to document
the damage. This is how Hurricane Sandy's devastation splashed across the
Internet. Snapshots captured on mobile phones via Instagram, an image-
sharing social network, served as graphic windows allowing glimpses of the
destruction. "Instagram bonded users together in a participatory, networked
public," blogged urban theorist Kazy Varnelis from New York (11/4/2012).[2]

Along the Atlantic coast, from Nova Scotia to South Carolina, residents
with power scanned the web for news and information, demonstrating the
Internet's resilience compared with other forms of information infrastructure. Prior to Sandy's landfall, Google had developed interactive maps to
track the path of the hurricane and provide localized support information,
including probable storm surge zones. A crisis map of Manhattan with links
via Facebook, Twitter, text, or e-mail connected those in trouble with local
evacuation centers and emergency shelters. This interactive crisis map was
designed expressly for mobile access and featured live feeds streaming evacuation information, and updates from Red Cross, the Federal Emergency
Management Agency (FEMA), and other municipal agencies. Later versions
of the map documented the extent of power outages, as well as grocery
store, gas station, pharmacy, charging station, warming center, and senior
service availability. Furthermore, the map traced subway, rail track, and
tunnel flooding, along with bridge and commuting information.

Emergency Twitter feeds also assisted in the coordination for those seeking help, shelter, and food. Mobile food trucks scrambled into operation,
microblogging their locations while distributing provisions to the cold and
famished. As mobile publics uploaded locational information, hybrid alliances formed between online and offline spaces. Broadcast news outlets
featured photographs and video footage shot and shared via mobile phones.
Accordingly *Time* magazine featured an Instagram image on one of its magazine
covers, while mainstream media featured amateur videos of the startling ex-
plosion at the Con Edison electric plant.[3] The proliferation of mobile devices
and applications, coupled with the ease and speed of online dissemination,
enable users to both witness and document the accidental or unexpected,
which has permanently changed the way we understand events around us.

As gathering places and sites of meaning for its members, networked
publics such as Facebook or Twitter can be understood as transient portable communities, cities on the go. In the case of Hurricane Sandy, a networked public, such as Instagram, can emerge as a crisis community, one
that is personal, mobile, controllable, and adaptable to personal, temporal
or geographic experience. Or in the case of the Boston marathon bombings,
housebound residents turned to Twitter for news and information updates.

That flexibility creates a resilient public sphere in which members choose
how to engage with one another. For most, social media cements strong
local bonds; for some, it connects through topical interests and affiliations;

Figure 6.1   New York City, NY. Instagram image of hurricane refugees looking for
Wi-Fi (2012).
Credit: M. Burger Calderon

and for others, it cultivates ties to a dispersed global community. In this way, a networked public, similar to a city in the physical world, displays a full spectrum of expressions, with varying levels of engagement and intimacy. As a nonplace community, each cluster or group allows for further individualized control over public-to-private accessibility. These self-organized enclaves represent a shift away from collective decision making to more control over conventions and protocols.

SOCIAL IMPLICATIONS

During the 1970s, counterculture politics and the rise of populist print media, along with DIY electronic culture and modem-based bulletin board systems (BSSes), contributed to the making of contemporary social media. By documenting this evolution, we can ascertain that technology is only one part of an exchange system; without participants, there is no public, nor any community. As a sociotechnical system, media, whether print, broadcast, or online, produces and perpetuates public space through interaction, participation, and user-generated content. A media space can also perform as a shared place where members can recognize each other's basic social equality, freely discuss collective issues, allow for conflicting opinions, come to common consent, and organize with agency. "A public," according to critical theorist Michael Warner, "is poetic world making."[4] That world is created through action, and it can be shared with others. Social media is constituted through regular, if not daily, intervals of publication—if there is no exchange, the public ceases to exist. By requiring reflexivity and circulation, a public is an ongoing space of encounter.[5]

Philosopher Jürgen Habermas examined the relationship between public opinion, print culture, and the powerful influence on political life. He posited that a media-reading audience, then, constitutes a public. As a result, many scholars came to define *publicness* as a social space created by the reflexive circulation of discourse and argumentation. This understanding makes the dispersed, networked public sphere we know today possible.

There are, nevertheless, some unresolved issues. A move toward more individualized and flexible forms of engagement within media environments counters the connective potential of the networks themselves. Over time, the consequences of niche media, filter bubbles, personalized feeds, and other outputs seem to lead toward increased social fragmentation by way of networked individualism.[6] While broadcast media documented audience fragmentation over the last ten or more years, the personalization of the Internet is also contributing to increasingly individualized forms of media engagement.[7] Algorithmic filtering, as well as online content curation, through self-selected Really Simple Syndication (RSS) feeds and sharing, retweeting, or repinning content, merely reinforces, rather than broadens, the existing conversation.[8]

Furthermore, the mass popularity of social software has not gone unnoticed by commercial interests. Market forces embed social software opportunistically for both political and commercial objectives. From game designers to online retailers, profit-seeking commercial entities are finding ways to leverage social media, and new cross-platformed applications pop up daily. Furthermore, the convergence of the Internet with mainstream broadcast television, by way of integrating Facebook updates and Twitter feeds into programs, signals mass media's move to restrategize and make itself relevant by integrating the participatory component of social media. These applications and services concurrently seek increasingly sophisticated ways to collect and monitor personal data. In addition, location-based mobile applications record information about everyday sociality, as the meta-data collected through user-generated content running on proprietary applications can also be commercially lucrative.[9] Just as demographic, geographic, social, and even biometric data form the economic base of fixed Internet conglomerates such as Facebook and Google, the additional geospatial data retrieved from mobile devices is associated with a significant market value. Moreover, these all have consequences to our individual privacy.[10] What appears to be an emphasis on customization at the user end is actually veiling the commercial practice of personal data mining on the provider end. Users perceive a gain in control, whereas they are constantly being monitored. "The extent, precision, and speed of this data gathering is unprecedented," according to Internet theorist Felix Stalder.[11] Thus, as our notions of the public are being reconfigured, so too is our understanding of individual privacy. There is also warranted concern over the surveillance of individual and collective actions, communications, and diaspora by governments. In addition to commercial data-mining practices, international agreements on Internet security prompted by the Arab uprisings are seeking to institutionalize surveillance practices worldwide.[12]

Despite these concerns, networked publics are important—if not vital— for the communication potential they afford to communities of people around the world. Some are crisis communities, as with those that emerged spontaneously during Hurricane Sandy, whereas others centered around fields of inquiry, activism, ethnic or identity politics, and/or religious beliefs are historically entrenched; the list is diverse. An important subgroup of these affinity-based communities uses online platforms with specific intent to organize and create agency in the physical world. In this way, subaltern counterpublics, defined as "parallel discursive arenas where members of subordinated social groups invent and circulate counter discourses to formulate oppositional interpretations of their identities, interests, and needs," create their own public spheres.[13] Where online conversations lead to real-world action (in the form of protests, boycotts, sit-ins, etc.), such action can have significant spatial implications. Although counterpublic populations may indeed be large (as with the 99%), their general lack of legislative presence situates their interests in the minority. A counterpublic's self-expression in practice and in appearance is restricted by local governmental policy, economic circumstances, religious orthodoxy, social structures, or media monopolies. Thus, the spatial practices of counterpublics tend to be circumscribed by the dominant hegemony in any given location. But Internet activism can supersede the limits of location, which points to the changing status of publicness. Social media provides opportunities for marginalized groups to create tactical communities, finding modes of survival by using and subverting the media infrastructure of the dominant culture. Within the context of activism, marginalized groups leverage social media to create a space of discourse for planning and organizational efforts.[14] These spaces transcend temporality and locality by bridging seemingly paradoxical categories of spatial identification. In these in-between spaces, disenfranchised groups are able to situate themselves in a unique community, both insulated from and connected to the world outside their physical situation.

Online counterpublics are not freely accessible as are public places; they exist in partial invisibility, which may work to their advantage. These nonproprietary communities of practice are less concerned with self-promotion and more concerned with the processes of information sharing and knowledge development. Within authoritarian countries, counterpublic leveraging of quotidian social networking platforms, such as Facebook or Twitter, enables minority groups to create new territory on the boundary line of established publics. Thus, social media can be understood as a reterritorialization of public space, one that affords an increased mode of interaction, contributing to wider accessibility and distribution throughout its intended community. The ad hoc repurposing of social networking tools offers creative opportunities that can result in actual empowerment on the ground.

While networked publics enable a new sphere of public discourse for marginalized groups, that new public sphere neither resembles, nor operates like, models of publicness in the past. As we discovered, online counterpublics are, first, heterogeneous publics. Second, they are provisional. Third, if they use proprietary platforms, they are commercially contaminated. And fourth, when online counterpublics find expression in physical space, it is often with strategic political objectives. While other demonstrations in the past might have been organized with potential news coverage in mind, they were not deployed with the same tactical precision and intentional global media dissemination. Thus, a circularity of content and action moves from online to offline space and back, completing a performative cycle.

While the Internet can provide a voice for marginalized groups, it does not necessarily mean that social media provides an idealized model for democratic discourse. Political processes are complex, and ultimately, there is no single media, nor simple technological solution, for collective decision making. How we, as a group, decide to adopt technology is what ultimately changes political practices. For now, the polyvalent possibilities of the Internet, as an alternative public sphere, have the potential to apply networked communication technologies for ad hoc political organization.

Whether or not social media will continue to be an effective organizational space remains to be determined; governments are rapidly attempting to put legislation in place that will eliminate many of the freedoms we have come to associate with social media platforms in general.[15]

The more ambitious project is less about the Internet's potential for democratic discourse and more concerned with its role in housing and facilitating the efforts of marginalized groups rallying for basic human needs and rights. The most important aspect about publicness is not the discourse but the political agency it affords—the politics of social justice finding everyday expression in the physical world.

URBAN IMPLICATIONS

Much of what has been discussed has occurred during a period of rapid technological innovation, and it is expected that social media will continue to evolve and change. As it stands today, however, social media is a complex assemblage of human actants and computational and physical resources. If social organizations are moving in the direction of more spatially distributed models characterized by individuality, mobility, and affinity, what might this mean for urban environments? A critical realization is that each of the topics— social media, public space, urban infrastructure, political activism, and privacy—can no longer be understood in isolation. Each entity is connected to the others vis-à-vis networked systems and wireless infrastructural integration. A pending convergence of high-speed networks, locative technologies, and environmental sensor systems is prompting a reconceptualization of the city, one where physical space is no longer understood as independent from digital space.[16] The two, physical and digital, are becoming increasingly intertwined. Whether accessed through smartphones or tablets, mobile networked publics are rapidly modifying, prototyping, and transforming urban practices.

This is where analysis of the effects of social media and ubiquitous computing technologies on existing spatial practices becomes instrumental to urban design. Within popular perception, a smartphone *is* an element of quotidian social practices, as it allows for messaging, coordination, navigation, geotagging, and so on. A mobile computing device, therefore, is evolving into a form of personal infrastructure, which potentially comes into conflict with previous notions of what is held in common or public.

What deserves additional attention, however, is the expansion of networked standards of surveillance into our physical lives through wireless network systems (WNS), global positioning systems (GPS), and other sensor systems. Physical space is being increasingly quantified, specified, and circumscribed by data. The ephemeral datascapes that defined initial encounters with the Internet are giving rise to a new media of geospatial information. What has become a matter of concern is that this future assemblage of wireless sensor networks and urban space has the capacity to instantiate an extensive applied control topology that braids sensors with data, social media, and mapping—in other words, context. In this way, we have come full circle from the placelessness of the early Internet to the present time, where every nodal point can be located, interconnected, and aware.

If the entire city effectively becomes a wireless sensor network system with data spontaneously generated from each point, individuals can then be geographically located and monitored at all times. The integration of social media into location-based protocols and the expropriation of that data to external sources raise serious questions about individual privacy. Thus, designers—both urban and software—have a shared responsibility: they should not only concentrate on problem solving, but also on the social, political, and environmental consequences of their design decisions.[17] While the focus of this study is not on infrastructural design per se, a humanistic approach—defined as an ethical perspective that emphasizes the value and agency of human beings, individually and collectively—as related to infrastructural design compels not only programmers but also architects, urbanists, public policy makers, and ordinary citizens to understand future challenges and opportunities.

The integration of networked technologies into everyday social practices compels us to reflect deeply on their protocols, platforms, and interfaces. The production of space is increasingly dependent on code, and code is written to produce space. Social media as a form of code is thus actively shaping sociospatial organization, processes, and economies, along with discursive and material cultures. These effects are set to become increasingly pervasive as more everyday practices are threaded through social media platforms.[18] While it is one thing to collect and model data in order to understand the complex interactions of a city, it is quite another to see how repressive governments might use those very same methods of data collection to discipline urban residents.

CONCLUSION

Social media is restructuring urban practices—through ad hoc experimentation, commercial software and application development, and communities of participation—yet this position is not meant to be confused with technological determinism. The objective of this book has been to look at these new conditions and reflect on how we can meaningfully engage with change and shape technology toward humanistic objectives. Empirical studies have demonstrated that social media may be designed to solve one problem, such as geographical separation, and in the process, it may cause another problem, such as psychological isolation. In spite of this fact, few want to return to pre-Internet technologies.

What has emerged vis-à-vis social media is a slippery public, full of ambiguities and contradictions, visible and invisible, contaminated by state controls and private infiltrations. And yet, as imperfectly formed and flawed as it is, for communities in crisis or those existing on the margins of society, social media can act as an alternative public with agency, proving effective in communication, organization, and activism—at least for the present.

Appendix A
Methodology for Online Research

> The problem is not that designers are lacking for creative ideas, but rather that they are frequently hampered by not having the time to search out appropriate people-based research.
>
> —Clare Cooper-Marcus

INTRODUCTION

If we look to history, public space has traditionally been the design province of architects. As world makers, architects possess a diverse set of interdisciplinary skills; hence, they are arguably uniquely qualified to contribute to the design of the public realm. We must also accept that definitions of public space are culturally relative and continually shifting, and that consequently today's understanding of public space may be quite different from that of the past.

A contested discourse exists on the differences between mediated and nonmediated publics, as do differing opinions on the importance of everyday public space in contemporary experience. The extent of the networked public population (over 1 billion on Facebook alone) necessitates additional research and a critical response. My objective with this study was to describe the actual social practices of the participants of networked publics through empirical research and to test the theory that, within popular perception, networked publics perform as alternative public spaces. Thus, the research project allowed for a systematic study that assists in a deeper understanding on the formative conditions and intertwined relationship between public space and online spheres.

EPISTEMOLOGICAL IMPLICATIONS

Before outlining my methodology for the online ethnographic study "Situated Networks: In Search of the Public," a brief discussion of research paradigms and their epistemological differences is necessary. Distinct research paradigms such as positivism or antipositivism imply the use of particular research methods in carrying out an investigation.[1] The choice of research methods has significant effects in shaping a research study and thus also influences the nature of results and conclusions.[2] Within the disciplines of architecture, urbanism, and new media, this question is particularly challenging because none of these fields has an intrinsic canon; thus, their research methodologies span disciplinary boundaries. Furthermore, when reflecting on the ontology of networked publics, one must conclude that there can be no one perfect ontology; interdisciplinary research is always working with multiple ontologies and epistemologies. This lack of a canon can prove challenging, especially when it is suggested that social entities or groups have a reality that is conception independent, meaning that the theories, models, and classifications used to study them may be objectively wrong—they may fail to capture the real history and internal dynamics of those entities.[3] Applying a mixed methodology may be the only way to capture the most salient factors of a given phenomenon.

As an example of how research paradigms shape results, in a recent study of online discussion groups, "Architecture without Architecture" (2009), the project investigator, Warren Sack of the University of California–Santa Cruz, developed an algorithm to count the number of times a particular word appeared in online discussion group activity. His assumption was that "the more times a word is used, the more meaning it has."[4] Because "Architecture without Architecture" employed a positivist research paradigm, the principal investigator (PI) applied a quantitative method to gather data: counting words, which is an efficient method when using computational instruments. However, such a quantitative method may ignore or neglect unmeasurable factors, which might also be the most salient ones. A crucial question remains unasked: "Is *quantity* equivalent to *meaning*?" In a word, no. Researchers may not fully understand the dynamics of an actual conversation or interaction containing qualitative factors that by their nature exist outside the research frame. The consequences can be serious because once words are counted, the collected data then shapes a PI's design of new software instruments for the collection of further quantitative data, which is then evaluated by further quantitative analysis. This type of methodological structure leads to a tautology, being able only to ensure that it verifies itself without necessarily ever addressing the research subject.

Unlike with a positivist research paradigm, my objective is to establish a realist and balanced approach in studying social phenomena, one that combines both quantitative and qualitative data.[5] According to Steven Eric Krauss, "Realism, as a philosophical paradigm, has elements of both positivism and constructivism."[6] While positivism concerns a single, concrete reality and interpretivism multiple realities, realism concerns multiple perceptions of a single, mind-independent reality.[7] (Constructivism posits that each individual constructs his or her own reality, hence multiple interpretations, also known as interpretivism.) Unlike positivist research, which claims to be value free, or interpretive research, which understands itself to be value laden, realism is instead *value cognizant*, conscious of the values of human systems and of researchers.[8] Realism recognizes that perceptions are imprecise and that there are differences between reality and perceptions of reality.[9] The critical realist agrees that our knowledge of reality is a result of social conditioning and thus cannot be understood independently of the social actors involved in the knowledge-derivation process.[10]

A realist approach understands social entities as autonomous, which is to say that they exist independently of the conceptions we have of them.[11] Each entity described may have at once an objective existence as a social organization (e.g., Facebook, Twitter, Instagram) and as a social practice (e.g., creating profiles, sharing images, texting, updating, lurking) that form the context of interactions between entities and referents. While it is acknowledged that the meanings of terms influence the terms' own referents, this only underscores the need for a realist initial approach and subsequent empirical research on a given topic.

New media in particular raises a daunting challenge due to its lack of disciplinary constraint and institutional tradition. There is no current orthodoxy outlining each step of the methodology, and so my method has been to borrow methods from other disciplines, even if only to critique them or use them as sites of departure. Any humanities study attempting to theorize the social practices of communal behavior relies on a heuristic model, which involves the interpretation of data. With graphical artifacts, heuristic methods drawn from visual and cultural criticism can aid in the interpretation.

As documented in Chapter Three "Origins" (this volume), networked publics, like other groups or institutions, are constructed through specific historical processes. Yet because networked publics are both social artifacts and mind-independent realities, they cannot be understood without the subjects' perceptions being taken into account.[12] Networked publics, as a form of social organization, have embedded values implicit in their definition and use. At the same time, networked publics are not imaginary, wholly subjective, or value laden because they are factual entities. In order to address these attributes, the research study was composed of two phases. The first was an objective stage of research wherein the relations of the social space and the structures of the field were examined. The second stage was a subjective analysis of social agents'(subjects') dispositions to act and categories of perception and understanding resulting from their inhabitation of the field.[13]

In the objective stage of research, I applied what is called a balanced or mixed methodology. Such approaches have various applications; for example, a mixed method can involve the use of quantitative methods within a global qualitative frame. A balanced method could employ qualitative methods to understand the meaning of the numbers produced by quantitative methods. In yet another potential application, it is possible to give precise and testable expression to qualitative ideas through quantitative instruments. The latter example most closely describes my application of a mixed or balanced methodology. I first use an objectivist/positivist approach by applying a quantitative method to a qualitative phenomenon (i.e., a survey or questionnaire for participants of networked publics). Next, to address any antipositivist concerns (i.e., those based in perspectives that emphasize a subjectivist approach to studying social phenomena), I employ a range of research techniques focusing on qualitative analysis: personal interviews, participant observations, accounts of individuals, and others.

RESEARCH QUESTIONS AND HYPOTHESIS

Before proceeding, I wish to emphasize that my research questions are not equivalent to my hypothesis. The research questions were developed around the limits of what empirical research could establish with a degree of certainty. The overarching question was whether, according to popular perception, networked publics constitute an alternative public realm. However, the work that transpired between Phase 1 and Phase 2 reflected an iterative and inductive process inherent to qualitative research. Over time I developed additional questions more concerned with understanding the relationship between an individual's online environment and the physical world. Further issues then arose: questions of the social extents of the online field of action—is the latter political (as in Habermas) or a recreation space (as with Bakhtin) or even a temporary autonomous zone (as for Bey)? I also wanted to know if the online participant was conditioned by the environment, or if the online environment is created by the participant.

While I developed the research questions, there persisted a strong theoretical tension within the notion of networked publics—do they act as "representational spaces" in the Lefebvrian sense? My ethnographic/participant observations had already documented the privileging of visuality in networked publics, for example, via text- and image-based exchanges occurring in a mediated physical space. Nevertheless, in this part of the study, my question aimed at something beyond representational issues—it could more be accurately stated as, What is the basis of knowledge that corresponds to a social reality, and how is that knowledge acquired and disseminated? While I will argue that networked publics are less material and less proximal, nonetheless, they *are* experiential. If visual knowledge is foregrounded, are networked publics' representations of the world and therefore representations of real-world public spaces? Why or why not? Or is it possible that they are abstracted and/or internalized by users and therefore more closely aligned with a broader theoretical definition of space, which is to say that public space is created and defined through social action and not only through physical constructs? In summary, is the phenomenon of networked publics competing with physical space, or is it an alternate mode of public interaction?

ONTOLOGICAL IMPLICATIONS

Unlike research questions, a research hypothesis is an attempt to describe what might be going on; it constitutes the ontological implications of a theoretical framework. A hypothesis then is the conceptualization of a question and operates as the statement of a tentative answer to the research questions.[14]

My hypothesis is that networked publics are created by the same social practices as other communities, whether online or off. As such, networked publics are neither a pure representation nor a simulation but a social expression existing within an environmental spectrum. Because network publics are embedded within everyday social practices, they are enmeshed in an actual, although comparatively less material, quotidian experience.

THEORETICAL FRAMEWORK SHAPES METHODOLOGY

In addition to a hypothesis, every researcher begins with certain goals and theoretical knowledge. In Chapter Two "Assembling the Publics" (this volume), I explained how these typically underscore particular problems and contribute to the development of a theoretical framework. Early, provisional questions frame the study in important ways; they guide decisions about methods and consequently influence, and are influenced by, the theoretical framework. David Harvey's theories on postmodern fragmentation and Manuel Castell's formulations on time/space alterations, contributed to a conceptualization of networked publics within a multiplicity of expressions. This overarching acknowledgment of multiplicity is what guided my research methods—forming an armature from which to design, develop, and test the methods. Finding agreement with Lefebvre that space is socially produced, my theoretical framework also draws on urban planner Melvin Webber's notion of the *urbane*, which conceptualizes many levels of communication space with varying degrees of proximity and publicness. Within an urbane spectrum, social clusters tend to emerge from previous proximal relations as well as from nonproximal special-interest groups (which may or may not find expression in physical space). Either way, both proximal and special-interest clusters describe, for Webber, a shared condition or community. As a sociotechnological system (per Latour), the Internet enables the formation of social bonds between clusters and nodes (sometimes place-based, sometimes not). However, *user interaction* through the movement of messages and information is what builds community and thereby creates a social space. Because both proximal and nonproximal publics share this aspect of social creation, networked publics cannot be understood as something separate from everyday physical publics. Online publics are mutually constituted with everyday social practices as an embedded feature thereof.

The actual processes of constructing *publics*, whether proximal or nonproximal, are similar.[15] What is different from previous modes of communication, however, is that social media, unlike earlier forms of one-way communication (e.g., telegraph, telephone, television), allows for many-to-many communication. Additionally, participants are actively engaged in producing public content; hence, online networked publics are interactive, creative social spaces. If space is being actively produced online and offline, the notion of a mutually constituted field of relations emphasizes not only the tenuousness of any absolute boundary but also the mutual dependency of entities.

These important aspects influenced how I shaped the methodology. Because I theorized that social media functions as part of a complex ecology and may contain new functional elements, the need is emphasized for qualitative methods—especially open-ended interviews wherein respondents are allowed to discuss in a less structured, personal way how networked publics can perform as sites of cultural meaning. The exploration of the perceptions of users of networked publics requires qualitative methods in order to capture the more salient elements of the phenomenon.

WHAT HAS BEEN DONE BEFORE

By looking at what is already known about social spaces and technology, it is evident there are a number of research projects that have contributed to this methodology. In the College of Environmental Design at the University of California–Berkeley, the cultural and historical geographer Clare Cooper-Marcus developed new ways to theorize and understand spatial practices.[16] Her research centered on the psychological and sociological factors of the built environment and on public space in particular. Arguing that design goals need to be balanced and merged with user preferences, she advocated a reversal of the design process so that designing could begin with research on people's motivations and behaviors.[17]

Cooper-Marcus's research is useful for a similar interrogation of online networked publics because it contains data-collection methods appropriate for studying the social and psychological aspects of the public realm. Arising from her work as a cultural geographer, her methodology is relevant in three ways: First, it examines people's perceptions of their surroundings; second, it analyzes the interrelatedness of environments in affecting behavior; and third, it addresses how the built environment can facilitate the creation of communities.[18] Cooper-Marcus's investigations of how human behavior and social activities both create and inform public environments contributed to the structure and design of my survey and focused interviews.

As explained in Chapter Five, I considered Internet ethnography of online communities as a suitable approach. Online research has been called by different terms: Internet ethnography, online ethnography, or simply, nethnography. Within the social sciences, online methodologies came into broader use as classical ethnographic inquiry moved away from defining fields as spatially defined localities and more toward sociopolitical locations, networks, or multisited approaches. Notions of fieldwork have had to contend with digital spaces, and this methodological transformation seems to be necessary. The development of social media and its effects *are* of immediate relevance to networked urbanism, political economy, public culture, migration and diasporas, transnational communities, mass media, and cultural studies, among others. Anthropologist Maximilian Forte emphasizes the importance of developing "an anthropological perspective on the processes through which grassroots visions . . . are being mobilized to link different countries, regions and localities."[19] That position acknowledges that some of the largest international mobilizations of protest have been coordinated and orchestrated *via social media.*

As to the question Why survey research?, "surveys are useful for descriptive, explanatory, or exploratory purposes," according to social scientist Earl Babbie. "They are chiefly used in studies that have individual people as the units of analysis. . . . Survey research is probably the best method available to the social scientist interested in collecting original data for purposes of describing a population too large to observe directly."[20] Furthermore, anonymous online interviews may tend to mitigate the so-called Bradley effect (i.e., the phenomenon of social desirability bias where interviewees may feel under pressure to provide an answer that is deemed to be publicly acceptable). In this case, net ethnography can be advantageous to direct observation. As anthropologist Annette Markham concludes, "Online or offline, all of us make sense of our experiences and tell the stories of our lives in self-centered and self-understood ways."[21] In summary, an online methodology was evaluated and considered appropriate for studying online cultures, in addition to methods of direct participation and observation.

MODES OF OBSERVATION

One of the drawbacks of previous net ethnographic studies is that none of them looked specifically at social media in relation to physical public space. Instead, the studies tended to focus on an isolated device or platform, which is only one part of a sociotechnical system. There is a separate thread of research that focuses on the role of shared objects in maintaining a social reality that can address this problem. Studies emerging from fields as diverse as Science, Technology & Society (STS), anthropology, psychology, and cultural studies foreground face-to-face interaction as a primary way in which societies and cultures are maintained.[22] Thus, I adapted their observational methods and interpretive analyses to my own research.

Clearly, when examining new phenomena, it would seem unwise to continue to follow old habits of thinking that include not only unacceptable dualisms but also fundamental category mistakes that might mislead our research and interpretations. Indeed, many problematic concepts are inseparable from problematic epistemologies.[23] While some of these studies' findings are outside the scope of my study, they nevertheless demonstrate that online social networks are culturally relative phenomena, and that, even within a particular culture, users frequently subvert or circumvent mainstream commercial objectives. What is important to emphasize, however, is that without any data obtained in the field (whether online or off), we cannot presume to know what is actually going on within a given phenomenon. Without empirical research, we will not be able to determine how these spaces are conceived and maintained within popular perception. Thus, while the results of this study are not by any means definitive, they provide at least a necessary beginning.

FIELD RESEARCH

Field research involves the collection of primary data or new information. At the College of Environmental Design, there is ample precedent for applying a social science methodology to learn about social spaces in the physical world, so it seemed logical to apply these same methods to online social media. Ethnography, participant observation, data collection, and survey research are all examples of field research, and these methods could be used to gather empirical data about online activities. However, what has complicated contemporary field research is that network technologies have completely disrupted the simple construction of a field site. Traditionally, ethnographers sought out physical sites and focused on the culture, peoples, practices, and artifacts present in geographically bounded contexts. This approach made sense because early anthropologists studied populations with limited mobility. Furthermore, there was also a collective understanding that culture and people were contained by a notion of place. Mobility and transience complicated matters, danah boyd explained, "but mediated technologies changed the rules entirely. In a networked society, we cannot take for granted the idea that culture is about collocated peoples."[24]

PHASE 1 OF A MULTIPHASE STUDY

After reviewing previous studies, I reflected on the various methods for collecting information through surveys and questionnaires. However, some methodological tension remained. Due to the qualitative aspects of my research, it was difficult to arrive at precise questions until I could make use of other components of the study. Some initial data collection and analysis needed to be done with provisional questions in order to be able to refine the questions later. Therefore, in order to develop and test the research instruments, the first phase of the multiphase study, a pilot study called Situated Networks, was initiated at Dalhousie University, Halifax, Nova

Scotia, between January and May 2008 (sixty-seven respondents). Then, as my research questions became more focused, they more closely informed the subsequent research instruments.

The Internet ethnographic data were derived from a multiphase study called Situated Networks: In Search of the Public initiated at Dalhousie University in Nova Scotia, Canada. As noted previously, a pilot study was conducted from January 5, 2008, through May 30, 2008; a second, primary study was conducted at the University of California–Berkeley from September 24, 2008, through June 1 2009, with an informal follow-up study completed on April 2, 2012. All data was anonymized. In this multiphase study, I collected 210 surveys: 67 surveys from the Phase 1 pilot study, 107 surveys from the Phase 2 primary study, and 36 surveys from the follow-up study. The studies were not merged.

MIXED METHODOLOGY

In this section, I describe the development of research techniques for a cross-sectional multiphase study and analysis, including data collection, data analysis, and research instruments: questionnaires and interviews.

When studying social media platforms both quantitative and qualitative data are important, but for different reasons. Quantitative or positivist research methods are systematic, scientific investigations of quantitative properties and phenomena and their relationships. The process of measurement is central to quantitative research because it provides the fundamental connection between empirical research and mathematical expression of quantitative relationships.[25] One method of collecting quantitative data is through the construction of a quantitative survey of human subjects. "Survey data collection is a method of obtaining information for the purpose of answering questions about the nature of social life."[26] A quantitative approach asks well-grounded, answerable questions: *who, what, where, when,* and *how much.* These types of questions would assist me in determining who was and who wasn't using networked publics, what they were being used for, and in what frequency. Such research is also useful for determining perceptions, attitudes, and motivations within large populations. I also hope to extrapolate these findings to learn about how people conceptualize their social relations in the public sphere more generally. In this respect, the information collected from survey data is far from sterile; it can produce incredibly complex portraits of a given phenomenon or a cultural group. Pierre Bourdieu's sociology studies, for example, used vast amounts of data to generate a cultural landscape.

In contrast to quantitative research, qualitative or constructivist research would assist me in answering questions such as How are networked publics being used as social gathering places and why? How do online practices relate to social practices in physical space? Most importantly, how does this mediated relationship change our conception of physical public space? Qualitative research would also address subjective questions regarding the popular perceptions of users within networked publics and their affordances and drawbacks. Less-constrained questions, structured within an open-ended interview, would allow users to discuss issues that might have been missed in the quantitative questions.

Such a combination of methods, as applied humanist research, can yield a rich and complex portrait of social practices mediated by new technologies. Although research paradigms have their own corresponding approaches and methods, as a design researcher, I have adopted methods that cut across research paradigms, reflecting the questions that I propose to answer.

HUMAN SUBJECTS PERMISSION

Formal permission applications involving human subjects were completed, filed, and approved with the University Research Ethics Boards according to the protocols of the National Commission for the Protection of Human Subjects at Dalhousie University and the Committee for Protection of Human Subjects (CPHS) at the University California–Berkeley. All collected data was anonymized.

INSTRUMENTS AND METHODS FOR MEASUREMENT

At the beginning of the project, my initial research questions were broader, having more to do with usage patterns and user motivations. With networked publics, what was of particular interest to me was studying the quality and frequency of online social practices in relation to offline activities. Observational studies and surveys seemed to be an effective way to observe these inherent connections and tensions in everyday online social groups. Yet even with my broad research questions in place, the development of research instruments immediately brought practical concerns to the forefront—specifically, identifying the methods that would best capture the types of data I sought. I therefore divided the study into two parts: The survey questions would first identify the things I needed to understand (quantitative data); my interview questions would then capture the information needed to understand those relationships (qualitative data).[27] From these real-world observations, my research team generated a series of questions that could later be applied to social media.

Developing Instruments for Phase 1 Pilot Study

1. Literature review + discussions on public/private, community, identity, modes of connection

2. Discussion + generation of models, theories, and hypotheses
3. Development of instruments and methods for measurement
4. Collection of empirical data
5. Analysis of data
6. Evaluation and interpretation of results (see Chapter Five, this volume)

Through collaboration with my research assistants, I drafted a series of questions that cross-referenced environmental behaviorist John Zeisel's criteria[28] with our own impressions of what was taking place in the field (although I emphasized restraint in forming assumptions about the users' experiences, for example, of isolation). It was important to maintain a balance between focus and open-endedness. Too little focus would not provide answers to the questions. Too much could create tunnel vision, leading to failure to obtain a wide enough range of data or to include important phenomena.[29] The first part of the survey contained questions with possible responses that could be easily quantified. After discussion of the results and numerous iterations, well-constructed, precise questions were developed for the questionnaire for the Dalhousie University pilot study.

OTHER CONSIDERATIONS

Why use the Internet as a means to survey individuals? Online research methods (ORMs) are ways in which researchers can collect data via the Internet. Many of these ORMs are related to existing research methodologies but reinvent them in the light of new technologies associated with the affordances of online use. Many individuals who participate in networked publics spend a significant amount of time online and consider doing so to be an important way of maintaining social and professional contacts. The conclusion was that if the topic under investigation was online activities, the best way to reach the sample group would be through a medium or mode readily accessible to the survey subjects.

However, the disadvantage of an online questionnaire was that it entailed the possibility of a low response rate. Not everyone has consistent access to the Internet, and many who do are not receptive to completing questionnaires online. How could the survey be distributed with a high response rate? Previous studies have indicated that responses to online questionnaire invitations are generally biased toward younger demographics, and since our target demographic was people under the age of thirty-four, that could be an advantage.

A questionnaire was designed for the study using survey software available online. Because the design and format of an online questionnaire can affect the quality of data gathered, aesthetics, along with verbal clarity, were considered carefully. "The physical layout of questions is sometimes as important as the wording of the questions themselves in assuring that the information elicited will be needed for the research purposes."[30] The overall visual composition, color, and font specifications were important elements that needed to be graphically unified. I designed the questionnaire to appear inviting, attractive, and not too long or dense.

The questionnaire needed to address the following considerations:

1. Measures: dependent variables, Internet Use

    a. Place where online.
    b. Time: number of hours per day of use.

2. Sample description

    a. How many responded out of how many contacted?
    b. What was each respondent's gender, age, and so on (percentages)?
    c. Propinquity: How far away was each respondent from home?

3. Similar interests

    a. Online groups (e.g., games, videos, music).
    b. Offline (e.g., special interests, sports, fan communities).

4. Contingency Questions: list filters.

5. Matrix questions (e.g., "Your Facebook profile _____"
    a. represents me.
    b. somewhat represents me.
    c. is only a small part of who I really am.)

6. Order of questions: Begin with less-controversial questions; one question per line.

The questionnaire was tested by my research assistants for aesthetics, clarity, ease, and total time; the questionnaire was finalized at 30 questions.

COLLECTING DATA ONLINE

In addition to my own observations and analysis, I wanted directly and anonymously to collect the responses of users of online social space. During the Canadian pilot study phase, the single largest networked public, Facebook, had a closed policy and was only open to students with the.edu suffix attached to their email addresses. Consequently, college student members of various networked publics were sampled. Another reason why college students were selected was that they were members of a familiar group, giving us a greater chance of gaining access to the publics. I was careful to account for relevant social groups within universities and included diverse groups of students and staff as well as the producers of the technologies they used.

At Berkeley, the sampling procedure began with a public announcement to all undergraduate and graduate students and staff in the Psychology Department. This was subsequently extended to include the College of Environmental Design, with a graduate sampling in the Planning Department and an undergraduate sampling in the Landscape Department.

GATEKEEPERS

What sites to choose? Which participants to select? What data to collect? In order to increase the rate of distribution and thereby the rate of response, the first step in accessing a given networked public was to contact and persuade a *gatekeeper* to allow permission to access community members.[31] There is of course a possibility that permission to gain entry will never be granted. In Canada, I attempted to survey different populations of networked publics in order to achieve a broad sample (see Chapter Five, this volume). My efforts to gain access from gatekeepers as documented previously for nonproprietary networked publics developed by the Canadian First Nations and a southwestern community college located near Austin, Texas, opened up a new conceptualization of the field. This very lack of response tended to verify that networked publics do indeed operate as alternative social spaces (for the First Nations) or as temporary autonomous zones (in the southwestern United States) for their members. The various reasons for this would have made for a research topic on their own.

While at the University of California–Berkeley, I met with the heads of three different departments to ask for their assistance in distributing the survey: director of student services, Psychology Department; chair of the City & Regional Planning Department; and chair of the Landscape Architecture Department. After we discussed the critical implications of the study, each of these individuals gave me permission to access their departmental listservs. The East Bay Chapter of the American Institute of Architects was also supportive of the study, but due to time considerations was unable to participate.

Once a gatekeeper had given permission to access a community's members, an announcement could be distributed online. Along with the background and human-subjects information, the announcement in this case included an embedded link connecting participants to the online survey. The announcement was distributed to undergraduate and graduate students at the Psychology Department and the College of Environmental Design (for urban planning and landscape architecture, disciplines that design public space). The questionnaire was distributed at or near the beginning of the fall 2008 and spring 2009 semesters so that the respondents would be less pressured by their studies and more likely to respond. In the first two phases of this multiphase study, I collected 174 surveys: 67 surveys from the Phase 1 pilot study and 107 surveys from the Phase 2 primary study.

In addition to the previously mentioned methods for gathering data, I was also curious about how people interacted with Facebook and how those practices then rippled through their everyday activities. After having a profile of my own for over seven years, I observed and collected others' profiles. A typical Facebook profile is analyzed using a standard set of criteria, discussed in Chapter Four, this volume. My intention was simply to observe objectively before designing and distributing the research instruments, although subjective impressions enter into the process.[32] I am still observing and maintaining my social media presence, which I have expanded into Instagram, Pinterest, Twitter, reddit and Tumblr.

The mobile interface Twitter came on the market as I began Phase 2. Twitter combines mobile Internet access with GPS information, which changed some of the variables in my study. The assumption had been that users accessed networked publics from fixed locations, usually their own desktops at home. Now, the increasing acceptance of smaller and more portable devices, specifically smartphones, provided individuals not only with mobile communication but also with computing, Internet access, image capture and sharing, and location tracking capabilities. In 2009, however, Twitter had a low adoption rate (1 percent); the sample group preferred texting from mobile phones or chatting from their laptops or fixed computers. By the follow-up study in 2012, Twitter had achieved a higher rate of use, and more people were accessing social media through mobile devices (36 percent). Instagram's adoption was faster and more widespread. The adoption of mobile technologies, Twitter and Instagram in particular, tends to reconfigure the way in which individuals interact in and engage with public space and, in effect, operates as a *remediation* of public practices.

DESIGN OF THE ONLINE INTERVIEW

For Phase 1, due to time limitations at the end of the semester, there were six interviews, conducted either by phone or face to face. With Phase 2, an alternative strategy was devised to increase our yield. The survey was distributed at the beginning of the semester, and participants were asked if they would consent to being interviewed anonymously (i.e., online, by telephone, or face-to- face), resulting in a much higher response rate. Out of 107 survey participants, 74 agreed to complete an online interview, with a different set of more open-ended questions than were asked in the survey. (There were no telephone or face-to-face interviews in Phase 2.) This is where some of the most interesting qualitative data appeared; due to anonymity, respondents felt comfortable frankly expressing many of their personal opinions. In this sense, an online instrument was more effective because it removed one of the traditional survey limitations: the relation between the observed and the observer. A researcher must acknowledge this dynamic as an influential factor in the study.[33]

SUMMARY OF RESEARCH METHODOLOGY

It is important to admit that every tool—even every research tool—has its bias.[34] In this case, both the online survey software and the HTML code used to create networked publics have their own particular biases. Computational methods are prescriptive; they bear the designer's reasoning and assumptions embedded within them—and these assumptions limit the choices of the users.

Another limitation is that, unlike those of scientific research, the results of social science research are not always exactly repeatable. In this respect, the study would have benefited from a larger sample demographic, including, for example, adults age thirty-four or older. Nevertheless, I have tried to outline a balanced yet systematic approach. Because networked publics are both site and context for the study, as well as social entities, a balanced approach will come closest to capturing multiple aspects of this single, mind-independent (or objective) reality.

CONCLUSION

In the first part of this appendix, the epistemological implications of various research paradigms were outlined; this was followed by a discussion of the numerous advantages of a balanced or mixed-method approach. The process of designing the research study was delineated, along with the challenges involved with developing qualitative instruments, the need for a pilot study to refine the survey questions, and finally the biases inherent within any given research method.

In the final analysis, design is always a form of social practice.[35] As a result, if popular perception suggests that concepts of publicness are changing, then it is of utmost importance that we, as researchers, attempt to understand that change more fully in order to provide designers with the information needed to make informed decisions in the design of the public realm—decisions that will support free and rational discourse rather than hidden commercial interests. This research project is one of the first attempts to do so.

Appendix B
Online Research Survey

In Appendix B, I present the research foundations for an Internet ethno-graphic methodology (the study's findings were discussed in Chapter 5, this volume). In this chapter, the quantitative survey results are presented. A pilot study that was conducted at Dalhousie University (2008), followed by a primary study I carried out at the University of California–Berkeley (2008–9), followed up by an informal study (2012). The surveys were administered to various demographics over a period of four years from January 2008 to April 2012. By its completion, there were 210 respondents, ranging in age from eighteen to forty-five and geographically dispersed from Halifax, Nova Scotia, to Austin, Texas, and from Berkeley, California, to Botswana. Full survey results are available online at [http://hdl.handle.net/2142/43983]

ONLINE SURVEY ANALYSIS

Who Is Online?

For the demographic data only, there were 174 + 36 total survey partici-pants. They were students and nonstudents (faculty, staff, and others not affiliated with a university) between the ages of eighteen and forty-five, al-though the majority were under the age of thirty-five. The pilot (Phase 1), primary study (Phase 2), and follow-up study results were not merged. This is because the pilot was set up to test the research instruments, and as a re-sult, the questionnaire was later changed. The total number of respondents for the Phase 2 primary study was 107 (Figure A1 and Figure A2).

N = 174 [2009] N = 36 [2012]	Female	Male
Pilot	61%	39%
Primary Study	83%	17%
Follow-up Study 2012	56%	44%

Figure A1 Sex of Respondents

N = 174	18–22 yrs	23–26 yrs	Over 35
Pilot	20%	50%	3%
Primary Study	69%	25%	6%
Follow-up Study 2012	8%	56%	8%

Figure A2   Age of Respondents

What follows are the results of the Phase 2 primary study only. Some respondents had multiple responses to the following questions; therefore, in some instances the totals will be greater than 100%.

Where Are You? And on Which Sites?

Most people access social media from home. Most said that they had "no special loyalty," but they preferred to belong to a networked public that their friends also belonged to.

N = 107 [2009] N = 36 [2012]	2009	2012
Facebook	96%	94%
My Space	12.6%	0%
Linkedin	0%	39%
Twitter	1%	22%
Other	12.6%	22%

Figure A3   Which social media platform?

What Are You Doing?

Almost all respondents belonged to a networked public primarily for social purposes (98%). Other reasons included professional activities and the activities of various special-interest groups.

N = 107	
Social purposes	98%
Professional activities	25%
Special interest groups -Television/film fan sites and music sites	15%
Special interest groups - Political	6%
Gaming, other	1%

Figure A4   Reasons for Belonging

Specific online activities were varied. Invitations were frequently handled online, and 75% of the respondents accepted or sent invitations for events or activities occurring in physical space. In this way, online use paralleled telephone use, in that both methods of communication facilitated or enabled activities in physical space.

Media sharing was as important as invitations, with 70% of all respondents sharing videos, photos, or links to online content. Sometimes the content was borrowed (illegally downloaded commercial content), but more often it was original content (user-generated) that often documented events that had happened previously in physical space: for example, photos taken at a party, while on a hike, or at a get-together.

The other most common activity within networked publics was regularly updating personal pages (65%). A wall page (where people can leave short messages) was the most heavily frequented (75%); the profile page (containing autobiographical content) was frequented to a lesser extent (65%). Both pages were in continual flux, with a flurry of photos and messages constantly loaded, exchanged, and downloaded. This often meant that within their social network, members shared what they had been doing recently or what they were currently doing in physical space.

How Often Are You Online and for How Long?

The average user checked his or her Facebook wall once or twice a day (44%) and spent about fifteen minutes online every time. As shown in Figure A5, only 17% of respondents spent more than an hour a day on Facebook or other social media site.

N = 107 [2009] N = 36 [2012]	2009	2012
Less than 30 minutes	59%	41%
30–60 minutes	25%	25%
1 hr or more	17%	36%

Figure A5 Total Length of Time Spent on Social Media Sites Per Day

How Public Are Social Media Sites?

There was also a full spectrum of responses when asked about the conditions for meeting a new online acquaintance in physical space. As shown in Figures A6–A13, replies ranged from "never!" to "right away!" and every possible response in between.

N = 107	
After corresponding for 4 or more weeks	71%
Never	20%
Immediately	3%

Figure A6   Conditions for Meeting a New Online Acquaintance in Physical Space

How well does your profile represent you?

N = 107	
It's accurate	22%
Somewhat accurate	37%
Only a small part of who I really am	41%

Figure A7   Profile Identity

How large is your immediate online community?

N = 107	
1 to 25	98%
25 to 50	8%
50 to 100	11%
100 to 200	21%
200 or more	43%

Figure A7   Size of online community

How long would you correspond with someone before meeting up with him or her in physical space?

N = 107	
Right away	2%
After a week	8%
After 2 to 3 weeks	18%
After a month or more	71%

Figure A8   Length of time before meeting in physical space

In your opinion, should online social protocols be more or less restrictive than in face-to-face interactions?

N = 107	
Less restricted	17%
Same as face-to-face	60%
More restricted	23.5%

Figure A9   Preference for online social protocol

Do your online activities lead to or relate to activities in physical space?

N=107	
Yes, just about every time I log in	10%
Frequently, a couple of times a week	37%
Hardly, a couple of times a month	53%

Figure A10   Overlapping spatial conditions

Have you ever resigned from an online social space?

N = 103	
Yes	44%
No	56%

Figure A11   Resignation from online publics

If so, did your social life decline?

N = 57	
Yes	44%
No	56%

Figure A12   Social implications of resignation

Would you consent to a confidential interview and to be quoted anonymously?

N = 105	
Yes	39%
No	61%

Figure A13   Participation in confidential interview

The purpose of the follow-up study was to verify that the findings of the Phase 2 primary study remained valid as of 2012. As was noted, the demographic shifted during the period; in 2012, more men participated in the survey (2009: 17% male; 2012: 41% male). Overall, the data were highly representative. Here is where the data deviated: As of 2012, people were spending more time on line. Participation on LinkedIn and Twitter had increased; hence, people were using mobile access in addition to fixed computers.

Do you access social media through phone or computer?

N = 36	2012
Mostly by mobile phone	23%
Equal between phone + computer	30%
Mostly by computer	49%

Figure A14   Mobile or fixed social media access

The full results of both surveys are available online at [http://hdl.handle.net/2142/43983]

Glossary

Alternative public   A subaltern public that is simultaneously (1) a space constructed through networked technologies and (2) an imagined community that emerges as an assemblage of diverse people, technologies, and practices.

Applied topology   Technically, a wireless network applied over an environment, whether urban, suburban, or rural.

Biopolitics   In the work of Michel Foucault, the style of government that regulates populations through biopower, or the application and impact of political power on all aspects of human life.

Campo   Italian for a secular public space; the term is derived from *field* or *commons*.

Civic media   Any form of communication that strengthens the social bonds within a community or creates a strong sense of civic engagement among its residents.

Civitas   The collective social body of citizens with rights and responsibilities; together a public entity or *res publica*.

Commons   The earliest definitions refer to land reserved for the use of the community, including grazing land, forests, and rivers. The commons can also include public goods such as public space or public infrastructure, which would include public education, health, and various infrastructures that allow a society to function (for example, roads, electricity, water delivery systems). More recently, the commons has related to cultural sphere. The cultural commons include literature, music, arts, design, film, video, television, radio, information, software, and sites of heritage. The open source movement is a contemporary example of the commons; it demonstrates new ways of cooperation and illustrates how economic value is not founded on exclusive possession, but rather on collective potentialities. Contemporary definitions extend the commons to a set of assets that have two characteristics: They are all gifts, and they are all shared. A shared gift is one we receive as members of a community, as opposed to individually. Examples of such gifts include air, water, environment, music, biosystems, and the Internet.

Communities of practice   Formed by people who engage in collective learning in a shared domain toward shared goals, for example, a group of software engineers or researchers trying to solve a complex problem.

Community   From the Latin *commūnitās*, equivalent to *common*. Later, old French, to *commune* or *communicate*. Today, *communities of associates* are no longer synonymous with the *communities of place*.

Contextual web   An applied networked topology overlaying an urban environment and made up of contributing mobile devices and/or sensors as dynamic nodes.

Counterpublic   Repressed and/or marginalized groups form subaltern counterpublics according to Nancy Fraser, described as parallel discursive arenas where members of subordinated social groups invent and circulate counterdiscourses to formulate oppositional interpretations of their identities, interests, and needs, Refer to: "Rethinking the Public Sphere: A Contribution to the Critique of Actually Existing Democracy," in *Habermas and the Public Sphere*, ed. Craig Calhoun (Cambridge: MIT Press, 1992), 122–23.

Fragmentation   In David Harvey's view, postmodern conditions reject attempts to represent immutable or ordered patterns and totalities in order to accept flux, fragments, and difference.

Media publics; mediated publics   Communication technologies across platforms such as print, radio, and broadcast. *A One-way mass media audience* means media across platforms (print, radio, broadcast).

Mobile applications   In common parlance, known as *apps*.

Mobile public network or PLMN   A public land mobile network (PLMN) is any wireless communications system intended for use by terrestrial subscribers in vehicles or on foot. Such a system can stand alone, but often it is interconnected with a fixed system such as the public switched telephone network (PSTN). The most familiar example of a PLMN end user is a person with a cell phone or tablet.

Networked counterpublics   Parallel discursive arenas; subaltern coalitions of marginal groups combating oppression from more dominant public spheres by way of distributed communication networks.

Networked public   A community that forms among some set of members of a social media site. Networked publics are publics that are restructured by networked technologies. "It is important to understand that social network sites are not only public they are *publics*," danah boyd explains. "However, it is insufficient to only call these publics, one must call them *networked publics*," which essentially means that it is spaces and audiences bound together through technological networks. Networked publics are affected by persistence, replicability, invisible audiences, and searchability. See danah boyd, *Taken Out of Context,* 2008)

Piazza   From the Greek and later Latin *platea*, meaning "courtyard, broad street." Also known as the sanctified space in front of a cathedral used for the performance of commonly held ceremonies and practices. In the 1640s, the term was mistakenly applied to the colonnade of Covent Garden, designed by Inigo Jones, rather than to the marketplace itself; hence, "the verandah of a house" (1724). Compare with *campos*.

Polis   From the Greek, the political life of a populace.

Post-bourgeois public sphere   Nancy Fraser revisits Habermas's historical description of the public sphere and argues that the bourgeois public sphere was in fact constituted by a number of significant exclusions. In contrast to Habermas's assertions on the disregard of status and inclusivity, Fraser claims that the bourgeois public sphere discriminated against women and lower social strata of society: "This network of clubs and associations—philanthropic, civic, professional, and cultural—was anything but accessible to everyone. On the contrary, it was the arena, the training ground and eventually the power base of a stratum of bourgeois men who were coming to see themselves as a 'universal class' and preparing to assert their fitness to govern." Thus, she stipulates a hegemonic tendency of the male bourgeois public sphere, which dominated at the cost of alternative publics (for example by gender, social status, ethnicity, and property ownership), thereby averting other groups from articulating their particular concerns. See "Rethinking the Public Sphere: A Contribution to the Critique of Actually Existing Democracy," in *Habermas and the Public Sphere*, edited by Craig Calhoun, 109–42 (Cambridge: MIT Press, 1992).

Public   Dictionaries confer different meanings on the word *public*. *Webster's* [Webster's Third New International Unabridged Dictionary, 3rd ed., 1981, SV "public"] defines *public* as a relationship, or an organization, in terms of accessibility, services, or place.

I. "Accessible to or shared by all members of the community" (e.g., water supply, public transportation system). What is public is supported by or for the benefit of people as a whole: *common*. What is public provides services to the people under some degree of state or civic control (e.g., railroads, Internet or other communication systems). What is public is open to, may be used by, or may or must be shared by all members of the community; it is not restricted to the private use of any person or persons and is generally accessible or available, used or enjoyed by all persons. Accessibility for public services or content is often associated with a fee (e.g., museum tickets, bus fare); therefore, accessibility has always been limited—not only by the cost of devices, but also by the cost to service providers. Perhaps the question about whether something is public should be this: Is the content conceivably available to all?

II. "Exposed to general view"; of an observable or perceptible nature; a place accessible or visible to all members of a community.

According to the *Oxford Dictionary, public* means "of or concerning the people as a whole"; whereas Gerald Hauser refers to the *populace* as publics formed by active members of society around issues.. Additional, related definitions are these: of, relating to, or affecting the people as an organized community: civic. Of, by, or directed to the people: *publics*; a group of people distinguished by common interests and characteristics: *fans*. The postmodern, postindustrial public is heterogeneous and fragmented. There is no one public that everyone identifies with; instead, there are many multiple *publics*.

B. Publication Communication (news or information) to the public; the act or process of issuing copies for general distribution; a published work.

Public space An extent or area set apart or available for use; an unobstructed area (e.g., parks, open spaces); a volume defined by architectural forms; a three-dimensional region (or representation of that region).

Public sphere The area over which something acts, exerts, influences, has its being or significance, or radiates; a domain or range of something as action, knowledge, or influence; a field of action or existence; province. The public sphere is an area in social life either physical, as in a café, or Internet enabled where individuals can come together to freely discuss and identify societal problems, and through that discussion influence political action; it is a sphere between private and government. Similar to the postmodern public, the postmodern sphere is composed of many intermediate dialogs among diverse peoples.

res publica The public affair: literally, the public entity (concrete as opposed to abstract); a commonwealth, sometimes a park.

Sensors Within machine-perception environments (robotics), it is instrumental to use sensors collectively to gather information about the condition of the environment. Mobile devices contain an average of seven sensors. While current phone sensors can track individuals as they move about the world, an emerging technology called *sensor fusion* uses information from multiple sensors and stitches it together to give mobile phones an understanding of its location and environment, in other words, context awareness. Sensor fusion might provide more information than one would typically assume. Mobile phones already know what building a person is in, and soon it will know what floor they are on, what room they are in, and what types of motion are going on.

Social media A variety of Internet mediums including networked publics, blogs, content-sharing sites such as YouTube, and collaborative content-production systems such as reddit.

Social media platform or social networking site A network such as Facebook or Twitter.

Spatial publics Material publics that are open to, accessible to, or shared by all members of the community (e.g., transportation systems, water supply, streets, public spaces). Spatial publics are supported by or for the benefit of the people as a whole, as in *common*. Spatial publics may also refer to the provision of services to the people under some degree of state or civic control (for example, railroads, Internet, Wi-Fi).

Spatial theory The interrogation of inherited notions of place and community resulting in the reformulation of *place* as an open set of relations. Critical spatial theories confront both conflicting and normative dimensions of urban landscape by situating the particulars of place within structural systems of organization and occupied space, a method that exposes the actual means of production and articulations of power.

Temporary autonomous zone (T.A.Z) The sociopolitical tactic of creating temporary spaces that elude formal structures of control. A pre-Internet concept that recognizes the controlling mechanisms that are placed on individuals and proposes a nonhierarchical system of social relationships by concentrating on the present, according to Hakim Bey.

Ubiquitous computing Also referred to as ubicomp, it is related to mobile computing, laptops, tablets, or pads; nondesktop computing. Defined as human-computer interaction (HCI) in which information processing has been thoroughly integrated into everyday objects and activities. Also known as pervasive computing.

Unmediated publics Areas with structurally defined boundaries. Access to visual and auditory information is limited by barriers; essentially, the audience has to be present in order to witness an action.

Urban *Urban*, similar to *public*, is an imprecise term. During the early seventeenth century, *urban* meant "relating to or characteristic of a town or city," from the Latin *urbanus*. [Oxford English Dictionary] Yet when compared with public, *urban* is a relatively new concept, not appearing in general use before the 1830s. The cultural theorist Raymond Williams suggests this is because the majority of the population lived in rural areas until the mid-nineteenth century; it was not until open land, the commons, became privatized that the corresponding notion of *urban* could come into being. See Williams, *The Country and the City* 1975: 97–100).

Notes

NOTES TO INTRODUCTION

1. David Harvey, *The Condition of Post-Modernity: An Enquiry into the Origins of Cultural Change* (Cambridge: Blackwell, 1989); Fredric Jameson, *Signatures of the Visible* (New York: Routledge, 1992); Manuel Castells, *The Rise of the Network Society*, 2nd ed. (Malden: Blackwell, 2000).
2. Richard Sennett, *The Fall of Public Man* (New York: W.W. Norton, 1974); Stephen E. Little, "Networks and Neighborhoods: Households, Community and Sovereignty in the Global Economy," *Urban Studies* 37, no. 10 (2000): 1813–25; Kazy Varnelis, *Networked Publics* (Cambridge: MIT Press, 2008).
3. Anthony Giddens, *The Constitution of Society: Outline of the Theory of Structuration*. (Cambridge: Polity Press, 1984); Stephen Graham and Simon Marvin. *Splintering Urbanism*. (New York: Routledge, 2001).
4. danah boyd, "Why Youth (Heart) Social Network Sites: The Role of Networked Publics in Teenage Social Life," in *MacArthur Foundation Series on Digital Learning: Youth, Identity, and Digital Media*, ed. David Buckingham,119–42 (Cambridge: MIT Press, 2007).
5. Bruno Latour, *Pandora's Hope: Essays on the Reality of Science Studies*. (Cambridge: Harvard University Press, 1999), 203–5, 214.
6. Craig Calhoun, "Community without Propinquity Revisited: Communications Technology and the Transformation of the Urban Public Sphere," *Sociological Inquiry* 68, no. 3 (1998): 374.
7. Ibid.

NOTES TO CHAPTER 1

1. According to Clay Shirky, if the dominant media is owned or controlled by authoritarian governments, with the earlier mass media model, a unidirectional endpoint-reception system made it simple to control and by controlling the core, i.e. state-owned television, radio and newspaper, the government controlled the end user. Unlike mass media's one-to-many transmission, social media allows for ad hoc, inexpensive and efficient many-to-many messaging so that individual multiple users act as nodes in a multidirectional endpoint system, providing efficient distribution of information.
2. Evgeny Morozov, "Facebook and Twitter Are Just Places That Revolutionaries Go," *Guardian,* March 7, 2011, accessed February 12, 2012, http://www.guardian.co.uk/commentisfree/2011/mar/07/facebook-twitter-revolutionaries-cyber-utopians.

3. Ibid.
4. Malcolm Gladwell and Clay Shirky, "From Innovation to Revolution: Does Social Media Make Protests Possible? *Foreign Affairs Journal* (March/April 2011), accessed April 30, 2011, http://www.foreignaffairs.com/articles/67325/malcolm-gladwell-and-clay-shirky/from-innovation-to-revolution.
5. Specifically, protesters demanded "higher wages, improved public services in the health, education, and transportation sectors, the elimination of government corruption, an end to police torture and arbitrary detainment, and the creation of a fair judiciary system." From Marina Ottaway and Amr Hamzawy, "Protest Movements and Political Change in the Arab World," *Carnegie Endowment for International Peace 5* (January 28, 2011): 3.
6. Malcolm Gladwell, "Small Change: Why the Revolution Will Not Be Tweeted," *New Yorker*, October 4, 2010.
7. Manuel Castells, *Networks of Outrage and Hope: Social Movements in the Internet Age* (Cambridge: Polity, 2012), 27.
8. Or the opposite, that governments pay bloggers to write positive commentaries about them.
9. Robert Asen, "Seeking the 'Counter' in Counterpublics," *Communication Theory* 10 (2000): 4, 424–46.
10. "Tiananmen Square 1989: The Declassified History," *National Security Archive*, accessed March 25, 2011, http://www.gwu.edu/~nsarchiv/NSAEBB/NSAEBB16/documents/index.html.
11. Many immigrants in France face social exclusion based on ethnicity. Rioting erupted on October 27, 2005, in the outskirts of Paris and continued for two weeks, spreading to 300 towns and cities throughout France. The rioting was sparked by the accidental deaths of two teenagers, one of French Arab and the other of French African descent, and grew into a violent protest against the high unemployment rates. "France: History, Geography, Government, and Culture," accessed December 10, 2010, http://www.infoplease.com/ipa/A0107517.html?pageno=7#ixzz1HdXUVbM4.
12. For example, the anti-Iraqi war protests in San Francisco (Feb 15, 2003) foregrounded political opposition to the international conflict that the U.S. administration had been ignoring.
13. For images refer to http://www.rawa.org/gallery.html.
14. Crabgrass is an open-source secure application for social networking and organizing platforms.
15. Trebor Scholz, *Collectivate*, accessed August 3, 2009, http://www.collectivate.net./.
16. "Old Technology Finds Role in Egyptian Protests," *BBC News*, January 31, 2011, accessed February 16, 2011, http://www.bbc.co.uk/news/technology-12322948.
17. The partnership of mobile technologies and social media networks such as Twitter allow multiple audience members increased agency. Case in point: Iran. In June 2009, general elections in Iran were scheduled to take place, allowing voters to participate in reform. Yet, when the elections were concluded and the results came back that Mahmoud Ahmadinejad had been reelected, people automatically claimed the elections were rigged. Soon after, pro-reform Iranians using their mobile phones and Twitter to begin mobilizing protests and demonstrations. The government quickly responded. "The day after the election, Iran closed the Internet down entirely for a half an hour, then slowly loosened its grip, as the authorities struggled to gain control," according to Jon Leyne (*BBC News*, February 11, 2010). The Iranian government continued to filter information on the web, control Internet speed, and organize intelligence to monitor dissenters online. Mehdi

Yahyanejad, the manager of a popular Farsi-language website, said as much to the *Washington Post* in 2010 "Here [in the United States], there is lots of buzz," he said. "But once you look, you see most of it are Americans tweeting among themselves." Golnaz Esfandiari points out that "good old-fashioned word of mouth was by far the most influential medium used to shape the post-election opposition activity" (*Foreign Policy,* June 7, 2010). Since then, Twitter and Iran have operated under precarious circumstances. Multiple reports illuminate Iran's use of Twitter to target pro-reformers and cease protests through the guise of antigovernment Tweets, according to Yaakov Lappin (*Jerusalem Post,* June 17, 2009). In response to these actions, pro-reformers are subverting Iranian filters by employing proxy addresses located on the West and changing their local times on their digital devices to non-Tehran time to circumvent government agents. In addition to supporters using Western proxy addresses, Iranian supporters abroad are supplying software providing unfiltered and anonymous access to Iranians so they can bypass government authorities and filters to websites such as Facebook and Twitter (*BBC News*, February 5, 2010). Yet, in December 2009, a group calling itself the Iranian Cyber Army, a pro-Iranian government supporter group, hacked Twitter by redirecting users to mowjcamp.org, where anti-American messages were displayed (*BBC News*, December 18, 2009). After an hour and fifteen minutes, Twitter regained control of the website, stating the group had "gained access to the inner workings of the site" (Ibid.).

18. Brent Scowcroft, a former national security advisor for President George H. W. Bush, discussing the Middle East situation said, "These devices like Facebook make it possible to organize a demonstration. You can contact a million people in thirty minutes to turn out in a square at 10 o'clock in the morning. This is unique, and I think that's the reason the immolation of a fruit peddler in Tunisia has swept the region. I think it's a new phenomenon that we're going to have to deal with from now on." Interview with Jim Lehrer, *PBS News Hour*, March 21, 2011.

19. The findings of my Internet enthnography documented in *Situated Networks: In [re]search of the Public* (2008–9), points out that for the majority of respondents, a Facebook page is a highly efficient planning and organizing tool—faster and less expensive than any other previous way of connecting geographically dispersed people. In contrast, Gladwell contends that political activism is not created by the affordances of social media but through strong personal bonds. The findings of my study confirmed this argument as well: For the majority of respondents, strong personal bonds were intrinsic to social media. The study verified that for most respondents, strong friendships were established in proximal space prior to joining a networked public such as Facebook. In other words, for the majority of the respondents, social media is actually mirroring their close physical world relationships. Gladwell further contends that networked organizations create weak links, although my study did not find evidence of this (refer to appendixes).

20. Castells, *Networks of Outrage and Hope*, 53–54.

21. Samantha M. Shapiro, "Revolution, Facebook-Style," *New York Times*, January 22, 2009, accessed March 20, 2011, http://www.nytimes.com/2009/01/25/magazine/25bloggers-t.html.

22. Ibid.

23. With access to a personal or public computer terminal or a smartphone.

24. Tierney, "Situated Networks."

25. The young, unemployed, and women make up a considerable number of those who were actively fighting against the military and using social media to get their points across, according to Mike Elkin, "Massive Protests Greet

Anniversary of Egypt's Revolution," *Washington Times*, January 25, 2012, accessed April 29, 2012, http://www.washingtontimes.com/news/2012/jan/25/massive-protests-greet-anniversary-of-egypts-revol/?page=all.

26. Castells, *Networks of Outrage and Hope*, 156–217.
27. Nezar Alsayyad, "The Virtual Square: Urban Space, Media, and the Egyptian Uprising," *Harvard International Review* (Summer 2012), 59.
28. Castells, *Networks of Outrage and Hope*, 193–94.
29. Steven Pinker, *The Stuff of Thought: Language as a Window into Human Nature*, (New York: Viking Press, 2007), 418–22.
30. Brandalism is the UK's street artists' practice of reappropriating billboard advertisements for social critique.
31. For more than two decades, the Internet has been strategic for planning and coordinating spatial interventions. In 1996 and 1997, Zapatistas and other activists met in mass in Chiapas and Spain to talk about their goals and ways of collaborating. This undoubtedly strengthened connections that had been formed online between participants by bringing them together in one physical location. However, the occurrence of these conferences also suggests that activists were not satisfied with operating entirely in a virtual space and found value in meeting face-to-face despite the significant effort required to do so. Refer to http://learn.bowdoin.edu/courses/soc022-richard-joyce/2010/04/zapatista-solidarity-online-a-case-study-of-internet-activism.
32. The endowment for Central European University was established by philanthropist George Soros, who is chairman of Soros Fund Management and founder of a global network of foundations dedicated to supporting open societies. Soros is Hungarian by birth.
33. Robert Boorstin, "Internet at Liberty Live Stream," *Google Policy Blog*, September 21, 2010, accessed March 10, 2011, http://googlepublicpolicy.blogspot.com/2010/09/internet-at-liberty-2010-live-stream.html; see also Brock N. Meeks, "Internet at Liberty Conference," *Center for Democracy & Technology*, September 21, 2010, accessed March 10, 2011, https://www.cdt.org/blogs/brock-meeks/internet-liberty-2010-promise-and-peril-online-free-expression.
34. Boorstin, "Internet at Liberty Conference."
35. David Nassar, "Google Convenes in Budapest on Internet Liberty," *Huffington Post*, September 24, 2010, accessed February 20, 2011, http://www.huffingtonpost.com/david-nassar/google-convenes-in-budape_b_738571.html.
36. Thanks to University of Illinois at Urbana-Champaign PhD candidate Shantel Martinez, who noted that some bloggers and activists were arrested at airports trying to reenter their homelands. Although many were arrested due to "old charges" from their digital activities, some believed it was their attendance at the conference that led authorities to locate them. One of the attendees, Mark Belinsky of *Digital Democracy*, noted, "The Chatham House Rule was enacted at the Conference, meaning that no one could be photographed or quoted without permission. I appreciate that Google made this simple but important gesture, given that many people were endangering their own lives to attend this conference. I'm often upset with the lack of caution taken when people take photos of friends who are dissidents in foreign countries. It's frightening what a little social network analysis can reveal for interested authorities. And it's a tool that is becoming less and less complicated and out of reach for some of the world's most repressive regimes." *Digital Democracy*, October 7, 2010, accessed February 23, 2011, http://digital-democracy.org/2010/10/07/googles-internet-at-liberty-conference/
37. "HRSI at the Google Conference," September 24, 2010, *Human Rights Initiative* blog, accessed March 12, 2011, http://hrsi.ceu.hu/blogs/krasznaya/2010-09-24/hrsi-at-the-google-conference.

38. The U.S. government, George Soros's *Open Society Foundation*, and Google funded these private events.

39. Morozov, "Facebook and Twitter Are Just Places That Revolutionaries Go."

40. Elsewhere I have written about nonproprietary networked publics and counterpublics; see Thérèse F. Tierney, "Disentangling Public Space: Social Media and Internet Activism," *Thresholds Journal* 41 (2013), 74–81.

41. Michael Gardiner, *The Dialogics of Critique: M. M. Bakhtin and the Theory of Ideology*, (London: Routledge, 1992), 3.

42. The importance of e-mail is in its potential democratic transmission: e-mail is an open protocol (RFC822). Everyone can implement it. E-mail is open for all potential users: Everyone who can buy a domain name can host an e-mail server and issue new e-mail addresses. Domain names are democratically controlled by IANA/IETF. Social media protocols are likewise open, but most people join proprietary platforms that their friends already belong to.

43. Samatha Shapiro, "Revolution, Facebook-Style."

44. Wael Ghonim, *Revolution 2.0* (New York: Houghton Mifflin Harcourt, 2012), 143.

45. Nezar Alsayyad, "The Virtual Square: Urban Space, Media and the Egyptian Uprising," *Harvard International Review* 33 (Summer 2012): 61; Castells, *Networks of Outrage and Hope*, 55, 59.

46. This refers not only to the technological digital divide but also to language literacy. English is almost required for Internet use; the majority of all web pages are written in English, although this trend is changing over time. In contrast, the use of a mobile device (smartphone) for Internet access is increasing among traditionally underrepresented groups and is often their only way of connecting to the Internet.

47. Felix Stadler, "Between Democracy and Spectacle: The Front End and the Back End of the Social Web," in *Social Media Reader* (New York: NYU Press, 2012), 249–50.

48. An exception is Zuccotti Park, a privately held public space (POPS) that Occupy Wall Street (OWS) used as a staging ground and campsite. The park's private status allowed for protesters to stay past municipal curfew hours.

49. The video was uploaded by an Egyptian blogger Wael Abbas who was involved in opposing torture in Egypt. Refer to Jennifer Preston's "Ethical Quandary for Social Sites," *New York Times*, March 27, 2011, http://www.nytimes.com/2011/03/28/business/media/28social.html?pagewanted=all&_r=0.

50. Subsequently, Facebook claimed the groups were in violation of terms and conditions, although discretion is usually involved in the implementation of policies. Nevertheless, consensus seems to point to the need for online publics to build open, decentralized social networks for self-hosted groups and events. Refer to http://www.opendemocracy.net/ourkingdom/guy-aitchison/political-purge-of-uk-facebook-underway (accessed December 3, 2012).

51. Joanne McNeil, "Occupy the Internet," *Occupy! An OWS-Inspired Gazette* Issue 1 (N+1) Rhizome, Nov 9, 2011, accessed June 8, 2012, http://www.nplusonemag.com/occupy-gazette.pdf.

52. Blocking access to a particular website cannot stop knowledgeable Internet users from employing virtual private networks or other technologies to access unbanned IP addresses outside the country as a means to access banned sites. In response to this problem, China shut down Internet access to all of Xinjiang Autonomous Region, the location of ethnic riots in Uigor in 2009. More recently, Egypt followed the same tactic for the entire country.

53. "Social Media as a Tool for Protest," *Stratfor Global Intelligence*, February 3, 2011, accessed February 25, 2013, http://www.stratfor.com/weekly/20110202-social-media-tool-protest.

54. "Department of Homeland Security Monitors Facebook, Twitter and News Sites for 'Situational Awareness," *Reuters Reporter*, 13 January 2012, accessed March 10, 2012, http://www.dailymail.co.uk/news/article-2085940/Facebook-Twitter-news-sites-monitored-US-Homeland-Security.html.
55. When a conventional cellular phone is turned on, it emits a signal. Cell phone companies can approximate cell phone locations by a triangulation system known as pinging. Cell phone companies can ping or contact the cell phone and locate the nearest tower the signal is coming from.
56. Brandon McGlone, office of the secretary of defense, interview with the author, May 23, 2012.
57. Sami Benn Gharbia, accessed September 1, 2012, http://nawaat.org/portail/2010/09/17/the-internet-freedom-fallacy-and-the-arab-digital-activism. Belinsky supported the U.S. stance to defend those freedoms, and "the more countries that stand to defend article 19 of the Universal Declaration of Human Rights stipulating information as a human right, the better."
58. Lothar Detemann, "Social Media Privacy: A Dozen Myths and Facts," *Stanford Technology Law Review*, accessed February 25, 2013, http://stlr.stanford.edu/pdf/determann-socialmediaprivacy.pdf.
59. "Department of Homeland Security Monitors Facebook, Twitter and News Sites for 'Situational Awareness."
60. Laurier Rochon, accessed September 3, 2012, http://pwd.io/guide.
61. Information has been coming out via WCITleaks.org, a website dedicated to disseminating classified documents for the meeting.
62. John Kampfer, "The Fight for Control of the Internet Has Become Critical," August 22, 2012, accessed February 25, 2013, http://www.guardian.co.uk/commentisfree/2012/aug/22/fight-control-internet-become-critical.
63. Somini Sengupta, "Censoring of Tweets Sets off #Outrage," *New York Times*, January 27, 2012, accessed March 10, 2011, http://www.nytimes.com/2012/01/28/technology/when-twitter-blocks-tweets-its-outrage.html.
64. For instance, in Germany pro-Nazi or Pro-Nazism tweets will be taken down in Germany but will still be accessible in other countries to view (*New York Times*, January 27, 2012). From the U.S. State Department to law professors and bloggers, those in favor of the changes agreed that Twitter is not above the law and must be held accountable to legal standards. "Previously, when Twitter erased a tweet, it vanished throughout the world. Under the new policy, a tweet breaking a law in one country can be taken down there and still be seen elsewhere. Twitter said it will post a censorship notice whenever a tweet is removed and will post the removal requests it receives from governments, companies and individuals at the website chillingeffects.org" (*Huffington Post*, January 27, 2012).
65. David Crary, "Twitter Censorship Policy Ignites Global Outrage," *Huffington Post*, January 27, 2012, accessed April 15, 2012, http://www.huffingtonpost.com/2012/01/27/twitter-censorship-policy-global-outrage_n_1238188.html.
66. Ibid.
67. Sengupta, "Censoring of Tweets Sets off #Outrage."
68. Crary, "Twitter Censorship Policy Ignites Global Outrage."
69. Rob Waugh, "Google Joins Twitter in Censorship Storm," *Daily Mail*, February 3, 2012, accessed April 29, 2012, http://www.dailymail.co.uk/sciencetech/article-2095328/Google-joins-Twitter-censorship-storm-Site-block-blog-posts-line-requests-repressive-governments.html?ITO=1490.
70. Ibid.
71. Ben Elgin and Vernon Silver, "Syria Disrupts Text Messaging of Protestors with Made-in-Dublin Equipment," *Bloomberg LP*, February 15, 2012,

accessed April, 29, 2012, http://www.bloomberg.com/news/2012-02-15/
syria-blocks-texts-with-dublin-made-gear.html.

72. Castells, *Networks of Outrage and Hope*; David Harvey, *Rebel Cities* (Brooklyn: Verso, 2012).

73. "To the extent that a society uses social media mundanely but deeply in everyday commerce and social interaction, it will be much harder for countries to effectively dismantle these without huge economic and social costs." From "Twitter, Facebook and YouTube's Role in the Arab Spring," *Social Capital Blog*, January 26, 2011, accessed December 3, 2012, http://socialcapital.wordpress.com.

74. Seeta Pena Gangadharan, "Tyrannies of Participation," panel discussion, ISEA, Sabanchi University, Istanbul, September 16, 2011.

75. Refer to Habermas, *The Structural Transformation of the Public Sphere* (1989) and Foucault *Discipline and Punish* (1977).

76. Sylvia Lavin has written extensively about electronically mediated atmospheres and environments. Lavin describes flickering as neither an open nor closed space but an environmental mode held together by a vast array of moving particulate matter ?ickering between on or off. Networked publics are flickering, unstable, not only due to electronic mediation, but also because as a communication platform, they are vulnerable to government clampdowns and the ever real possibility of Facebook suspending activist accounts and group pages.

77. James Bohman, "Expanding Dialogue: the Internet, the Public Sphere and Prospects for Transnational Democracy," in Nick Crossley and John Michael Roberts, eds., *After Habermas: New Perspectives on the Public Sphere* (Oxford: Blackwell, 2004), 134.

78. According to Laurier Rochon, there is an idea circulating in Western discourse that the Internet has a natural inclination to produce a specific brand of Western democracy.

79. Wael Ghonim, quoted in an interview with Wolf Blitzer, *CNN*, February 11, 2011.

NOTES TO CHAPTER 2

1. *Oxford Dictionary*, 2nd ed., s.v. "public"; *Webster's Third New International Unabridged Dictionary*, 3rd ed., 1981, s.v. "public."

2. Stephen Carr, Mark Francis, Leanne G. Rivlin, and Andrew M. Stone, *Public Space* (Cambridge: Cambridge University Press,1992), 52–55.

3. Raymond Williams, *Culture and Society 1780–1950* (New York: Columbia University Press, 1987), 75.

4. Richard Sennett, *The Fall of Public Man* (New York: W.W. Norton, 1974), 16.

5. Piazza is defined as "sanctified place," designating the space in front of churches; campo is derived from "field," referring back to the secular commons— a public field commonly shared among members of the community.

6. Carr et al., *Public Space*, 24.

7. The eighteenth century's public infrastructure of plazas and boulevards, as well as the nineteenth century's shopping arcades, became a site of bourgeois display.

8. According to the architectural theorist Sylvia Lavin (1991) municipal laws prescribed how and when the lower classes could frequent public parks, and where they could and could not venture.

9. *Spatial theory* interrogates inherited notions of place and community, resulting in the reformulation of *place* as an open set of relations. Critical spatial theories confront both conflicting and normative dimensions of urban landscape by situating the particulars of place within structural systems of organization and occupied space, thus exposing the actual means of production and articulations of power.

10. Martina Low developed the notion of a *relational* model of space, which focuses on the orderings of living entities and social entities; it also examines how space is constituted in processes of perception, recall, or ideation to manifest itself as societal structure.

11. Henri Lefebvre, *The Production of Space*, trans. Donald Nicholson-Smith (Oxford: Wiley-Blackwell, 1992).

12. The Situationists included Guy Deborg, Henri Lefebvre, and Constant Nieuwenhuys, among others. In the *Critique of Everyday Life* (1947), Lefebvre proposed that architecture could instigate the creation of new situations. The actions of the Situationists vis-à-vis performance, installations, and films were said to have contributed to 1968 Paris student demonstrations.

13. Economic pressures, for Lefebvre, pervade and shape space, resulting in an economic notion of space as a product. Space is commodified as well as consumed. Refer to *The Production of Space*,85.

14. I draw on mathematician and philosopher Alfred North Whitehead's explicit definition of context—no entity can be what it is in isolation from all other entities, and that no entity is entirely determined by these other entities. Steven Shaviro describes it thus: The margin of indetermination, which is the freedom of the individual entity, is better described as a contingent decision than as a set of properties. Whitehead also introduced space and time as a dynamic model into the equation by distinguishing between actual entities and what he calls societies, or aggregations of entities that possess spatial extent and temporal duration (whereas the actual entities themselves in a certain sense *produce* temporality and spatiality, rather than being located within them).

15. Everyday practices are *metis*, ways of operating, or in psychological terms, schemata of action. Michel De Certeau applies the concept of appropriation, explained through his example of colonized cultures: Indigenous peoples were forced to consume the colonizer's rituals, and appropriated these same rituals, representations and laws, while concurrently subverting them. They did this not by rejecting or altering them, but by creating different meanings or using them toward different cultural objectives than their conquerors intended. De Certeau is concerned here with the difference between the original producers of a representation and the secondary users of a representation because it shows how an appropriation or reappropriation of a dominant culture can be channeled to a marginalized group's interests and rules. We see this also with sociologist Pierre Bourdieu's theory of social practices, where the makeshift, a technique of bricolage, results in ad hoc manipulations of spaces, or in operators of networks. According to de Certeau, "Culture articulates, conflicts, and alternately legitimizes, displaces or controls the superior force." Refer to *The Practice of Everyday Life* (Berkeley: University of California Press, 2002), xvii.

16. "As a science of human settlements, Ekistics offered a vehicle for analyzing and understanding urban landscapes as complex matrices of mutable and evolving networks of information." Nataly Gattegno, "Building in the Inevitable City of the Future," paper presented at the conference on Constantinos A. Doxiadis and His Work, Athens, Greece, January 2007.

17. Mark Wigley, "The Architectural Brain," in *Network Practices: New Strategies for Architecture and Design*, ed. Anthony Burke and Thérèse Tierney (New York: Princeton Architectural Press, 2007), 36–40, 43.

18. Melvin Webber, "Order in Diversity: Community Without Propinquity," in *Cities and Space: The Future of Urban Land*, ed. Lowdon Wingo (Baltimore: Johns Hopkins Press, 1963), 23–54.
19. Reynar Banham, *Los Angeles: The Four Ecologies* (New York: Harper & Row, 1971).
20. Melvin Webber, "The Urban Place and the Non-Urban Realm," in *Explorations into Urban Structure* (London: Oxford University Press, 1964), 116.
21. Webber described it more closely: "A city is not described by the buildings, but by the social relations which bind the city together." Refer to "Order in Diversity: Community without Propinquity," in *Cities and Space*, 29.
22. "Never before in human history has it been so easy to communicate across long distances. Never before have men (*sic*) been able to maintain intimate and continuing contact with others across thousands of miles; never has intimacy been so independent of spatial propinquity" with the capability to unite all places at almost the same time. Webber also viewed the automobile as "an important instrument of personal freedom." Refer to Webber, "The Urban Place and the Non-Urban Realm," 40
23. David Harvey suggests that postmodernism is an intensification of modernism.
24. Public space, for example MacArthur Park in Los Angeles, exhibits complex usage patterns. Various groups habituate spatial territory at specific times of the day in specific ways. Refer to Gerardo Sandoval's *Immigration and the Revitalization of Los Angeles: Development and Change in MacArthur Park* (Amherst: Cambria Press, 2009).
25. Larry Busbea, *Topologies: the Urban Utopia of France 1960–1970* (Cambridge: MIT Press, 2007), 11.
26. John Walton, "Urban Sociology: The Contribution and Limits of Political Economy," *Annual Review of Sociology* 19 (1993): 301–20
27. Manuel Castells, *The Rise of the Network Society*, 2nd ed. (Malden: Blackwell, 2000), 12.
28. Manuel Castells, *The Informational City: Information Technology, Economic Restructuring, and the Urban Regional Process* (Oxford, UK; Cambridge, MA: Blackwell, 1989), 146.
29. David Walters and Linda Brown, *Design First: Design-Based Planning for Communities* (London: Architectural Press, 2004), 23.
30. Stephen Graham and Simon Marvin, *Splintering Urbanism* (New York: Routledge, 2001), 43–45.
31. Castells, *The Rise of the Network Society*, 1–76.
32. Walters and Brown, *Design First*, 23.
33. Webber, "Order in Diversity: Community without Propinquity," 29.
34. Ibid.
35. Richard Florida, *The Rise of the Creative Class* (Cambridge, MA: Basic Books, 2002), 223–33.
36. Florida, *The Rise of the Creative Class*, 223–33.
37. Reynar Banham believed that Los Angeles represents a new urban model. At the same time, places that have natural assets, what Florida terms non-transportable on-site amenities, will only become more valued real estate; examples include Silicon Valley, Boston's east corridor, and the locales immediately north of New York City.
38. Kenneth Goldberg, *The Robot in the Garden* (Cambridge: MIT Press, 2000), 3–14.
39. Uricchio, William, "Historicizing Media in Transition," *Rethinking Media Change* (Cambridge: MIT Press, 2003), 30.

40. Yehuda Kalay, New Media Research Methods Seminar, University of California–Berkeley, May 3, 2007.
41. CITRIS Lecture, University of California–Berkeley Jena Burrell "Co-Evoluation of the mobile phone and users in Rural Uganda" February 11, 2009 and "mobile flagship" program at the World Bank consisting of studies related to mobile services and applications in selected sectors, including "Mobile Banking Users and Non Users Behavior Study," "Extending Mobile Applications in Africa through Social Networking," and "Mobile Applications for Sectoral Development," accessed March 20, 2011, http://go.worldbank.org/2Y63OQHOG0.
42. Lucien Febvre, Henri-Jean Martin, and David Gerard, *The Coming of the Book: The Impact of Printing 1450–1800* (New York: Verso, 1997).
43. As an example of how technology is embedded in social contexts that may make its various potentials unrealizable, consider the discovery of gunpowder in China in 1040.
44. Joshua Meyrowitz, *No Sense of Place: The Impact of Electronic Media on Social Behavior* (New York: Oxford Press, 1985).
45. Ibid.
46. danah boyd, "Taken Out of Context: American Teen Sociality in Networked Publics," PhD diss., University of California–Berkeley, 2008.
47. James Bohman, "Expanding Dialogue: The Internet, the Public Sphere and Prospects for Transnational Democracy," in *After Habermas: New Perspectives on the Public Sphere*, ed. Nick Crossley and John Michael Roberts (Oxford: Blackwell, 2004), 134.
48. Granville Ganter, "Review of Publics and Counterpublics," *St. John's University Humanities Review* 1, no. 1 (March 2003),1, accessed April 15, 2009, http://facpub.stjohns.edu/ganterg/sjureview/vol1–1/publics.html.
49. In the United States, individuals such as Randolph Hearst bought up newspapers and controlled public opinion. According to Granville Ganter, when Tom Brokaw addresses the U.S. "public" on the evening news, that news is filtered and arranged by the megacorporations that own the television stations that also promote the war for Iraqi oil.
50. Michel Foucault, *Des Espaces Autres*, "Of Other Spaces" (1967): *Heterotopias. Architecture/Movement/Continuities* 5 (October 1984): 46–49.
51. Michael Gardiner, "Wild Publics and Grotesque Symposiums: Habermas and Bakhtin on Dialogue, Everyday Life and the Public Sphere," in *After Habermas: New Perspectives on the Public Sphere*, ed. Nick Crossley and John Michael Roberts (Oxford: Blackwell, 2004), 29.
52. Jenkins's view aligns with theories advanced by sociologist Rob Shields in "The Virtual" (2002).
53. Place serves as a *"place* where ideas, values, and shared experiences are constructed [as a center of meaning]." Refer to Paul Adams, "Television as Gathering Place," *Annals of the Association of American Geographers* 82, no. 1 (1992): 119–20.
54. One-way transmission originates from one source such as telegraph, radio, film, or television.
55. Adams, "Television as Gathering Place," 119–20.
56. Edmund Carpenter, *They Became What They Beheld* (E. P. Dutton,1970), 63.
57. Anthony Giddens, *The Constitution of Society: Outline of the Theory of Structuration* (Cambridge: Polity Press, 1984), 170, 264.
58. *Random House Webster's Unabriged Dictionary,* 2nd ed 2001., s.v. *"civitas."*
59. Harold Innis, *Changing Concepts of Time* (Toronto: University of Toronto Press, 1952), 83.
60. Concerns can be traced back to classical philosophy. For Plato, writing is once removed from its author. Unlike face-to-face conversation, one cannot

query a text if there is a misunderstanding. Texts are often read in isolation, creating an individuated state of mind.

61. In "Science in Action: How to follow scientists and engineers" (1987), the sociologist Bruno Latour emphasized the importance of context and/or relations, with the belief that to remove any thing from its context is to change it entirely. With "What is Philosophy?" (1994), the philosophers Gilles Deleuze and Felix Guattari described this relationship as a "plane of immanence." Mathematician and philosopher Alfred North Whitehead in "Process and Reality" (1929) explicitly described context—no entity can be what it is in isolation from all other entities, and that no entity is entirely determined by these other entities.

62. Wikipedia definition: The term *Web 2.0* is associated with social media applications that facilitate interactive information sharing, interoperability, and user-generated content on the World Wide Web. A Web 2.0 site allows users to interact and collaborate with each other as co-creators in an online community. This is in contrast with other websites where users are limited to the passive viewing of content. Examples of Web 2.0 include social networking sites, blogs, wikis, video sharing, web applications, mashups, and folksonomies. The term Web 2.0 refers to cumulative changes in the ways in which software developers and end users use the Web. Refer to http://en.wikipedia.org/wiki/Web_2.0.

63. According to cultural theorist James Donald. Refer to *Imagining the Modern City*, (Minneapolis, MN: University of Minnesota Press, 1999).

64. Nezar AlSayyad, *Cinematic Urbanism: A History of the Modern City from Reel to Real* (London: Routledge, 2006), 1.

65. George Herbert Mead, "The Community and the Institution," Section 34 in Mind Self and Society from the Standpoint of a Social Behaviorist, ed. Charles W. Morris (Chicago: University of Chicago Press,1934), 271.

66. Catherine R. Squires, "Rethinking the Black Public Sphere: A Vocabulary for Multiple Public Spheres," *Communication Theory* 12, no.4 (2002), 450.

67. In the 1820s, Frances Wright toured the United States and provoked attacks as she lectured against slavery and for women's rights, birth control, and worker rights. Refer to Michael Warner, "Public and Private" in *Publics and Counterpublics* (New York: Zone Books, 2002), 21–63.

68. On a public scale, what is perceived as an *outsider perspective* by psychologists at least is defined by the media (whether Twitter or other)—if the media presents certain ideas as skewed, those with minority opinions hold back, feel marginalized, and will continue to hold back, with the result that they marginalize themselves even more. Thus, when Twitter uses algorithms to select top topics based on their business criteria, minority voices may be censored.

69. Joanne McNeil, *Occupy! An OWS-Inspired Gazette* Issue 1 (N+1) Rhizome Nov 9, 2011: 24–25, accessed June 8, 2012. http://www.nplusonemag.com/OCCUPY-GAZETTE.pdf.

70. Nancy Fraser, "Rethinking the Public Sphere: A Contribution to the Critique of Actually Existing Democracy," in *The Cultural Studies Reader*, ed. Simon During (London: Routledge, 2nd ed, 1999), 527.

71. Ganter, "Review of Publics," 1.

72. Michael Warner, *Publics and Counterpublics*, 119.

73. Mike Featherstone, "The Heroic Life and the Everyday Life," *Theory Culture and Society* 9, no.1 (1992):159–82.

74. Christian Fuchs, "Class, Knowledge and New Media," *Media Culture & Society* 32, no. 1 (2010): 141.

75. Ibid.

76. In "What They Know," the *Wall Street Journal* developed an exposure index that determines the degree to which each free site, such as Dictionary.com, exposes visitors to monitoring. Refer to http://blogs.wsj.com/wtk.
77. Fuchs, "Class, Knowledge and the New Media," 146, 149.
78. Social marketing firms, for example uSocial, offered paid services that finds Twitter and Facebook followers and recommends them to follow the individual or business that purchased the service. Legal action is on-going. Refer to http://gigaom.com/2009/08/17/twitter-wants-to-shut-down-usocial-but-why-cant-it.
79. Rachel O'Dwyer, "Network Media: Exploring the Sociotechnical Relations Between Mobile Networks and Media Publics," conference paper, ISEA Conference, Istanbul, 2011.
80. The algorithms applied in OpenSocial, OpenGraph, and GraphRank automate the so-called sense-making processes of what content is relevant to a particular user. Refer to Taina Butcher, http://www.culturemachine.net/index.php/cm/article/view/470/489.
81. Sanford Kwinter, "The Tragedy of the Commons," *Log* 25 (Summer 2012): 143.
82. Rachel O'Dwyer, "Network Media" 2011.
83. Squires, "Rethinking the Black Public Sphere," 458.
84. Giddens, *The Constitution of Society*, 170, 264.
85. De Certeau, *The Practice of Everyday Life*, 36–37, 117–18.
86. Bohman "Expanding Dialogue," 134.
87. Sociologist Gary Marx acknowledges, "Powerful forces work against any easy assumption that a decent society is self-perpetuating or that once set in motion, progress must continue. The masthead of a black civil rights newspaper in Sun Flower County, Mississippi reads, 'Freedom Is a Constant Struggle.' . . . There are no permanent victories in the liberties business. Liberty and individualism are fragile and historically the exception rather than the rule. There is no guarantee that hard won rights will stay won or be extended, in the face of continual social and technical challenges. But vigilance, knowledge and wisdom are likely to help." Refer to *Privacy and Technology*, http://web.mit.edu/gtmarx/www/privantt.html.

NOTES TO CHAPTER 3

1. "How Twitter Engineers Outwitted Mubarak in One Weekend," *Guardian*, accessed February 25, 2011, http://www.guardian.co.uk/technology/2011/feb/06/twitter-speak-tweet-mubarak-networker.
2. Michael Warner, *Publics and Counterpublics* (New York: Zone Books, 2002), 8.
3. While other sites of emergence occurred, I have chosen to concentrate on these three.
4. Bruno Latour, *Reassembling the Social: An Introduction to Actor-Network-Theory* (Oxford: Oxford University Press, 2005).
5. WordNet® 3.0., Princeton University, accessed March 27, 2009, http://dictionary.reference.com/browse/internet.
6. Clay Shirky, *Corante: Many 2 Many: a group weblog on social software* (2006), accessed February 26, 2013, http://many.corante.com/archives/2006/12/12/second_life_what_are_the_real_numbers.php.
7. By comparison, a conference call is expensive, difficult to arrange, time-consuming, and useless for large groups.

8. danah boyd and Nicole Ellison "Social Network Sites: Definition, History, and Scholarship," *Journal of Computer-Mediated Communication*, 13, no. 1 (2007), article 11: page 4, accessed November 1, 2008, http://jcmc.indiana.edu/vol13/issue1/boyd.ellison.html.
9. Through Stewart Brand's publications, he trained a generation of media journalists, such as Kevin Kelly, who eventually went on to found the San Francisco–based *Wired* magazine.
10. Silicon Valley, accessed March 20, 2011, http://svsf40.icann.org/about.
11. Fred Turner, *From Counterculture to Cyberculture: Stewart Brand, the Whole Earth Network, and the Rise of Digital Utopianism*, (Chicago: University of Chicago Press, 2006), 70.
12. Later documented in the film "Ecological Design: Inventing the Future" (1994).
13. Andrew Kirk, *Counterculture Green* (Lawrence: University of Kansas Press, 2007), 47.
14. Ibid., 48.
15. The address was 558 Santa Cruz Avenue, Menlo Park, CA 94025, although the Truck Store was once located adjacent to San Francisquito Creek.
16. Turner, *From Counterculture to Cyberculture*, 79.
17. Gareth Branwyn, *The Whole Earth Review* (1998), accessed December 18, 2012, http://www.streettech.com/bcp/BCPtext/CyberCulture/WholeEarth Review.html.
18. Turner, *From Counterculture to Cyberculture*, 72–73.
19. The journalist Donald C. Hoefler wrote for *Electronic News*, a weekly tabloid. He first used the phrase "SiliconValley" in 1971 to describe the congeries of electronics firms mushrooming in Santa Clara County as a distinct community.
20. Sean Nelson, interview by the author with a former programmer at NASA Ames Research Lab, Moffett Field, CA; Mill Valley, CA, December 13, 2008.
21. Al Alcorn, cofounder of Atari with Nolan Bushnell, interview with PodTech.net, July 22 2006. The video can be accessed at http://www.podtech.net/home/?p=881.
22. Refer to http://indiatoday.intoday.in/story/india-visit-gave-a-vision-to-steve-jobs/1/154785.html.
23. Turner, *From Counterculture to Cyberculture*, 18.
24. The content of *CQ* often wandered through science fiction and popular culture. Besides giving space to unknown, but provocative writers, Brand presented articles by many highly respected authors and thinkers, including Howard T. Odum, Witold Rybczynski, Karl Hess, Christopher Swan, Orville Schell, Ivan Illich, Wendell Berry, Ursula K. Le Guin, Gregory Bateson, Amory Lovins, Hazel Henderson, Gary Snyder, Lynn Margulis, Eric Drexler, Gerard K. O'Neill, Peter Calthorpe, Sim Van der Ryn, Paul Hawken, John Todd, J. Baldwin, Kevin Kelly (future editor of *Wired* magazine), and Donella Meadows.
25. Turner, *From Counterculture to Cyberculture*, 129.
26. Theodor Nelson, *Computer Lib: You Can and Must Understand Computers Now* (N.p.: Nelson, 1974).
27. Ibid.
28. David Harvey, *The Condition of Post-Modernity* (Cambridge: Blackwell, 1990), 23.
29. Harvey, *The Condition of Post-Modernity*, 150.
30. Furthermore, production is now decreasingly situated in large economies of scale where all production is done in one site, and is increasingly

decentralizing itself, where a company's product is designed and composed of numerous parts that are made in various places around the world.

31. Manuel Castells, *The Rise of the Network Society* (Malden: Blackwell, 1996), 151–200.
32. AnnaLee Saxenian, *Regional Advantage: Culture and Competition in Silicon Valley and Route 128* (Cambridge: Harvard University Press, 1994), 35.
33. Naomi Leonard, "Flocks and Fleets: Collective Motion and Sensing Networks in Nature and Robotics," Mobile Millennium lecture, University of California Berkeley, November 5, 2008.
34. Harvey, *The Condition of Post-Modernity*, 171.
35. For more on the importance of informal social networks to employment in the region during this period, see AnnaLee Saxenian, *Regional Advantage: Culture and Competition in Silicon Valley and Route 128.*
36. The Berkeley Community Memory Project (1972) operated much as a regular bulletin board did: You could leave a message on it, and only the people standing in front of it could read the message. Created by Efrem Lipkin, Mark Szpakowski, and Lee Felsenstein, this bulletin board, called "Community Memory," allowed users to sit down at an ASR-33 teletype located inside Leopold's Records in Berkeley, California, and type in a message—or read messages left by other people at that location. Early messages included queries on how to make ethanol, ads for taxi services, and questions about finding decent bagels in Berkeley. The teletype linked to a remote XDS-940 time-sharing computer running custom software in San Francisco. The messages were limited in audience to those who used the sole terminal at the record store. Actually this terminal was soon followed by a glass teletype at the Whole Earth Access Store on Shattuck Avenue in Berkeley, a terminal at a high school in the Mission district in San Francisco, and one at the Village Design house on Ashby in Berkeley, all connected to the same XDS-940 host at Project One in San Francisco, according to Mark Szpakowski, *Resource One Newsletter*, No 2, April 1974, accessed January 5, 2013, http://www.well.com/~szpak/cm/index.html.
37. Nelson, interview by the author with a former programmer at Ames Research Lab, Moffett Field, CA.
38. Later came X-Modem developed by Christenson and Suess, one of the first standard protocols for error-free file/data exchange. Soon Chicago BBS CBBS and other bulletin boards added upload/download libraries with X-Modem support. Refer to http://www.portcommodore.com/dokuwiki/doku.php?id=larry:comp:bbs:a_bbs_history.
39. Refer to http://www.wired.com/culture/lifestyle/news/1999/03/18175.
40. Jason Scott Sadofsky, director, "Baud," *BBS: The Documentary*, (2005), film, disc 1 DVD.
41. A BBS is a computer system: a computer/CPU, with a bespoke BBS software program installed on it, plus a printer, modem (plus terminal [command line] software), and a phone line. In 1978, pre-Windows, many computers were still command-line driven; there was no graphical user interface (GUI) allowing users to interact with electronic devices using images rather than text commands. In some cases, communication did not occur on screen; it was printed out on paper at 30 characters per second. Examples of home computers included Commodore 64, back in the halcyon days of 8-bit computing, Intel 8080, Motorola 6800, and TSR 80 CPU with a 16K memory board.
42. Jennings, Tom, email message with author, April 25, 2013. As to the name Fido, Jennings wrote: "Fido was originally the name of a computer I had in the late 70's. I was working for a friend's consulting company (Microft

Inc, Falmouth MA) and we were using my computer, which was in a four foot high rack: 18 slot chassis with 14 cards (4MHz Z80, CPU 64K memory, bootstrap ROM card (six cards so far\dots), 8'' floppy, DC-300 tape drive, and a BASF 6172 8-inch Winchester tape drive which was as fast as it was unreliable. (It had a progressive and degenerative disease we called "the whoops"; the voice-coil head positioner make the customary chirping sounds; the BASF's favorite failure mode was to lose track of where it's head was at (quite literally) and instead of the familiar chirping sounds as it seeked up and down the disk, it made a sort of whooping sound, like a falling siren, followed by a KLUNK as the positioner hit it's backstop. You had to power it down to reset it. Most annoying.) The rear door was a rack of fans to keep it all cool. It was extremely large and complex, and when it ran (most of the time) quite powerful. It ran PDOS (a rather nice CP/M-80 compatible OS) and we did "C" (BDS and Whitesmiths) and assembly work on it. It had so many parts\dots{} I called it a mongrel. I had taken to calling it "Fido." Debbie took a business card, whited-out the name and wrote in "Fido, Office Computer." The name stuck."

43. CompuServe Information Service (1979). The first two consumer online services—The Source and CompuServe Information Service—debuted in 1979. CompuServe offered features such as online news, shopping, encyclopedia and database access, electronic mail, and message boards. In 1980 CompuServe debuted CB Simulator (a name that capitalized on the Citizens' Band radio craze of the time). As the first nationwide online chat service, CB Simulator worked much like Internet Relay Chat, which debuted eight years later. Of the two 1979 services, CompuServe endured longer, eventually becoming a part of AOL. Today, CompuServe exists as a value ISP that only vaguely resembles its former self. Usenet (1980) allowed users on different systems across a network to converse publicly through posts in topic-themed newsgroups. Tom Truscott and Jim Ellis created Usenet at Duke University and linked it to other machines nationwide via ARPANET. Any topic was fair game for discussion on Usenet, including movies, politics, religion, and eventually, drugs, sex, and pornography. Usenet grew quickly and became one of the most popular message systems on the early public Internet of the 1990s. The mighty AOL got its start as Quantum Link (or Q-Link for short), a 1985 dial-up online service for Commodore 64 computers. It provided features similar to CompuServe at the time, including message boards, news, shopping, file downloads, and chat. It also had early online multiuser games and was home to Habitat, a pioneering experiment in online virtual worlds. The service changed its name to America Online in 1991, and it stopped supporting Commodore computers in 1995.

44. For example, on December 31, 1994, the global New Year's Eve party on the Internet was initiated by WELL members and supported by The WELL. Live and cyber sites around the world and across five time zones came together to celebrate. Contrary to popular perception, a layered or hybrid space connected BBSes' online practices with physical space.

45. In the1970s there were commercial subscription services (ISP). At that time, the Internet was entirely a dial-up modem service, for example, with CompuServe, Prodigy, GEnie, or even Quantum Link, which eventually became America Online (AOL), and the costs were prohibitive for most users. If you wanted to interact with others online, the only alternative was dial-up BBSes, which were free, although some provided premium services that might require payment. Users were responsible for the long-distance costs billed to the phone lines.

46. Michel de Certeau, *The Practice of Everyday Life* (Berkeley: University of California Press, 2002), 117.

47. Ibid., 97.

48. Larry Brilliant, a physician and epidemiologist, was the developer of the cholera vaccine.

49. Stewart Brand, in conversation with the author, March 16 2009, Berkeley, CA.

50. From 1994 to 1999, Bruce Katz, founder of Rockport, a manufacturer of walking shoes, owned the WELL. Since April 1999 Salon.com has owned it; several of Salon's founders, including Scott Rosenberg, had previously been regular participants on the WELL.

51. Bruno Latour, *We Have Never Been so Modern*, trans. Catherine Porter. (Cambridge: Harvard University Press, 1993), 120.

52. Rachel O'Dwyer, "Network Media: Exploring the Sociotechnical Relations Between Mobile Networks and Media Publics," conference paper, ISEA conference, Istanbul, 2011.

53. Stephen E, Little "Networks and Neighborhoods: Household, Community and Sovereignty in the Global Economy," special issue Intelligent Urban Development, *Urban Studies* 37, no. 10 (2000), 1811–23.

54. "What Is an 'Internet Forum'?" video by Ethan Feerst and Dylan Stewart Group,
http://www.videojug.com/interview/internet-communities-and forums-2#what-is-an-internet-forum

55. Refer to Mitch Kapor, http://www.theatlantic.com/technology/archive/2012/07/what-the-wells-rise-and-fall-tell-us-about-online-community/259504; see also http://www.kapor.com/writing/MarkoffReview.htm.

56. Nelson, interview by the author with a former programmer at Ames Research Lab, Moffett Field, CA.

57. Howard Rheingold, *Virtual Community: Homesteading on the Electronic Frontier* (Cambridge: MIT Press, 1993)

58. Also refer to http://www.zdnet.com/blog/perlow/when-bbs-sysops-ruled-the-earth/16548.

59. Nelson, interview by the author with a former programmer at Ames Research Lab, Moffett Field, CA.

60. Ibid.

61. Nick Crossley and John Michael Roberts, *After Habermas: New Perspectives on the Public Sphere* (Oxford: Blackwell, 2004), 28–48.

62. Stewart Brand in conversation with the author, March 16, 2009, Berkeley, CA.

63. Felix Stalder, "Between Democracy and Spectacle: The Front-end and Back-end of the Social Web," in *Social Media Reader* (New York: New York University Press, 2012), 242–56.

64. Contrasting the physical sites in which the digital and the network operate illuminates the difference between the two. The site for the former is the desktop microcomputer, displaying information through a heavy CRT monitor, connected to the network via a dial-up modem or perhaps through a high-latency first-generation broadband connection. In 2013, there is no such dominant site. A Wi-Fi-enabled laptop is now the most popular computing platform, but the mobile smartphone and tablet compete with and complement it. What unites these machines is their mobility and interconnectivity, making them ubiquitous, key interfaces to global telecommunication networks. A supercomputer, smartphone, laptop, iPod, wireless router, Xbox game platform, Mars rover, video surveillance camera, television set-top box, and automobile computer are essentially the same device, running—or capable of running—operating systems derived from UNIX, such as Linux or VxWorks, and becoming specific only in terms of scale and their mechanisms

for input and output, for sensing and acting upon the world. Instead, the new technological grail for industry is a universal, converged network, capable of distributing audio, video, Internet transmissions, voice, text, chat—and of undertaking any other conceivable networking task.

65. Malcolm McCullough, "On Ambient Information," in *Inscribing the Square: Urban Data as Public Space*, ed. Dietmar Offenhuber and Katja Schechtner, (Vienna: Springr-Verlag, 2012), 14–17.
66. David Sarno, "Jack Dorsay on the Twitter Ecosystem, Part II," *Los Angeles Times*, February 19, 2009.
67. Ibid.
68. Ibid.
69. David Sarno, "Twitter Creator Jack Dorsey Illuminates the Site's Founding Document, Part I," *Los Angeles Times*, February 18, 2009.
70. Jose Garcia-Montes, Domingo Caballero-Munoz, and Marino Perez-Alvarez, "Changes in the Self Resulting from the Use of Mobile Phones," *Media, Culture & Society* 28, no. 1 (2006): 72.
71. Gilles Deleuze and Claire Parnet, *Dialogues II* (New York: Columbia University Press, 1987),70.
72. Christen Fuchs, "Class, Knowledge, and New Media," in *Media, Culture & Society* 32, no. 1 (2010): 141–50.

NOTES TO CHAPTER 4

1. Pew Research Center, *Social Network Sites and Our Lives* (2012), accessed October 7, 2012, http://pewinternet.org/Commentary/2012/March/Pew-Internet-Social-Networking-full-detail.aspx.
2. Ibid.
3. danah boyd completed a study on teenage use of online social networks: *Taken Out of Context: American Teen Sociality in Networked Publics*, PhD dissertation, University of California–Berkeley, 2008, accessed September 20, 2009, http://www.danah.org/papers.
4. danah boyd, "Why Youth (Heart) Social Network Sites," in *MacArthur Foundation Series on Digital Learning: Youth, Identity, and Digital Media*, ed. David Buckingham (Cambridge: MIT Press, 2007).
5. Kazy Varnelis, *Networked Publics* (Cambridge: MIT Press, 2006).
6. Sherry Turkle, *Alone Together* (New York: Basic Books, 2011).
7. Refer to Wendy Hui Kyong Chun, *Control and Freedom: Power and Paranoia in the Age of Fiber Optics* (Cambridge: MIT, 2006) and Turkle, *Alone Together*.
8. Wi-Fi-enabled mobile technologies (e.g., laptops, tablets, mobile phones) are triggered by user location and deliver multimedia and other content directly to the user of the mobile device. Almost all cellular phones can be located in space through global positioning systems (GPS), which enable the receiver to be located through a series of spatial coordinates; locational content is then transmitted via simple SMS messages.
9. Refer to danah boyd and Nicole Ellison, "Social Network Sites: Definition, History, and Scholarship," *Journal of Computer-Mediated Communication* 13, no. 1 (2007), accessed November 1, 2008, http://jcmc.indiana.edu/vol13/issue1/boyd.ellison.html. 1.
10. Ibid., 2007
11. Ibid., 2007
12. Mizuko Ito et al., *Hanging Out, Messing Around, Geeking Out: Living and Learning with New Media* (Cambridge: MIT Press, 2008), 79.

13. Ito et al., *Hanging Out, Messing Around.*
14. Ori Schwartz, "Who Moved My Conversation? Instant Messaging, Intertextuality and New Regimes of Intimacy and Truth," *Media Culture & Society* 33, no. 1 (2011), 71.
15. David Buckingham, *Children Talking Television* (London: Falmer Press, 1993); Henry Jenkins, *The Children's Culture Reader* (New York: New York University Press, 1998); Ellen Seiter, *Sold Separately: Children and Parents in a Consumer Culture* (Chapel Hill: Rutgers University Press, 1993).
16. For QR codes and mobile media, refer to Thérèse Tierney, "Situated Networks," course website, Dalhousie University, 2008, http://arch6513.architecture.dal.ca/.
17. According to Don Bannister and Joyce Agnew, to construe is "to interpret or translate," "The Child's Construing of Self," in *Nebraska Symposium on Motivation 1976: Personal Construct Psychology* 24, edited by James K. Cole and Alvin W. Landfield. (Lincoln: University of Nebraska Press, 1977).
18. Bruno Latour, *Science in Action: How to Follow Scientists and Engineers* (Cambridge: Harvard University Press, 1987).
19. W. Bijker, T. P. Hughes, and T. J. Pinch, *The Social Construction of Technological Systems: New Directions in the Sociology and History of Technology* (Cambridge: MIT Press, 1987), 34. Also refer to J. Walvin, Leisure and Society, 1830–1950 (London: Longman, 1978), 93.
20. Nezar AlSayyad, *Cinematic Urbanism: A History of the Modern City from Reel to Real* (London: Routledge, 2006), 42.
21. Cognitive models are culturally acquired and learned habits that operate as "a system of dispositions, lasting, acquired schemes of perception, thought and action." Refer to Pierre Bourdieu, "Structures, Habits, Practices," in *The Logic of Practice* (Stanford: Stanford University Press, 1990), 52–79. For example, personal perceptions regarding shared rituals of friendship formation fall into this category.
22. AlSayyad, *Cinematic Urbanism,* 1–3.
23. Graham Dawson, *Soldier Heroes: British Adventure, Empire and the Cult of Masculinity* (London: Routledge, 1994), 48.
24. Ibid.
25. Heather Horst, "From My Space to Facebook: Coming of Age in a Networked Public Culture," in Ito et al., *Hanging Out,* 92–116.
26. Eric Gordon and Adriana de Souza e Silva, *Net Locality: Why Location Matters in a Networked World* (Malden: Wiley-Blackwell, 2011), 177–78.
27. According to Jeremy Schiff, University of California–Berkeley Electrical Engineering and Computer Sciences, MMORPGs, and MUDS often cultivate a rhetoric of community and sense of belonging and develop some normative order. Most members remain anonymous (or use pseudonyms), and MUD use remains primarily an entertainment-competitive activity, in which commitment levels are low and intense participation is episodic.
28. AlSayyad, *Cinematic Urbanism,*15.
29. Melvin M. Webber, "Order in Diversity: Community without Propinquity," in *Cities and Space: The Future of Urban Land,* ed. Lowdon Wingo, (Baltimore: Johns Hopkins Press, 1963), 23–54.
30. Yochai Benkler and Aaron Shaw, "A Tale of Two Blogs: Discursive Practices on the Left and the Right," Berkman Center for the Internet, Harvard University, April 27, 2010, accessed December 7, 2012, http://cyber.law.harvard.edu/publications/2010/Tale_Two_Blogospheres_Discursive_Practices_Left_Right.
31. Cameron Marlow, "The Structural Determinants of Media Contagion," PhD dissertation, MIT, 2005, accessed August 3, 2009, http://cameronmarlow.com/papers.

32. Pew Research Center, April 13, 2012, accessed June 8, 2012, http://pewresearch. org/pubs/2240/internet-adoption-digital-online-broadband-mobile.
33. Mobile technologies tend to have a higher penetration rate and have a potential in the developing world to bridge the digital/internet gap. Killian Fox, "Africa's Mobile Economic Revolution," *The Guardian,* July 23, 2011, http://www.guardian.co.uk/technology/2011/jul/24/mobile-phones-africa-microfinance-farming
34. Eszter Hargittai, "Whose Space? Differences among Users and Non-Users of Social Network Sites." *Journal of Computer-Mediated Communication* 13, no.1, article 14 (2007), accessed February 10, 2009, http://jcmc.indiana.edu/vol13/issue1/hargittai.html.
35. Hargittai, "A Framework for Studying Differences in People's Digital Media Uses," in *Cyberworld Unlimited,* ed. Nadia Kutscher and Hans-Uwe Otto (Berlin: VS Verlag für Sozialwissenschaften/GWV Fachverlage GmbH, 2007), 121–37.
36. Eli Paiser, *The Filter Bubble* (New York: Penguin Group, 2011), 142–43.
37. Wenhong Chen and Barry Wellman. "Minding the Cyber-Gap: The Internet and Social Inequality," in *Blackwell Companion to Social Inequalities,* ed. Mary Romero and Eric Margolis (Oxford: Wiley Blackwell, 2005), 4–9, http://homes.chass.utoronto.ca/~wellman/publications/digidiv/cybergap.pdf.
38. Hargittai, "A Framework for Studying Differences," 121–37.
39. Tierney, "Situated Networks."
40. Shantel Martinez, PhD candidate, University of Illinois at Urbana-Champaign, in discussion with the author, April 2012. Refer to Mary L. Gray, *Out in the Country: Youth, Media, and Queer Visibility in Rural America* (New York: NYU Press, 2009). Gray references such scholars as Martin Monalansan, David Valentine, Eve Sedgwick, John D'Emilio, and Clifford Geertz in her analysis.
41. Gray, *Out in the Country,* 15.
42. Gray, *Out in the Country,* 17.
43. Michal Daliot-Bul, "Asobi in Action: Contesting the Cultural Meanings and Cultural Boundaries of Play in Urban Japan from the 1970s to Present," Cultural Studies 23, no. 2 (2009), 1–26.
44. In that sense, the imaginary is not necessarily real as it is an *imagined* concept contingent on the imagination of a particular social subject. Nonetheless, there remains some debate among those who use the term (or its associated terms, such as *imaginaire,* as to the ontological status of the *imaginary.* Some, such as Henry Corbin understand the *imaginary* to be quite real indeed, while others ascribe to it only a social or imagined reality. John B. Thompson, *Studies in the Theory of Ideology* (Berkeley: University of California Press, 1984), 6.
45. Whereas the term *friend* can refer even more narrowly to those shared practices that grow out of close relations in given local social worlds, an interesting evolution is occurring: Recent years have found users friending widely. For example, the media artist and designer Alexander Gelman has 2,767 friends (and counting). As long as someone is a friend of a friend, he will ask to friend them; these connections culminate in mass invitations to international events.
46. Jessica Helfand, *Scrapbooks: An American History* (New Haven: Yale University Press, 2008).
47. In the autobiographical genre, there is an accepted contract between author and reader requiring honesty and truth from the author. Although readers accept that any autobiographical content is constructed (and edited), the literary form demands the illusion of truth. If falsity is discovered, the autobiography is of no value. Benvenuto Cellini (1500–71), prefacing his own autobiography, wrote, "No matter what sort he is . . . if he cares for

truth and goodness, [he] ought to write the story of his own life in his own hand." Younger Facebook users, along with many others of their generation, place an especially high value on honesty and transparency (Tierney *Situated Networks:In [re]search of the Publics,* 2009).

48. Protopop was a precursor to the Pop Art movement of the 1960s and 1970s and used *as found* cultural objects, including mundane objects culled from American commercial products and advertising design.

49. Hertha Wong, "Visual Autobiography," unpublished manuscript (Berkeley: University of California–Berkeley, 2006).

50. Jessica Helfand, *Scrapbooks.*

51. Referring to America and the myth of the self-made man (*sic*).

52. David Harvey, *The Condition of Post-Modernity: An Enquiry into the Origins of Cultural Change* (Cambridge MA: Blackwell, 1990), 302.

53. Irene Chen, conversation with the author, University of California–Berkeley, May 2009.

54. Much of Facebook can be critiqued as originating from Mark Zuckerberg's adolescent inclinations; nonetheless, the platform offers an open framework. Many of the ideological biases that appear to be built into Facebook can be dealt with by modifying framework and/or content, fixes that are available through gamer communities.

55. Refer to the incredible example of Bert from *Sesame Street* appearing with Osama Bin Laden: http://en.wikipedia.org/wiki/Bert_is_Evil.

56. boyd, "Why Youth (Heart) Social Network Sites."

57. Lawrence Lessig, *Remix: Making Art and Commerce Thrive in the Hybrid Economy* (New York: Penguin, 2008).

58. Melvin Webber, "The Urban Place and the Non-Urban Realm," in *Explorations into Urban Structure* (London: Oxford University Press, 1964), 109.

59. Richard Sennet, *The Fall of Public Man* (New York: W.W. Norton,1974), 14–15.

60. Craig Calhoun, "Community without Propinquity Revisited: Communications Technology and the Transformation of the Urban Public Sphere," *Sociological Inquiry* 68, no. 3 (1998), 381.

61. These considerations apply to the social construction of teenagers and youth culture more generally. Refer to Mizuko et al., *Hanging Out.*

62. According to survey data, the majority of social media users are either multitasking or are online in lieu of watching television. Nic Newman, William Dutton, Grant Blank, "Social Media in the Changing Ecology of News," *International Journal of Internet Science 7, no.1,(2012),* 18.

63. Daliot-Bul, "Japan's Mobile Technoculture: The Production of a Cellular Playscape and Its Cultural Implications," *Media, Culture & Society* 29, no. 6 (2007), 961.

64. However, even in places such as Europe and South America where there is less mobility and students may continue to live in parents' homes, social networks have also seen a huge increase.

65. Erik Adigard, "Re: BAM symposium," E-mail to the author, July 7, 2008.

66. Sherry Turkle, *Alone Together.*

67. Harvey, *The Condition of Post-Modernity,* 302

68. Ibid., 302.

69. The author, narrator, and protagonist must be the same–the contract that Philippe Lejeune defines. In our case, the author/narrator and the portrait/photographic image must be the same. For Lejeune, the self is produced in the performance of writing a life; autobiography is manifest through an enactment rather than bound by an agreement. It is a cultural performance. Philippe Lejeune 'The Autobiographical Contract' In *French Literary Theory*

Today ed. by Tzvetan Todorov, trans. by R. Carter (Cambridge: Cambridge University Press, 1982), 202. Excerpted from the French original Le pacte autobiographique by Philippe Lejeune (Paris: Editions de Seuil, 1975).

70. In adolescent development, according to psychologist Erik Erickson's observations, there appears to be more experimentation with personal identity.

71. The Berg beats Mount Rushmore!! According to the actual Facebook survey, Berlin's The Berg is more popular than Mount Rushmore, South-Dakota; refer to http://www.facebook.com/pages/Mount-Rushmore/23093812575 The Berg now challenges the Niagara Falls.

72. James Donald, "This, Here, Now: Imagining the Modern City," in *Imagining Cities: Scripts, Signs, Memories*, ed. Sallie Westwood and John Williams (London: Routledge, 1997), xii.

73. Rob Shields, *The Virtual* (London: Routledge, 2002), 47.

74. Jakob Tigges, architect of The Berg. The project can also be interpreted as satire aimed at local Berlin politicians for their lack of imagination in determining a future for the Tempelhof airport property; refer to website and proof, accessed June 8, 2012, http://www.the-berg.de/proof.html.

75. Stewart Hicks, "Slipstream," unpublished paper (November 2011).

76. William Mitchell, *E-Topia: "Urban Life, Jim—But Not as We Know It"* (Cambridge: MIT Press, 1996), 24.

NOTES TO CHAPTER 5

1. danah boyd, "How Can Qualitative Internet Researchers Define the Boundaries of Their Projects: A Response to Christine Hine," *Internet Inquiry: Conversations about Method*, ed. Annette Markham and Nancy Baym (Los Angeles: Sage, 2008), 27.

2. William Mitchell, *Beyond Productivity: Information Technology, Innovation and Creativity* (Washington: National Academies Press, 2003) and Melvin Webber, "The Urban Place and the Non Urban Realm," in *Explorations into Urban Structure* (London: Oxford University Press, 1964), 79–153; Jürgen Habermas, *The Structural Transformation of the Public Sphere: An Inquiry into a Category of Bourgeois Society*, trans. Thomas Burger (Cambridge: Polity, 1989); Mikhail Bakhtin, *Rabelais and His World*, trans. Hélène Iswolsky (Bloomington: Indiana University Press, 1993); Henry Jenkins, *Convergence Culture: Where Old and New Media Collide* (New York: New York University Press, 2006).

3. Maximillian C. Forte, "Another Revolution Missed? The Anthropology of Cyberspace," Anthropology News 43, no. 9(2002).

4. Earl R. Babbie, *The Practice of Social Science Research* (Florence: Wadsworth, 2003), 315–16.

5. According to Annette Markham, "Truth is an elusive term in any context"; from *Life Online* (Walnut Creek: Altiamira Press, 1998), 210.

6. This second phase was adapted from Clare Cooper Marcus's studies on public space, completed at the University of California–Berkeley.

7. From her "Taken Out of Context: American Teen Sociality in Networked Publics," PhD diss., University of California–Berkeley, 2008.

8. danah boyd, "Why Youth (Heart) Social Network Sites," in *MacArthur Foundation Series on Digital Learning: Youth, Identity, and Digital Media*, ed. David Buckingham (Cambridge: MIT Press, 2007), 18.

9. Claire Procopio and Steven Procopio, "Do You Know What It Means to Miss New Orleans? Internet communication, Geographic Community and

Social Capital in Crisis," *Journal of Applied Communication Research* 35, no. 1 (2007): 67–81.

10. Thomas Schweizer, "Embeddedness of Ethnographic Cases," *Current Anthropology*, 38 no. 5 (1997): 739–60. See also Thomas Schweizer and D. R. White, *Kinship, Networks, and Exchange: Structural Analysis in the Social Sciences* (Cambridge: Cambridge University Press, 1998).

11. Heather Horst and Daniel Miller, "From Kinship to Linkup: Cellphones and Social Networking in Jamaica," *Current Anthropology* 46, no. 5 (2005): 755.

12. Refer to http://www.comscoredatamine.com/2012/02/more-than-half-of-people-that-access-social-networks-on-their-smartphone-do-so-on-a-near-daily-basis. accessed February 29, 2012.

13. Jena Burrell, "Co-Evolution of the Mobile Phone and Users in Rural Uganda," Center for Information Technology Research in the Interests of Society (CITRIS) lecture, University of California–Berkeley February 11, 2009.

14. "The Next Billion Geeks: How the Mobile Internet Will Transform the BRICI countries," *Economist*, September 2, 2010, accessed March 7, 2011, http://www.economist.com/node/16944020.

15. "There are over five billion mobile phones in the world today; add to this tablets, laptops, medical devices and wireless sensors, and the numbers are staggering," says Hari Balakrishnan, Fujitsu Professor of Electrical Engineering and Computer Science, chair of Wireless @MIT. Wireless and mobile research applications include transportation, health care, education, collaboration, and environmental sustainability. Projects already underway include safe and efficient road transportation, autonomous driving, wireless medical implants, mobile video delivery, multiparty wireless videoconferencing, and energy harvesting. (*MIT News,* Oct. 11, 2012)

16. Manuel Castells, *The Rise of the Network Society,* 2nd ed. (Malden: Blackwell, 2000), 1–76.

17. This connected condition can be conceptualized as a flattened ontology of relations. A flat ontology applies to whatever we encounter in lived experience, since every relationship is a society. Here I borrow from Alfred North Whitehead's definition of society: an aggregation of entities that possesses spatial extent and temporal duration.

18. Memes, in the social media context, are popular ideas, usually in a visual format, that are shared collectively with others.

19. "hooking up: To have any form of intimacy with a member of the preferred sex that you don't consider a significant other. Usually, when said by modern youth it means to make out, and when said by people between the ages of 20 and 35 it generally means to have sex, and if a very old person says it, it probably means to simply spend time with somebody." *Urban Dictionary*, accessed April 23, 2010, http://www.urbandictionary.com/define.php?term=hooking%20up.

20. The shortened graphical format of Facebook's wall was adopted by Twitter for mobile phones.

21. Analysis indicates that Twitter's own website accessed from desktops, not mobile devices, is the largest platform overall, representing 27.6% of all activity worldwide. But collectively it is mobile clients (including iPad software) that are most used; they represent about 61% of all tweets, with Twitter's own mobile apps and mobile web presence accounting for 74% of that, according to Ingrid Lunden on Techcrunch, July, 31, 2012, accessed November 15, 2012, http://techcrunch.com/2012/07/31/twitter-may-have-500m-users-but-only-170m-are-active-75-on-twitters-own-clients.

22. This is a pattern that danah boyd observed with under-eighteen-year-olds (often under close parental supervision) and documented in her dissertation research: refer to danah boyd, "Taken Out of Context."

23. "Offline rules of etiquette no longer seem to apply," notes Ashley Wick of Wick Communications. There is another downside to connectivity: "If you text a friend that you can't make dinner because you're sick, and then a picture of you dancing . . . shows up on someone's Instagram feed, you just got caught," explains writer Derek Blasberg (*New York Times, Nov. 16, 2012*).

24. Anthropologist Cynthia Joba suggested another possibility for future research: to compare Myers-Briggs personality test results with online behavior. Email correspondence with author, March 19, 2011.

25. For example Sherry Turkel, *Life on the Screen: Identity in the Age of the Internet* (New York: Simon & Schuster, 1995).

26. Babbie, *The Practice of Social Science Research*, 315–16.

27. A potlatch is a gift-giving festival and primary economic system practiced by indigenous peoples of the Pacific Northwest coast of Canada and the United States; refer to Aldona Jonaitis, *Chiefly Feasts: The Enduring Kwakiutl Potlatch* (Seattle: University of Washington Press, 1991).

28. The cultural differences between the indigenous peoples of North America (First Nations, Native Americans) and immigrant Europeans caused extensive political tension, ethnic violence, and social disruption for hundreds of years, tensions that are not easily erased.

29. Nancy Fraser, "Rethinking the Public Sphere: A Contribution to the Critique of Actually Existing Democracy," in *Habermas and the Public Sphere*, ed. Craig Calhoun (Cambridge: MIT Press, 1992), 122–23.

30. Mark Frankel and Sanyin Sang, "Ethical and Legal Aspects of Human Subjects Research on the Internet," AAAS Workshop Report, June 10–11, 1999, accessed February 25, 2013, http://www.aaas.org/spp/sfrl/projects/intres/report.pdf.

31. Horst and Miller, "From Kinship to Linkup," 755.

32. Granville Ganter, review of *Publics and Counterpublics* by Michael Warner, *St. John's University Humanities Review*, 1, no1 (March 2003), accessed May 23, 2012, http://facpub.stjohns.edu/ganterg/sjureview/vol1-1/publics.html.

33. Dayna Cunningham in conversation with Henry Jenkins, "Can African Americans Find their Voice in Cyberspace?" (March 2, 2009), accessed May 20, 2009, http://henryjenkins.org/2009/03/can_african-americans_find_the.html

34. Questions of territory, land, associated identity, and ancestral roots are certainly not obsolete concepts at the individual scale. As my research developed, it started to become clear that social media allows diasporas to organize across political borders. Social media platforms, of which Facebook is only one of thousands, have strong meaning and membership for deterritorialized groups: international students, immigrants, and ethnic and other minorities. For example, Google marketing manager Wael Ghonim was not living in Egypt when he (along with others) set up the Facebook page, "We Are All Khaled Said," in 2011 but was in fact residing in the United Arab Emirates.

35. Dimitri Milioni, "Probing the Online Counterpublic Sphere: the Case of Indymedia Athens," *Media, Culture & Society* 31 (May 2009): 409–31.

36. David Ronfeldt, John Arquilla, Graham Fuller, and Melissa Fuller, "The Zapatista 'Social Netwar' in Mexico," accessed December 1, 2012, http://www.rand.org/pubs/monograph_reports/MR994.html.

37. Michael E. Gardiner, "Wild Publics and Grotesque Symposiums: Habermas and Bakhtin on Dialogue, Everyday Life and the Public Sphere," in *After Habermas: New Perspectives on the Public Sphere*, ed. Nick Crossley and John Michael Roberts (Oxford: Blackwell, 2004), 29.
38. Michael Gardiner, "Wild Publics and Grotesque Symposiums," 30.
39. See Henry Jenkins's "Photoshop for Democracy" in *Convergence Culture: Where Old and New Media Collide* (New York: New York University Press, 2006), 206–239.
40. Mikhail Bakhtin, "Forms of Time and of the Chronotope in the Novel," in *The Dialogic Imagination: Four Essays*, ed. Michael Holquist, trans. Caryl Emerson and Michael Holquist (Austin: University of Texas Press, 1981), 385.
41. Ulrich Beck, *Community. Seeking Safety in an Insecure World* (London: Polity, 2001),144.
42. Clay Shirky, *The Power of Crowds*, NPR TED Radio Hour, accessed December 1, 2012, http://www.npr.org/2012/05/16/152866680/the-power-of-crowds.

NOTES TO CHAPTER 6

1. "Humans of New York and Tumblr Sandy Fundraiser: Brandon Stanton's Photos Inspire Viral Campaign," *Huffington Post*, November 20, 2012, accessed December 21, 2012, http://www.huffingtonpost.com/2012/11/19/humans-of-new-york_n_2161537.html?utm_hp_ref=new-york.
2. Kazy Varnelis, "The Instagram Storm and the City," *Network Culture* (blog), November 4, 2012, accessed Nov. 22, 2012, http://varnelis.net/blog/the_instagram_storm_and_the_city.
3. Instagram CEO Kevin Systrom indicated that users of the photo-sharing service uploaded more than 800,000 photos tagged with the hashtag #Sandy last week, and said that it was "probably the biggest event to be captured on Instagram." *Gigaom* (blog), November 5, 2012, accessed November 6, 2012 http://gigaom.com/2012/11/05/instagram-ceo-sandy-was-probably-instagrams-biggest-moment/
4. Michael Warner, *Publics and Counterpublics* (New York: Zone Books, 2002), 64.
5. Warner, *Publics and Counterpublics*, 67–118.
6. Benedict Anderson, Imagined Communities: Reflections on the Origin and Spread of Nationalism,2nd ed. (London: Verso, 2006); Eli Parser, The Filter Bubble (New York, Penguin Press, 2011); Sonia Livingstone, "The Changing Social Landscape," in *Handbook of New Media: Social Shaping and Social Consequences of ICTs*, ed. Leah Lievrouw and Sonia Livingstone (London: Sage, 2002), 17–21.
7. The Pew Research Center for the People & the Press, accessed August 2, 2009, http://people-press.org/report/?pageid=203.
8. Nicholas de Monchaux, in conversation at University of California–Berkeley lecture, 2012.
9. Information gleaned from mobile wireless networks includes those we come into contact with and for how long; what value we, as individuals, offer as a node in the network; and broad mobility dynamics concerning our movements as a group. These are all important data for determining the reconfigurable topology and routing protocols implemented by the network as well as its efficiency, and overall performance.

10. Rachel O'Dwyer, "Network Media: Exploring the Sociotechnical Relations Between Mobile Networks & Media Publics," conference paper, ISEA conference, Istanbul, 2011.
11. Felix Stalder, "Between Democracy and Spectacle: The Front-end and Back-end of the Social Web," in *Social Media Reader* (New York: New York University Press, 2012), 250.
12. Leo Kelion, "UN Internet Regulation Treaty Talks begin in Dubai," accessed December 21, 2012, http://www.bbc.co.uk/news/technology-20575844.
13. Nancy Fraser also proposed the notion that contrary to opening up the political realm to everyone, the Habermasean public sphere actually shifted political power from a repressive mode of domination to a hegemonic one. Rather than rule by power, there was now rule by the majority ideology. To deal with this hegemonic domination, Fraser argues that repressed groups form subaltern counterpublics. Refer to Nancy Fraser, "Rethinking the Public Sphere: A Contribution to the Critique of Actually Existing Democracy." In *The Cultural Studies Reader*, edited by Simon During, 518-36. New York: Routledge, 2nd ed, 1999.
14. Robert Asen and Daniel C. Brouwer, *Counterpublics and the State*, (Albany: SUNY Press, 2001).
15. Refer to http://thehill.com/blogs/hillicon-valley/technology/270541-this-week-in-tech-nations-meet-to-rewrite-un-internet-treaty, (accessed December 21, 2012).
16. Labels range from ubiquitous computing and urban informatics to the Internet of Things, from smart dust and ambient intelligence to sensor topologies. In 2012 the city of San Francisco commissioned Paradox Engineering to deploy a pilot industrial wireless network to manage urban infrastructure, effectively creating a Internet of Things (IoT) at the urban scale.
17. Barry Katz, "Design and the Human Condition: An Untimely Meditation," lecture, the Hewlett Foundation, Menlo Park, CA, February 14, 2008.
18. As social geographers Rob Kitchen and Martin Dodge argue, urban policy making requires an interdisciplinary approach. Today GIS software, digital modeling programs, and wireless sensor information make it possible to build a model of the city from user interaction and understand movement and circulation patterns in new ways. This enables designers and planners to study the city from the bottom up—from actual everyday social practices of urban residents.

NOTES TO APPENDIX A

1. In its broadest sense, positivism is a rejection of metaphysics. It advances the position that the goal of knowledge is simply to describe the phenomena that we experience. The purpose of science is simply to stick to what we can observe and measure. Knowledge of anything beyond that, a positivist would hold, is impossible Positivists, therefore, separate themselves from the world they study, while researchers within other paradigms acknowledge the need to participate in real-world life to some extent so as to better understand and express its emergent properties and features. Refer to William M. Trochim, *The Research Methods Knowledge Base,* accessed March 21, 2013, http://anatomyfacts.com/Research/ResearchMethodsKnowledgeBase.pdf
2. T. D. Cook and C. S. Reichardt, eds., *Qualitative and Quantitative Methods in Evaluation Research* (Beverly Hills: Sage Publications, 1979), 8.

3. Manuel DeLanda, *A New Philosophy of Society* (New York: Continuum Books, 2006), 1.
4. Warren Sack, "Architecture without Architecture," CITRIS lecture, University of California–Berkeley, March 18, 2009.
5. As a research paradigm, realism has other descriptors, including critical realism, postpositivism, and neopostpositivism.
6. Steven Krauss, "Research Paradigms and Meaning Making," *Qualitative Report* 10, no. 4 (2005): 761, accessed April 25, 2009, http://www.nova.edu/ssss/QR/QR10-4/index.html.
7. Marilyn Healy and Chad Perry "Comprehensive Criteria to Judge Validity and Reliability of Qualitative Research within the Realism Paradigm," Qualitative Market Research 3, no. 3 (2000),118–26.
8. Yvonna Lincoln and Egon Guba, *Naturalistic Inquiry* (New York: Sage, 1985), 42.
9. Bisman, J. E. "The critical realist paradigm as an approach to research in accounting." Poster presentation at the Accounting Association of Australian and New Zealand Annual Conference, Perth, Australia. (July 2002)
10. Krauss, "Research Paradigms," 761–62.
11. DeLanda, *A New Philosophy of Society*, 1.
12. Ian Hacking, *The Social Construction of What?* (Cambridge: Harvard University Press, 1999).
13. Pierre Bourdieu, "The Corporatism of the Universal: The Role of Intellectuals in the Modern World," *TELOS* 81 (Fall 1989): 327.
14. Joseph Maxwell, *Qualitative Research* (Thousand Oaks: Sage Pub, 2005), 69.
15. Melvin Webber, "Order in Diversity: Community without Propinquity," in *Cities and Space: The Future Use of Urban Land*, ed. Lowdon Wingo (Baltimore: Johns Hopkins Press, 1963), 29.
16. Clare Cooper-Marcus and Wendy Sarkissian, *Housing as if People Matter: Site Design Guidelines for Medium-Density Family Housing* (Berkeley: University of California Press, 1986).
17. Cooper-Marcus applies a social science methodology first, which requires a reversal of the design process so that it begins with people's motivations and behaviors. Because users of space differ in age, gender, ability, and interest, these differences need to be addressed in the design of spaces. What do people need psychologically? Will users of mobile technologies subvert traditional urban practices? Or is there a way in which one can approach design with a new knowledge of user preferences that have not yet been usurped by commercial interests and thus influence the development of these technologies?
18. Cooper-Marcus and Sarkissian. Housing as if People Mattered.
19. Maximillian C. Forte, "Another Revolution Missed? The Anthropology of Cyberspace," Anthropology News 43, no. 9 (2002): 21
20. Earl R. Babbie, *The Practice of Social Science Research* (Florence: Wadsworth, 2003), 315–16.
21. According to Markham, "Truth is an elusive term in any context," from *Life Online* (Walnut Creek: Altiamira Press, 1998), 210.
22. Bruno Latour and Steve Woolgar, *Laboratory Life: The Social Construction of Scientific Facts.* (Beverly Hills: Sage Publications, 1979) ; Bruno Latour, *Pandora's Hope: Essays on the Reality of Science Studies* (Cambridge: Harvard University Press, 1999); Paul Rabinow and William Sullivan, *Interpretive Social Science: A Second Look* (Berkeley: University of California Press,1987); Mustafa Emirbayer and Jeff Goodwin (1994), "Network Analysis, Culture, and the Problem of Agency," *American Journal of Sociology*, 99, no. 6 (1994), 1411–54.

23. Robert Mugerauer, "Toward a Theory of Integrated Urban Ecology: Complementing Pickett et al." *Ecology and Society* 15, no. 4 (2010), 31.
24. danah boyd, "How Can Qualitative Internet Researchers Define the Boundaries of Their Projects: A Response to Christine Hine," in *Internet Inquiry: Conversations about Method*, ed. Annette Markham and Nancy Baym (Los Angeles: Sage, 2008), 27.
25. Babbie, *The Practice of Social Science Research,* 349.
26. Ibid.
27. Joseph Maxwell, *Qualitative Research* (Thousand Oaks: Sage, 2005), 77.
28. John Zeisel, *Inquiry by Design: Tools for Environment Behavior Research* (New York: W. W. Norton, 1981), 157–77.
29. Maxwell, *Qualitative Research*, 66.
30. Babbie, *The Practice of Social Science Research*, 349–50.
31. Babbie, *Survey Research Methods*, 2nd ed. (New York: Wadsworth, 1990), 18.
32. Robert Kozinets, "The Field behind the Screen: Using Netnography for Marketing Research in Online Communities," *Journal of Marketing Research* 39, no.1 (2002): 63–67.
33. John Zeisel, *Inquiry by Design: Tools for Environment Behavior Research* (Belmont CA: Wadsworth, Inc.,1981), 143.
34. William Mitchell, *Beyond Productivity: Information Technology, Innovation and Creativity*. (Washington: National Academies Press, (2003), 3.
35. Luomir Popov, "Architecture as Social Design: The Social Nature of Design Objects and the Implications for the Profession," *Journal of Design Research* 2, no. 2 (2002); see also Cooper-Marcus and Wendy Sarkissian, *Housing as if People Matter.*

Selected Bibliography

Aarseth, Espen J. *Cybertext: Perspectives on Ergodic Literature.* Baltimore: Johns Hopkins University Press, 1996.

Adams, Paul. "Television as Gathering Place." *Annals of the Association of American Geographers* 82, no. 1 (1992): 117–35.

Adorno, Theodore. "The Culture Industry Revisited." In *Media Studies: A Reader*, edited by Paul Marris and Sue Thornham, 31–37. New York: New York University Press, 2000.

Alcorn, Allan. Interview by PodTech. July 22, 2009.

Alexander, Christopher. "A City Is Not a Tree." In *Design after Modernism,* edited by John Thackara, 67–84. London: Thames and Hudson, 1988. Accessed October 7, 2012. http://www.rudi.net/books/200.

Al Sayyad, Nezar. *Cinematic Urbanism: A History of the Modern City from Reel to Real.* London: Routledge, 2006.

Anderson, Benedict. *Imagined Communities: Reflections on the Origin and Spread of Nationalism.* 2nd rev. ed. London: Verso, 2006.Arendt, Hannah. *The Human Condition.* Chicago: University of Chicago Press, 1958.

Auslander, Philip. *From Acting to Performance: Essays in Modernism and Postmodernism.* London: Routledge, 1997.

Babbie, Earl R. *The Practice of Social Science Research.* Belmont, CA: Wadsworth Thomson Learning, 2001.

———. *Survey Research Methods.* 2nd ed. Belmont: Wadsworth Pub, 1990.

Bakhtin, Mikhail. "Forms of Time and of the Chronotope in the Novel." In *The Dialogic Imagination: Four Essays*, edited by Michael Holquist, 84–258. Translated by Caryl Emerson and Michael Holquist. Austin: University of Texas Press, 1981.

Bakhtin, Mikhail. *Rabelais and His World.* Translated by Hélène Iswolsky. Bloomington: Indiana University Press, 1993.

Balakrishnan, Hari. "MIT's CSAIL launches new center to tackle the future of wireless and mobile technologies." In *MIT News,* Oct. 11, 2012), accessed March 30, 2012, http://web.mit.edu/newsoffice/2012/wireless-research-center-founded-1011.html

Banham, Reynar. *Los Angeles: The Four Ecologies.* New York: Harper and Row, 1971.

Bannister, Don, and Joyce Agnew. "The Child's Construing of Self." In *Nebraska Symposium on Motivation 1976: Personal Construct Psychology 24*, edited by James K. Cole and Alvin W. Landfield. Lincoln: University of Nebraska Press, 1977.

Barthes, Roland. *Camera Lucida: Reflections on Photography.* Translated by Richard Howard. 2nd ed. New York: Hill and Wang, 1981.

Bateson, Gregory. *Naven: A Survey of the Problems Suggested by a Composite Picture of the Culture of a New Guinea Tribe Drawn from Three Points of View.* 2nd ed. Stanford: Stanford University Press, 1958.

Baudrillard, Jean. "Simulacra and Simulations." In *Jean Baudrillard: Selected Writings.* Edited by Mark Poster, 169–87. Translated by Jacques Mourrain. 2nd ed. Stanford: Stanford University Press, 2002.

Bazin, André. *What Is Cinema? Volume II.* Translated by Hugh Gray. Berkeley: University of California Press, 1971.

Becker, Carl. "What Is Evidence?" In *The Historian as Detective: Essays on Evidence,* edited by Robin Winks, 7–21. New York: Harper, 1968.

Beer, David. "Social Network(ing) Sites . . . Revisiting the Story So Far: A Response to danah boyd and Nicole Ellison." *Journal of Computer-Mediated Communication* 13, no. 2 (2008): 516–29.

Benjamin, Walter. "On Language as Such and on the Language of Man." In *Walter Benjamin: Selected Writings, Vol. 1, 1913–1926.* Edited by Michael W. Jennings and Marcus Bullock, 62–74. Cambridge: Belknap Press, 1996.

———. "The Work of Art in the Age of Mechanical Reproduction," 1936. Accessed November 1, 2012. http://design.wishiewashie.com/HT5/WalterBenjamin TheWorkofArt.pdf.

Berg, Bruce L. *Qualitative Research Methods for the Social Sciences.* 2nd ed. Boston: Allyn and Bacon, 1995.

Bergon, Henri. *Creative Evolution.* Translated by Arthur Mitchell. New York: H. Holt and Company, 1913.

Berkeley, George. *Treatise Concerning the Principles of Human Knowledge,* 1710. Accessed November 1, 2012. http://www.uoregon.edu/~rbear/berkeley.html.

Bey, Hakim. *T.A.Z.: The Temporary Autonomous Zone, Ontological Anarchy, Poetic Terrorism.* 2nd ed. Brooklyn: Autonomedia, 2003.

Bijker, Wiebe, Thomas P. Hughes, and Trevor J. Pinch, eds. *The Social Construction of Technological Systems: New Directions in the Sociology and History of Technology.* Cambridge: MIT Press, 1987.

Bohman, James. "Expanding Dialogue: The Internet, the Public Sphere and Prospects for Transnational Democracy." In *After Habermas: New Perspectives on the Public Sphere,* edited by Nick Crossley and John Michael Roberts, 131–55. Oxford: Blackwell, 2004.

Boulding, Kenneth. *The Image: Knowledge in Life and Society.* Ann Arbor: University of Michigan Press, 1969.

Bourdieu, Pierre. "The Aristocracy of Culture." In *Distinction: A Social Critique of the Judgment of Taste,* 11–17. Translated by Richard Nice. Cambridge: Harvard University Press, 1984.

———. "The Corporatism of the Universal: The Role of Intellectuals in the Modern World." *TELOS* 81 (Fall 1989): 99–110.

———. "Structures, Habitus, Practices." In *The Logic of Practice,* 52–65. Stanford: Stanford University Press, 1990.

boyd, danah. "Facebook's 'Privacy Trainwreck': Exposure, Invasion, and Drama." *Apophenia Blog.* September 8, 2006. Accessed April 11, 2009. http://www. danah.org/papers/FacebookAndPrivacy.html.

———. "How Can Qualitative Internet Researchers Define the Boundaries of Their Projects: A Response to Christine Hine." In *Internet Inquiry: Conversations about Method,* edited by Annette Markham and Nancy Baym, 26–32. Los Angeles: Sage, 2008.

———. "Taken Out of Context: American Teen Sociality in Networked Publics." PhD diss., University of California–Berkeley, 2008.

———. "Why Youth (Heart) Social Network Sites: The Role of Networked Publics in Teenage Social Life." In *MacArthur Foundation Series on Digital Learning:*

Youth, Identity, and Digital Media, edited by David Buckingham, 119–42. Cambridge: MIT Press, 2007.
boyd, danah, and Nicole Ellison. "Social Network Sites: Definition, History, and Scholarship." *Journal of Computer-Mediated Communication* 13, no. 1 (2007): 210–30. Accessed September 17, 2008. http://jcmc.indiana.edu/vol13/issue1/boyd.ellison.html.
Brand, Stewart. Interview with the author. March 16, 2009. Berkeley, CA.
Braudel, Fernand. *La Méditerranée et le monde méditerranéen à l'époque de Philippe II*. Paris: Editions de Fallois, 1949.
Brill, Michael. "An Ontology for Exploring Urban Public Life Today." *Places* 6, no. 1 (1989): 24–31.
———. "Transformation, Nostalgia and Illusion in Public Life and Public Place." In *Public Places and Spaces*, edited by Irwin Altman and Ervin Zube, 7–30. Vol. 10, *Human Behavior and Environment*. New York: Plenum Press, 1989.
Buckingham, David. *Children Talking Television*, London: Falmer Press, 1993.
Budd, Jonathan 2008. "Public Space and Architecture." *World Architecture Community*. Accessed May 16, 2009. http://www.worldarchitecture.org/theory-issues/mn/public-space-and-architecture-architecture-theory-issues-pages.
Burke, Anthony, and Therese Tierney, eds. *Network Practices: New Strategies for Architecture and Design*. New York: Princeton Architectural Press, 2007.
Burrell, Jena. "Co-Evolution of the Mobile Phone and Users in Rural Uganda." Lecture presented at CITRIS, University of California–Berkeley, February 11, 2009.
Burroughs, William. "The Future of the Novel." *In Multimedia Form: Wagner to Virtual Reality* eds Randall Packer and Kenjordon, 293–296, Newyork: Norton, 2001.
Busbea, Larry. *Topologies: The Urban Utopia of France 1960–1970*, Cambridge: MIT Press, 2007.
Bush, Vannevar. "As We May Think." *Atlantic Monthly* (July 1, 1945): 52–79.
Calhoun, Craig. "Community without Propinquity Revisited: Communications Technology and the Transformation of the Urban Public Sphere." *Sociological Inquiry* 68, no. 3 (1998): 373–97.
Carpenter, Edmund. *"Oh What a Blow That Phantom Gave Me!"* New York: Holt, Rinehart and Winston, 1973.
———. *They Became What They Beheld*. New York: E. P. Dutton,1970.
Carr, Stephen, Mark Francis, Leanne Rivlin, and Andrew Stone. *Public Space*. Cambridge: Cambridge University Press, 1992.
Castells, Manuel. *The Rise of the Network Society*. 2nd ed. Malden: Blackwell, 2000.
Chun, Wendy Hui Kyong. *Control and Freedom: Power and Paranoia in the Age of Fiber Optics*. Cambridge, MA: MIT Press, 2008.
———, and Thomas Keenan Eds. *New Media/Old Media: A History and Theory Reader,* New York: Routledge, 2006.
Clifford, James. *The Predicament of Culture: Twentieth-Century Ethnography, Literature and Art*. Cambridge: Harvard University Press, 1986.
Cooper Marcus, Clare, and Carolyn Francis, eds. *People Places: Design Guidelines for Urban Open Space*. 2nd ed. New York: John Wiley and Sons, 1997.
Cooper Marcus, Clare, and Wendy Sarkissian. *Housing as if People Matter: Site Design Guidelines for the Planning of Medium-Density Family Housing*. Berkeley: University of California Press, 1986.
Coward, L. Andrew, and Nikos Salingaros. "The Information Architecture of Cities." *Journal of Information Science* 30, no. 2 (2004): 107–18.
Crossley, Nick, and John Michael Roberts, eds. *After Habermas: New Perspectives on the Public Sphere*. Oxford: Blackwell, 2004.
Crouse, Jeff, and Stephanie Rothenberg. *Invisible Threads*. Mixed-reality performance installation. January 27, 2008.

———. *10 Simple Steps to Your Own Virtual Sweatshop.* Video, 2008.

Cuff, Dana. *Architecture: The Story of Practice.* Cambridge: MIT Press, 1991.

Daliot-Bul, Michal. "Japan's Mobile Technoculture: The Production of a Cellular Playscape and Its Cultural Implications." *Media Culture Society* 29, no. 6 (2007): 954–71.

Deborg, Guy. *Society of the Spectacle.* New York: Zone Books, 1995.

de Certeau, Michel. *The Practice of Everyday Life.* Berkeley: University of California Press, 2002.

DeLanda, Manuel. "Does Convergence Imply Homogenization?" Paper presented at European Media Master Forum, Stuttgart, Germany, April 1999.

———. *A New Philosophy of Society: Assemblage Theory and Social Complexity.* Continuum: New York, 2006.

———. *A Thousand Years of Non-Linear History.* Cambridge: MIT Press, 2000.

Deleuze, Gilles, and Guattari, Felix. *A Thousand Plateaus: Capitalism and Schizophrenia.* Translated by Brian Massumi. Minneapolis: University of Michigan Press, 1987.

Derrida, Jacques. "Structure, Sign and Play in the Discourse of the Human Sciences." In *Writing and Difference*, edited by Jacques Derrida, 278–93. Chicago: University of Chicago Press, 1978.

Diamond, Jared. *Guns, Germs, and Steel: The Fates of Human Societies.* New York: W.W. Norton, 1997.

Donald, James. "This, Here, Now: Imagining the Modern City." In *Imagining Cities: Scripts, Signs, Memories*, edited by Sallie Westwood and John Williams, 181–201. London: Routledge, 1997.

Doniger, Wendy. *Splitting the Difference: Gender and Myth in Ancient Greece and India.* Chicago: University of Chicago Press, 1999.

Durkheim, Emile. *Professional Ethics and Civic Morals.* London: Routledge, 1992.

Eco, Umberto. *Travels in Hyperreality.* New York: Harcourt, Brace & Jovanovich, 1986.

Featherstone, M. "The Heroic Life and the Everyday Life." *Theory, Culture and Society* 9, no. 1 (1992): 159–82.

Findlay, John. *Magic Lands: Western Cityscapes and American Culture after 1940.* Berkeley: University of California Press, 1992.

Florida, Richard. *The Rise of the Creative Class.* New York: Basic Books, 2002.

Foucault, Michel. *The Archeology of Knowledge and the Discourse of Language.* Translated by A. M. Sheridan Smith. New York: Pantheon Books, 1972.

———. *Discipline and Punish: The Birth of the Prison,* New York: Random House, 1975.

———. *Foucault Live: Interviews 1961–1984.* Edited by Sylvere Lotinger. New York: Semiotext(e), 1996.

———. *The Order of Things: An Archeology of the Human Sciences.* New York: Vintage Books, 1966.

Frasca, Gonzalo. "Videogames of the Oppressed: Critical Thinking, Education, Tolerance, and Other Trivial Issues." In *First Person: New Media as Story, Performance, and Game*, edited by Noah Wardrip-Fruin and Pat Harrigan, 85–94. Cambridge, MIT Press, 2004.

Fraser, Nancy. "Rethinking the Public Sphere: A Contribution to the Critique of Actually Existing Democracy." In *The Cultural Studies Reader*, edited by Simon During, 518–36. New York: Routledge, 2nd ed, 1999.

Fuchs, Christian. "Class, Knowledge and New Media." *Media Culture and Society* 32, no. 1 (2010): 141–50.

Galison, Peter. "War against the Center." *Grey Room* 4 (Summer 2001): 5–33.

Gangadharan, Seeta Pena. "Tyrannies of Participation." Panel discussion presented at ISEA, Sabanchi University, Istanbul, September 16, 2011.

Ganter, Granville. "Review of Publics and Counterpublics." *St. John's University Humanities Review* 1, no. 1 (2003). Accessed July 25, 2009. http://facpub.stjohns.edu/~~ganterg/sjureview/vol1–1/publics.html.

Garcia-Montes, Jose, Domingo Caballero-Munoz, and Marino Perez-Alvarez. "Changes in the Self Resulting from the Use of Mobile Phones." *Media Culture Society* 28, no. 1 (2006): 67–82.

Gardiner, Michael. *The Dialogics of Critique: M. M. Bakhtin and the Theory of Ideology*. London: Routledge, 2002.

———. "Wild Publics and Grotesque Symposiums: Habermas and Bakhtin on Dialogue, Everyday Life and the Public Sphere." In *After Habermas: New Perspectives on the Public Sphere*, edited by Nick Crossley and John Michael Roberts, 28–48. Oxford: Blackwell, 2004

Geertz, Clifford. "Deep Play: Notes on the Balinese Cockfight." In *The Interpretation of Cultures: Selected Essays*, edited by Clifford Geertz, 412–53. New York: Basic Books, 1973.

Giddens, Anthony. *The Constitution of Society: Outline of the Theory of Structuration*. Cambridge: Polity Press, 1984.

Goldberg, Ken, ed. *The Robot in the Garden: Telerobotics and Telepistemology in the Age of the Internet*. Cambridge: MIT Press, 2000.

Gombrich, Ernst H. *Art and Illusion*. Oxford: Phaidon Press, 2002.

Gordon, Eric, and Adriana de Souza e Silva. *Net Locality: Why Location Matters in a Networked World*. Malden: Wiley-Blackwell, 2011.

Goulder, A. "Sociology and the Everyday Life." In *The Idea of Social Structure: Papers in Honor of Robert K. Merton*, edited by Lewis A. Coser, 417–32. New York: Harcourt Brace Jovanovich, 1975.

Graham, Stephen, and Simon Marvin. *Splintering Urbanism*. New York: Routledge, 2001.

Grosz, Elizabeth. *Architecture from the Outside: Essays on Virtual and Real Space*. Cambridge: MIT Press, 2001.

Habermas, Jürgen. *The Structural Transformation of the Public Sphere: An Inquiry into a Category of Bourgeois Society*. Translated by Thomas Burger. Cambridge: Polity, 1989.

Hacking, Ian. *The Social Construction of What?* Cambridge: Harvard University Press, 1999.

Hajer, Maarten, and Arnold Reijindorp. *In Search of the New Public Domain*. Amsterdam: NAI, 2001.

Hansen, Mark B.N. *New Philosophy for New Media*. Cambridge: MIT Press, 2004.

Haraway, Donna J. "Situated Knowledges: The Science Question in Feminism and the Privilege of Partial Perspective." In *Simians, Cyborgs, and Women: The Reinvention of Nature*, 183–202. Routledge: New York, 1991.

Hargittai, Eszther. "Whose Space? Differences among Users and Non-Users of Social Network Sites." *Journal of Computer-Mediated Communication* 13, no. 1. (2007): 276-97.

Harvey, David. *The Condition of Post-Modernity: An Enquiry into the Origins of Cultural Change*. Cambridge: Blackwell, 1989.

Hawley, Amos H. *Human Ecology: A Theoretical Essay*. Chicago: University of Chicago Press, 1986.

Hayles, N. Katherine. "Simulated Nature and Natural Simulations: Rethinking the Relation between the Beholder and the World." In *Uncommon Ground: Toward Reinventing Nature*, edited by William Cronon, 409–25. New York: W.W. Norton, 1995.

Marilyn Healy and Chad Perry "Comprehensive Criteria to Judge Validity and Reliability of Qualitative Research within the Realism Paradigm," *Qualitative Market Research* 3, no. 3 (2000),118–26.

Helfand, Jessica. *Scrapbooks: An American History*. New Haven: Yale University Press, 2008.

Hobson, Janel. "Digital Whiteness, Primitive Blackness: Racializing the 'Digital Divide' in Film and New Media." *Feminist Media Studies* 8, no. 2. (2008): 111–26.

Ingraham, Catherine. "Lines and Linearity: Problems in Architectural Theory." In *Drawing/Building/Text*, edited by Andrea Kahn, 63–84. New York: Princeton Architectural Press, 1991.

Innis, Harold. *Changing Concepts of Time*. Toronto: University of Toronto Press, 1952.

Jacobs, Jane. *The Death and Life of Great American Cities*. New York: Random House, 1961.

James, Clifford. *The Predicament of Culture: Twentieth-Century Ethnography, Literature and Art*. Cambridge: Harvard University Press, 1986.

Jameson, Fredric. *Signatures of the Visible*. New York: Routledge, 1992.

Jasper, James M. *Restless Nation: Starting over in America*. Chicago: University of Chicago Press, 2000.

Jenkins, Henry. *Convergence Culture: Where Old and New Media Collide*. New York: New York University Press, 2006.

———. Personal blog. Accessed June 8, 2009. http://civic.mit.edu/watchlistenlearn/henry-jenkins-on-what-is-civic-media.

———. *Textual Poachers: Television Fans & Participatory Culture*. London: Routledge, 1992.

Jordon, Tim. *Hacking: Digital Media and Technological Determinism*. London: Blackwell, 2008.

Katz, Barry M. *Technology and Culture: A Historical Romance*. Stanford: Stanford Alumni Association, 1990.

Kay, Alan, and Adele Goldberg. "Personal Dynamic Media." In *The New Media Reader*, edited by Noah Wardrip-Fruin and Nick Montfort, 391–404. Cambridge: MIT Press 2003.

Kelly, Kevin. "The Whole Earth Blogalog." *Conceptual Trends, Current Topics* (blog). Accessed May 14, 2009. http://kk.org/ct2/2008/09/the-whole-earth-blogalog.php.

Kelty, Christopher M. "Culture's Open Sources: Software, Copyright, and Cultural Critique." *Anthropological Quarterly* 77, no. 3 (2004): 499–506.

Kelty, Christopher, and Hannah Landecker. "A Theory of Animation: Cells, L-Systems, and Film." *Grey Room* 17 (Fall 2004): 30–63.

Kent, Fred. *Project for Public Spaces*. Accessed April 26, 2009. http://www.pps.org/about/team/fkent/.

Kirk, Andrew. *Counterculture Green: The Whole Earth Catalog and American Environmentalism*. Lawrence: University of Kansas, 2007.

Kollock, Peter, and Marc Smith. "Managing the Virtual Commons: Cooperation and Conflict in Computer Communities." In *Computer-Mediated Communication: Linguistic, Social, and Cross-Cultural Perspectives*, edited by Susan Herring, 109–28. Amsterdam: John Benjamins, 1996.

Koffka, Kurt. "Perception: An Introduction to the Gestalt-Theorie." *Psychological Bulletin* 19, no. 10 (1922): 531–85.

Kostof, Spiro. *A History of Architecture: Settings and Rituals*. Edited by Gregory Castillo. 2nd ed. Oxford: Oxford University Press, 1995.

Kosuth, Joseph. "1975." In *Conceptual Art: A Critical Anthology*, edited by Alexander Alberro and Blake Stimson, 334. Cambridge: MIT Press, 2000.

Krauss, Steven Eric. "Research Paradigms and Meaning Making: A Primer." *Qualitative Report* 10, no. 4 (2005): 758–70.

Kriem, Maya. "Mobile Telephony in Morocco: A Changing Sociality." *Media Culture Society* 31, no. 4 (2009): 617.

Latour, Bruno. *Pandora's Hope: Essays on the Reality of Science Studies.* Cambridge: Harvard University Press, 1999.

———. *Reassembling the Social: An Introduction to Actor-Network-Theory.* Oxford: Oxford University Press, 2005.

———. *Science in Action: How to Follow Scientists and Engineers through Society.* Cambridge: Harvard University Press, 1987.

———. *We Have Never Been So Modern.* Translated by Catherine Porter. Cambridge: Harvard University Press, 1993.

Laurel, Brenda. *Utopian Entrepreneur.* Cambridge: MIT Press, 2001.

Lavin, Silvia. "In the Names of History: Quatremère de Quincy." *Journal of Architectural Education* 44, no. 3 (1991): 131–37.

Lefebvre, Henri. *The Critique of Everyday Life* translated John Moore. London: Verso, 1991 (1947).

———. *The Production of Space,* translated Donald Nicholson-Smith. Oxford: Basil Blackwell, 1991 (1974).

Lejeune, Philippe. 'The Autobiographical Contract' In *French Literary Theory Today* ed. by Tzvetan Todorov, trans. by R. Carter (Cambridge: Cambridge University Press, 1982) Excerpted from the French original Le pacte autobiographique by Philippe Lejeune (Paris: Editions de Seuil, 1975).

Lennard, Suzanne H. Crowhurst, and Henry L. Lennard. *Public Life in Urban Places: Social and Architectural Characteristics Conducive to Public Life in European Cities.* South Hampton: Gondolier Press, 1984.

Lessig, Lawrence. "In Defense of Piracy." *Wall Street Journal,* October 11, 2008.

Lewin, Kurt. *Field Theory in Social Science: Selected Theoretical Papers.* Edited by Dorwin Cartwright. New York: Harper & Row, 1964.

Little, Stephen E. "Networks and Neighborhoods: Households, Community and Sovereignty in the Global Economy." *Urban Studies* 37, no. 10 (2000): 1813–25.

Livingstone, Sonia. "The Changing Social Landscape". In *Handbook of New Media: Social Shaping and Social Consequences of ICTs,* edited by Leah A. Lievrouw and Sonia Livingstone, 17–21. London: Sage, 2002.

MacDorman, Karl F., and Hiroshi Ishiguro. "The Uncanny Advantage of Using Androids in Cognitive Science Research." *Interaction Studies* 7, no. 3 (2006): 297–337.

MacKinnon, Rebecca. *"Race to the Bottom": Corporate Complicity in Chinese Internet Censorship.* New York: Human Rights Watch, 2006.

Michael Mandiberg, ed. *Social Media Reader.* New York: New York University Press, 2012.

Manovitch, Lev. *The Language of New Media.* Cambridge: MIT Press, 2001.

Marlow, Cameron. "The Structural Determinants of Media Contagion." PhD diss., MIT, 2005.

Martin, Reinhold. *The Organization Complex: Architecture, Media, and Corporate Space.* Cambridge: MIT Press, 2003.

Massumi, Brian. *Parables for the Virtual: Movement, Affect, Sensation.* Durham: Duke University Press, 2002.

Matsuda, Misa. "Mobile Communication and Selective Sociality." In *Personal, Portable, Pedestrian: Mobile Phones in Japanese Life,* edited by Mizuko Ito, Daisuke Okabe, and Misa Matsuda, 123–42. Cambridge: MIT Press, 2005.

Maturana, Humberto R., and Francisco J. Varela. *Autopoiesis and Cognition: The Realization of the Living.* Boston: Reidel, 1980.

Maxwell, Joseph. *Qualitative Research: An Interactive Approach.* 2nd ed. Thousand Oaks: Sage, 2005.

McArthur, J.A. "Digital Subculture: A Geek Meaning of Style." *Journal of Communication Inquiry* (October 2008): 1–13.

McCullough, Malcolm. *Digital Ground: Architecture, Pervasive Computing and Environmental Knowing.* Cambridge: MIT Press, 2004.

McGetrick, Brendan, and Rem Koolhaas, eds. *Content.* Cologne: Taschen, 2004.

McLuhan, Marshall. *The Gutenberg Galaxy: The Making of Typographic Man.* Toronto: University of Toronto Press, 1962.

———. *Understanding Media: The Extensions of Man.* Cambridge: MIT Press, 1964.

———. "The Medium is the Message." In *The Essential McLuhan,* edited by Eric McLuhan and Frank Zingrove, 151–60. New York: Basic Books, 1995.

McLuhan, Marshall, and Bruce R. Powers. *The Global Village: Transformations in World Life and Media in the 21st Century.* Cambridge: Oxford University Press, 1989.

McNeil, Joanne. "Occupy the Internet." *Occupy! An OWS-Inspired Gazette* Issue 1 (N+1) Rhizome Nov 9, 2011: 24–25. Accessed June 8, 2012. http://www.npluso nemag.com/OCCUPY-GAZETTE.pdf.

Mead, George Herbert. *Mind Self and Society: From the Standpoint of a Social Behaviorist,* Chicago: University of Chicago Press,1934.

Meyrowitz, Joshua. *No Sense of Place: The Impact of Electronic Media on Social Behavior.* New York: Oxford Press, 1985.

Miller, Peggy J., Randolph Potts, Heidi Fung, Lisa Hoogstra, and Judy Mintz. "Narrative Practices and the Social Construction of Self in Childhood." *American Ethnologist* 17, no. 2 (1990): 292–311.

Mitcham, Carl. *Metaphysics, Epistemology, and Technology: Research in Philosophy and Technology.* Toronto: Jai Press, 2000.

Mitchell, William J. *Beyond Productivity: Information Technology, Innovation and Creativity.* Washington: National Academies Press, 2003.

Mitchell, William J. *Me++: The Cyborg Self and the Networked City.* Cambridge: MIT Press, 2004.

Morozov, Evgeny, panel discussion by Bridget Kendall, *The Forum: A World of Ideas,* BBC radio July 28, 2009.

Mumford, Lewis. *Technics and Civilization.* Fort Washington: Harvest Books, 1963.

Murmur. Archival audio project website, Toronto. Accessed August 24, 2007. http://murmurtoronto.ca.

Nelson, Sean. Interview with a former NASA Ames Research Lab programmer. Moffett Field, CA, Mill Valley, CA. (December 13, 2008).

Nichols, Vincent. "The Overuse of E-mails and Texts." *Irish Times,* August 3, 2009. Accessed June 17, 2012 http://www.irishtimes.com/newspaper/world/2009/0803/1224251929001.html.

Nickell, Joe. "Return of the Living BBS." *Wired* (March 1, 1999): 7.

Nyanthi, Kelvin. "Authenticity of Online Social Relationships." Unpublished paper, Dalhousie University, Halifax, Nova Scotia, 2008.

Offenhuber, Dietmar, and Katja Schechtner, eds. *Inscribing the Square: Urban Data as Public Space.* Vienna: Springr-Verlag, 2012.

Ong, Walter J. *Orality and Literacy: The Technologizing of the Word.* New York: Routeledge, 1982.

Ottaway, Marina, and Amr Hamzawy. "Protest Movements and Political Change in the Arab World." *Carnegie Endowment for International Peace 5* (January 25, 2011): 1–14.

Pariser, Eli. *The Filter Bubble: What the Internet Is Hiding From You.* New York: Penguin Press, 2011.

Pearson, Roberta E., and William Uricchio. "Corruption, Criminality, and the Nickelodeon." In *Hop on Pop: The Politics and Pleasures of Popular Culture,* edited by Henry Jenkins, Tara McPherson, and Jane Shattuc, 376–87. Durham: Duke University Press, 2002.

Phillips, Amy K. "The Image of the Simulated City: Sim City 2000 and Popular Perceptions of the City." Master of Architecture thesis. University of California-Berkeley, 1993.

Picon, Antoine, and Alessandre Ponte, eds. *Architecture and the Sciences: Exchanging Metaphors*. Princeton: Princeton Architectural Press, 2004.

Popov, Lubomir. "Architecture as Social Design: The Social Nature of Design Objects and the Implications for the Profession." *Journal of Design Research* 2, no. 2 (2002). Accessed April 30, 2013. http://www.inderscience.com/jdr/back files/articles/issue2002.02/article4.html

Procopio, Claire H., and Steven T. Procopio. "Do You Know What it Means to Miss New Orleans? Internet Communication, Geographic Community and Social Capital in Crisis." *Journal of Applied Communication Research* 35, no. 1 (2007): 67–87.

Protzen, Jean-Pierre. "Reflections on the Fable of the Caliph, the Ten Architects, and the Philosopher." *Journal of Architectural Education* 34, no. 4 (1981): 2–8.

Putnam, Robert D. "Bowling Alone: America's Declining Social Capital." *Journal of Democracy* 6, no. 1 (1995): 65–78.

Raban, Jonathan. *Soft City*. New York: Harvill Press, 1974.

Rabinow, Paul, and William M. Sullivan, eds. *Interpretive Social Science: A Second Look*. Berkeley: University of California Press, 1987.

Rheingold, Howard. *Virtual Community: Homesteading on the Electronic Frontier*. Cambridge: MIT Press, 1993.

Rittel, Horst W. J. "On the Planning Crisis: Systems Analysis of the 'First and Second Generations.'" *Bedrifts Oekonomen* 8 (October 1972): 35–41.

Rittel, Horst W. J., and Melvin M. Webber. "Dilemmas in a General Theory of Planning." *Policy Sciences* 4, no. 2 (1973): 155–69.

Rodowick, D. N. *Reading the Figural, or, Philosophy after the New Media*. Durham: Duke University Press, 2001.

Rosch, Eleanor. "The Environment of Minds: Toward a Noetic and Hedonic Ecology." In *Cognitive Ecology*, edited by Morton P. Friedman and Edward C. Carterette, 3–23. San Diego: Academic Press, 1996.

———. "If You Depict a Bird, Give it Space to Fly: Eastern Psychologies, the Arts, and Self-knowledge." *SubStance* 30, nos. 1 and 2 (2006): 236–51.

Rush, Michael. *New Media in Late 20th-Century Art*. London: Thames and Hudson, 1999.

Sadofsky, Jason Scott. *BBS the Documentary*. Film, 2005, copy in DVD format, disks 1–3.

Saxenian, Anna Lee. *Regional Advantage: Culture and Competition in Silicon Valley and Route 128*. Cambridge: Harvard University Press, 1994.

Schon, Donald A. "From Technical Rationality to Reflection-in-Action." In *The Reflective Practitioner: How Professionals Think in Action*, 21–75. New York: Basic Books, 1983.

Schwartz, Ori. "Who Moved My Conversation? Instant Messging, Intertexuality and New Regimes of Intimacy and Truth." *Media Culture and Society* 33, no. 1 (2011): 71–87.

Searle, John R. *The Construction of Social Reality*. New York: Free Press, 1995.

———. *Intentionality: An Essay in the Philosophy of Mind*. Reprint. Cambridge: Cambridge University Press, 1999.

Seiter, Ellen. *Sold Separately: Children and Parents in a Consumer Culture*. Chapel Hill: Rutgers University Press, 1993.

Sennett, Richard. *The Fall of Public Man*. New York: W.W. Norton, 1974.

Sharp, Willoughby. "Worldpool: A Call for Global Community Communications." *Only Paper Today* (December 1978): 8–9.

Shields, Rob. *The Virtual*. London: Routledge, 2002.

Shirky, Clay. *Here Comes Everybody*. New York: Penguin Press, 2008.

———. "Social Software and the Politics of Groups." *Networks, Economics, and Culture mailing list* (March 9, 2003). Accessed June 9, 2007, http://shirky.com/writings/group_politics.html

Sorkin, Michael. *Variations on a Theme Park: The New American City and the End of Public Space*. New York: Hill & Wang, 1992.

Squaresoft. *Final Fantasy X*. PS2. Costa Mesa, CA: Square EA, 2001.

Squires, Catherine R. "Rethinking the Black Public Sphere: An Alternative Vocabulary for Multiple Public Spheres." *Communication Theory* 12, no. 4 (2002): 446–68.

Stallabrass, Julian. "Just Gaming: Allegory and Economy in Computer Games." *New Left Review* 198 (March-April 1993): 83–106.

Thorburn, David, Henry Jerkins, and Brad Seawell, eds. *Rethinking Media Change: The Aesthetics of Transition*. Cambridge: MIT Press, 2003.

Thurston, Thomas. "Building Social Networks with Computer Networks: A New Deal for Teaching and Learning." *History Teacher* 34, no. 2 (2001): 175–81.

Tierney, Thérèse [as 510 Collective] 2010. Project: "Los Angeles REDcar" in *A NEW INFRASTRUCTURE: Innovative Transit Solutions for Los Angeles*. Edited by Peter Zellner. New York: The Architect's Newspaper: New York Architecture and Design, p 117.

———."In [re]search of the Public: Reality and Representation in Online Social Sites," Unpublished ethnographic study, Dalhousie University, Halifax, Nova Scotia, May 30, 2008.

———."Situated Networks: In [re]search of the Public." PhD diss., University of California-Berkeley, 2009. ProQuest 580127461

Toffler, Alvin. *Future Shock*. New York: Random House, 1970.

Tsagarousianou, Roza, Damian Tambini, and Cathy Bryan, eds. *Cyberdemocracy: Technology, Cities and Civic Networks*. London: Routledge, 1998.

Turkle, Sherry. *Alone Together*. New York, Basic Books, 2011.

———. *Life on the Screen: Identity in the Age of the Internet*. New York: Simon & Schuster, 1995.

Turner, Fred. *From Counterculture to Cyberculture: Stewart Brand, the Whole Earth Network, and the Rise of Digital Utopianism*. Chicago: University of Chicago Press, 2006.

———. "Where the Counterculture Met the New Economy: The WELL and the Origins of Virtual Community." *Technology and Culture* 46, no. 3 (2005): 485–512.

Varela, Francisco J., Evan Thompson, and Eleanor Rosch. *The Embodied Mind: Cognitive Science and Human Experience*. Cambridge: MIT Press, 1991.

Varnelis, Kazy. *Networked Publics*. Cambridge: MIT Press, 2008.

Vesely, Dalibor. *Architecture in the Age of Divided Representation*. Cambridge: MIT Press, 2004.

Virilio, Paul. *The Vision Machine*. Bloomington: Indiana University Press,1994.

Wark, McKenzie. *A Hacker Manifesto [Version 4.0]*. Cambridge, MA: Harvard University Press. 2004. Accessed August 24, 2007. http://subsol.c3.hu/subsol_2/contributors0/warktext.html.

———. *Virtual Geography: Living with Global Media Events*. Bloomington: Indiana University Press, 1994.

Warner, Michael. *Publics and Counterpublics*. New York: Zone Books, 2002.

Webber, Melvin. "Order in Diversity: Community without Propinquity." In *Cities and Space: The Future Use of Urban Land*, edited by Lowdon Wingo, 23–54. Baltimore: Johns Hopkins Press, 1963.

———. "Planning in an Environment of Change, Part II: Permissive Planning." *Town Planning Review* 39, no. 4 (1969): 282–84.

———. "The Urban Place and the Non Urban Realm." In *Explorations into Urban Structure*, edited by Webber, et al, 79–153. Philadelphia: University of Pennsylvania Press, 1964.

Weiner, Norbert. *The Human Use of Human Beings: Cybernetics and Society*. New York: Avon Books, 1986.

Wellman, Barry, and Bernie Hogan. "The Immanent Internet." In *Netting Citizens: Exploring Citizenship in a Digital Age*, edited by Johnston McKay, 54–80. Edinburgh: St. Andrew Press, 2004.

White, Lynn. *Medieval Technology and Social Change*. Oxford: Clarendon Press, 1963.

Whitehead, Alfred North. *Process and Reality*. Edited by David Ray Griffin and Donald W. Sherburne. Corrected ed. New York: Simon and Schuster, 1978.

Whyte, William H. *The Social Life of Small Urban Spaces*. Washington: Conservation Foundation, 1980.

Wigley, Mark. *Constants New Babylon, The Hyper Architecture of Desire*. Rotterdam: Uitgeverij, 1998.

Williams, Raymond. *The Country and the City*. Oxford: Oxford University Press, 1975.

Winograd, Terry, and Carlos F. Flores. "Using Computers: A Direction for Design." In *Understanding Computers & Cognition: A New Foundation for Design*, 163–80. Norwood: Ablex, 1986.

Wong, Hertha. "Visual Autobiography." Unpublished manuscript, 2006.

WordNet® 3.0. Princeton University. Accessed March 27, 2009. http://dictionary.reference.com/browse/internet.

Xie, Bo. "The Mutual Shaping of Online and Offline Social Relationships." *IR Information Research* 13, no. 3 (2008): 4.

Zeisel, John. *Inquiry by Design: Tools for Environment Behavior Research*. Belmont, CA: Wadsworth, Inc.,1981.

Zucker, P. *Town and Square: From the Agora to the Village Green*. New York: Columbia University Press, 1959.

Index

Note: Page numbers in *italics* indicate figures.

9 781138 649309